Rare Birds
A gamekeeper's memories

Brian Aston

HAYLOFT

First published 2004

Hayloft Publishing Ltd, Kirkby Stephen,
Cumbria, CA17 4DJ

tel: (017683) 42300
fax. (017683) 41568
e-mail: books@hayloft.org.uk
web: www.hayloft.org.uk

© 2004 Brian Aston

ISBN 1 904524 26 5

A catalogue record for this book is available
from the British Library

Apart from any fair dealing for the purposes of research or private study, or criticism
or review, as permitted under the Copyright, Designs & Patents Act, 1988, this
publication may only be reproduced, stored or transmitted, in any form or by any means,
with the prior permission in writing of the publishers, or in the case of reprographic
reproduction in accordance with the terms of the licenses issued by the
Copyright Licensing Agency.

Produced, printed and bound in the EU

Contents

I	The early years	5
II	Life on the farm	74
III	Down the mines	116
IV	National Service and Germany	122
V	Game keeping in Yorkshire	132
VI	Game keeping in Kent	159
VII	Game keeping in Wiltshire	176
VIII	Game keeping in Lancashire	186
IX	Game keeping in Cumbria	198

The author at Edenhall with his daughters

I
THE EARLY YEARS

The Beginning

Our doctor was Irish, mother always called him Doctor 'Marny', anyway that was what it sounded like, he said that I was to do much travelling in my life and travel I did. My little life started on the 25 June 1932, and I lived at Bank Top until I was eighteen years old. Mother always said our address was Raynors Yard, Bank Top, Earlsheaton. It appears that I was a sickly child and was almost given up for dead a few times, evidently I was made of strong stuff as later I was to prove.

The view from our window was on the left side of an ancient barn, sandstone built with a flagged roof, a really huge building dating back to the 17th century. Directly in front of us there was the yard gateway, and a row of four very old cottages standing slightly lower than our house. Outside our door there was just a dirt yard with ruts in it so that when it rained, these ruts formed small streams down which I sailed my matchbox boats.

One down and two up was our house, the next door being the same, they being quite modern, built about 1900. The Oldroyds, our neighbours, were called Harry, Anna and daughter, Emma, who was crippled from birth. Over the years they were very good to us. I was always in trouble or hurting myself. Anna was always at hand to treat my many cuts and bruises, she having been a nurse in the 1914-1918 war. As I grew stronger and started wandering about, I soon found my way into the old barn. Even today when I think back over the years, it is one of my earliest recollections.

Two brothers, the Riley Brothers, were renting the barn - everyone called it the garage as it was used to house the two Morris Commercial lorries that they used in their haulage business. Every morning, six days a week, the lorries were out at their work then I had the whole great building to explore. In one part of the gable end inside were beehives made of straw wound round ropes, then formed into a domed shape. I believe there were six of them, all sitting in recesses in the wall. They must have been ancient in those days. An old Austin 10 stood in a corner. I would sit inside it and pretend I was driving it. Many hours I sat there dreaming, everything covered in thick dust. I must have been muck up always!!

Mother made all my clothes from bits and pieces, sometimes an old coat was cut up and used. I was not fussy.

The main barn doors were really tall. Going inside was to me like being in a cathedral. There was much timber work, huge baulks on stone piers that carried the trusses of the roof, it being built the same way as the old tithe barns I have seen in the south of England. A flight of rickety stairs led to the lofts of which I shall write later.

At the gable end of the barn farthest from our house, stood the blacksmith's hearth. Around this hearth was some wooden flooring and six standings for heavy horses along the back wall, with a kind of floor above them to keep horse feed and hay. What a place it was, always small noises from birds, rats, mice or could be anything, in the gloomy place.

Outside the old barn, on what we called the front, a lot if it was covered with ivy, very thick with many years of growth. Lots of sparrows and starlings nested there. In spring a flowering cherry tree would bloom, it was only a small tree which I climbed many times.

At the far end of the building lived Mr and Mrs Leak, their son Jeffery and Brenda, their young daughter. They lived in what would have been the farmhouse, down one step into the living room with a cast iron range for the cooking. At the back there was a big wash house with a set pot to boil things in. The Jacob's Ladder led up to two bedrooms - they were very small - a Jacob's Ladder being just the treads and no risers at the back of them. Outside the door of this farmhouse, right under the upstairs windows grew a lilac tree. It was lovely to see it in the spring when it flowered, the smell very fragrant, ho, the memories.

Many was the time when Mrs Leak locked herself out of the house and I was sent to climb up and through one of the bedroom windows to open up the door. Mr Leak was a fireman. He had a very old Jowett car, one that the roof folded back to make it a touring car. They were both small people and very homely.

Back to the barn - at the end nearest our house was a small paddock and a pig sty as well, an ideal place to hide and right under their noses. This old barn was the setting for my early life and even today, 65 years later, I think of it and wish it were still there.

A hawthorn tree stood to the left side of the track that led to the front of the barn and Leak's cottage. Mother used to walk the few paces to this tree and throw the leaves from her teapot there and occasionally an odd mushroom would appear about where the leaves fell. The very old wall holding back the remains of a field was covered with convolvulus in summer, the big white trumpets with bees and other insects about them.

Charley Jackson's shop was just over the wall, the brick foundations built high to bring the shop level with the road that ran in front of it. In the corner nearest the barn was a gallows with two great big old floor beams standing upright. They were about twenty feet high; they must have been well dug into the ground and about ten feet apart. Another beam or cross head rested on the two uprights. Two sets of block and tackle, one on each side of the cross head, hung down and from them the back part of an old furniture van hung. Underneath this contraption was a space high enough for a lorry to reverse under the old van back. The box-like van was then lowered down onto the lorry and fastened with ropes. It was used for furniture removals.

Being Stitched After the Bread Pot Broke
I would have been three years old and must have been getting about a bit where the food was kept, the pantry, we called it. You had to go down about three steps to the cold slab. Halfway down the steps stood a large stone bread crock with a wooden lid on it. I was in the habit of climbing up on the lid so as to look out of a small window into the back yard.

One day as I stood on my perch, the pot broke under me and as I fell. A piece of broken pot stuck up still attached to the base - I landed upon this and was cut in my right groin. It was a nasty cut and needed stitching. I remember vividly being held down upon the table, my legs and arms pinned down, while the doctor stitched me and no anaesthetic was used 'ether'.

The neighbours said that my screams could be heard all over Bank Top. My mother was terrified - what would father say when he arrived home at night? Evidently, had the wound been a little nearer the artery, it could have been fatal. That was my first accident - more were to follow in later years.

At the top of our stairs was a small landing window. Now, if I had misbehaved and was put to bed, I would get a bedroom chair and climb out of the window. It was quite a feat to do as the window was high in the wall and I had to go out head first, as it wasn't large enough to turn round in and the drop on the outside onto the coal house roof was about six feet. I soon learned to roll over on landing on the roof. The rest was easy. Returning home again was harder, my dad would be awaiting me!!

Sammy Lister
He was an old horse even when I first remember him. Sammy's knees were scarred by many a fall on the icy roads. Sharps or studs were hammered into his shoes in bad weather to help the shoes to get a better grip.

Sammy Lister, as my mother called him, was yoked in Edmund Lister's milk float; morning and evening together they hawked milk. Heath Farm was Sammy's home - a small farm that had seen many changes over the years. I would say that, originally, the farm had started as a sheep farm, because of the name Heath. Many small farms had milk rounds to supplement their incomes. I took bits of bread to Sammy as he stood awaiting Edmund Lister to make his deliveries.

Old Bank was a bad road, it tilted towards our yard steeply and at times could be lethal when covered with ice. It was the old stagecoach road. I had been at Aunt Evelyn's one day and on my way home I met Sammy. Snow was on the ground and the road was slippery. Sammy was stood by Tempest's shop. I stopped to stroke him, he looked tired and his knees were bleeding. Poor Sammy he had been down again.

Horses, like people, depend on their legs; if our legs cannot carry us we are done for. Sammy's legs were so knocked about he could no longer draw the float. Sammy's days were over. I believe he was put out to grass as I remember him in the fields by the farm.

Charley Jackson's Shop
In Coronation Year 1937, Charley Jackson was selling tin cap pistols at one penny each in his little shop. He sold green groceries mainly and sometimes Mrs Jackson, Charley's mother, looked after it while he was away. She was always dressed in Victorian clothes, mostly black, a bit frightening sometimes as the shop was dimly lit. I remember the Coronation of George VI - there was a party in front of our house with tables, chairs, flags and streamers from the windows. All our neighbours helped and there were sandwiches, buns and pop for the kids and holiday from school. Weeks after it was

all over, on a shelf in Jackson's shop, was a small toy State Coach with all the white horses and liveried footmen. I would stand and stare at it and think about the party in our yard and wonder what it was all about.

I started school when I was about four years old. We all went together, my sister, Joan, she was about three years older than me; Ernest Dawson, my mate; Jean and David Carroll; the Keir brothers; Betty Exley and more. We had to go along a path at the bottom of the park, where amongst the trees was a pond. One day, on our way, Ernest Dawson stopped at this pond. Evidently I took off my coat, anyway he chucked the coat into the water and I, not wanting to lose my coat, walked in after it, up to my middle. I remember my mother pulling me from the water, I holding on to the coat. There was no school for me that day as I was wearing corduroy pull ups. They were very heavy with water in them.

And so growing up was a busy time for me and my mother and father. He was always busy either at work or in our allotment. We had a big piece of ground and a decent sized greenhouse with a coke fired boiler to heat it.

Dad grew tomatoes on staging inside and, underneath the staging was a bed specially made for growing mushrooms, with sacking hanging down to keep out the light. I used to go with my father in the evening to stoke up the boiler so that it kept warm all night.

We had a dog, a smooth coated fox terrier, called her Dinky. My dad got her from Tom Walker. Mr Walker was a small made man who used to cobble shoes and upholster chairs in a wooden cabin at the bottom of his garden. I chose Dinky when she was a pup.

Dinky was my mate as soon as we met, she being only a tiny pup. She looked just like her mother, only Dinky had a brown face with a white blaze parting her head right to her nose, and a lovely big brown saddle in the middle of her back, just where a saddle should be. What times she and I were to have together. Dinky slept in one of grandad's big easy chairs. The house had been my grandad's but he went away to work when my grandma died.

I do not remember seeing my gran. Grandad had a moustache and was a good looking man with a fiery temper as I found out later. My mother's mother died in 1929 so, after grandad went away to Coventry to work on the big contracts that were being done at the time, my mother took over the house and all its contents.

Rats

Down the yard in front of our house, there was an ash pit where folk threw their cinders and rubbish. The council scavengers came to empty them about once a month. Anyway, these middens had half doors, the top half always open so that people could throw the rubbish in. I, have grown a bit by now, could, with a bit of luck, just see inside and afore long, saw what was happening there - rats. Aye, rats - sometimes we would seem them out of our window; mother always blamed the old barn for them.

Well, now I had seen the rats, I was very interested indeed, and so was Dinky, my dog. I soon found out from my dad how to go about catching them rats, and where they liked to live, under old sacking and piles of wood, or under almost any old stuff that lay about.

One day someone called at our house to say that a rat had just gone into the old wall by the pig sty. I got some old bits of material and pinched some matches from the shelf and out I went, stuffing rags into the likely holes in the wall. When I had used all the rags, I got Dinky and set the rags alight. Soon they started to smoulder and in a short while smoke was coming from all over the wall. Out came the rat and by luck, it came out the same side as my dog. It made for the old midden, but being quick enough, Dinky had it nipped and then gave it a right good shake. I was shouting, 'Go on, shake it' and jumping about. I was so pleased at what we had done.

By now a few of the neighbours, wondering what I was shouting about, came down to have a look and to see who was responsible for the smoke, they seemed pleased to see the rat king dead. So that was the start of my rat catching, my very first rat. Little did I think that what had happened that day would affect my life and set me wanting to be amongst nature for the rest of my life.

Summer times before the War were good. We had picnics in the Kirk Baulks fields, played in the beck by the little stone bridge where the water always tasted of salt. I suppose it was salty because it came from far down in the earth, it was pumped out of the mines thereabouts.

I loved picnics, especially with Aunt Evelyn; she was good to my sister Joan and I, and had a lovely nature to her, she not having children of her own. Uncle William had died quite young.

We made daisy chains and I looked for bird's nests. I was fascinated with the different kinds I found. I was told not to take the eggs but I, being a young, inquisitive lad, had to gather a few and, therefore, I started a collection. The older boys showed me how to blow them, but if the eggs had been sat on for some time, it was impossible to get all the insides out of the shell.

I remember being lifted up to be shown a song thrush sitting on her nest, in a very tall hawthorn hedge, which more like trees. Little did I know that years later, I would work on that farm and help Uncle Walter to cut and lay that very same hedge. Dad worked at Pilldacre Mill in those days. It belonged to some people called Filton. Dad did some gardening for them when he could spare the time.

We - mother, sister Joan and I - would walk through the village, mother stopping to talk to folks she knew, for she had lived there before she married dad. Sometimes we would be invited into someone's cottage - mother would sit and talk, we children usually outside looking about or playing with the other bairns.

We would arrive at the mill where dad was, and we would all sit in the field. If mother had cooked a steak and kidney pudding, the basin it was done in was usually wrapped in a cloth

Pilldacre

It was lovely to be among the haycocks, I rolling about in the hay. There were fields and farms all around the mill. Dad took me and showed me the new dam full of lovely clear water, somebody had put goldfish in there.

I was told that a kingfisher often sat watching for small sticklebacks. A few years later, I swam in the dam with some more lads; it was nice clean water from a beck. On these outings we did not take Dinky, as mother was too busy looking after the pair of us, me in particular. Later we would walk home, tired out but having enjoyed every minute of it, with me asking mother when we could go again.

Dad's family came from Thorne Hill or Thornhill Lees. There were five of them, three boys and two girls - Harold, William, Herbert my father, Aunt Evelyn and Aunt Mary. Dad's mother died when he was quite young. I believe his father, my grandfather, moved away, I did not recollect him. My great grandfather was killed in 1914, in a boiler explosion at the forge, along with many more men. Many a time I have heard out family talk of Steven, my great grandfather who lived to 81 years.

Rare Birds

More rats

I found a big wooden rat trap of the type called a 'nipper' trap, which was much the same as the usual mousetrap. I had seen a large rat go under the wooden flooring at the blacksmith's hearth one day and I decided to catch him. So, placing a piece of bacon rind on the sharp metal spike of the trap, I strained to get the spring over and then lock it in place with the long pin. Anyway I managed to do that, goodness knows what would have happened if the pin had slipped, the trap was a good strong one. It could have given me a nasty injury or broken the fingers of a six year old boy.

I kept the trap by the broken floor and thought no more of it. The next morning I went out to the barn. As I got near where the trap had been set, I could not see it. The light was not very good, so I went right up to the hearth and could just see a bit of tail sticking out under the boards. Being careful and thinking this rat could still be alive, I got a bit of wood and poked about and managed to get the rat and trap out. 'Bloody hell!' I thought, the rat was a whopper with a great thick tail - he was a beaut. He was quite dead. Away I went and showed him to everybody. Boy, was I proud - he was my second victim and the biggest.

Well, that was it. I was hooked on rat catching. I had got started in good time. I was six years old and had caught my first two rats. I started to go in Scott's field; it was all rough grass, ideal for voles and mice. Dinky was as keen as I. Voles are quite easy to dig out and my dog was very sharp, nipping them as fast as they bolted. Sheets of old, galvanised iron, lying flat, were ideal places to find them. Many a day we hunted the Tenter fields over, then round the frog pond and back home to pay a visit to the old barn to see how my trap was.

By now I had acquired a wire rat trap, one that catches them alive. I was into the ash pits, around the old privies, anywhere there was a rat, I was there. I did play with other children, cricket and kicking a ball about, but I think I liked to be out and about on my own at that period of my life.

Old Tebby Gibson had some hens on a rough bit of ground and I sometimes saw him going there with his double barrel gun. He too was after the rats. There are nearly always some vermin where poultry are kept. Now and then I would hear a shot and know that was one rat I would not get. Tebby was a small man and not very sociable. There were some old stables where I too went and hovered about in my search for rats.

Mr Illingworth lived directly opposite our house. Next door to him was Sara Oldroyd and next to her the Walton family. Clifford Walton worked in the mines; he must have been at the coal face, as he was very black when he arrived home. He had to get bathed in front of the fire in a tin bath like we all did in those days.

Mrs Walton was called by the neighbours, 'Addy Oddy'. Why, I don't know. She had a bit of a two wheeled cart with shafts. She used to gad about selling eggs, and she wore a beret and gabardine coat and wellington boots. She was thin and quite tall. Sheila Walton was an only child. Once a month a load of coal would arrive at the Walton's home and would lie there waiting until Mr Walton got home, then they would all start to get it shovelled into the coal house.

Old Mr Illingworth sat alone in semi-darkness; the sun didn't get into his house. He sat in the corner by the range. He always wore a black bowler hat and scarf and a fawn gabardine raincoat, and he was difficult to see in the gloomy room, the only room in the house. There was never much of a fire in the grate and there was an old sideboard with stuffed birds under a glass dome and other ornaments. There were some chairs of various kinds and a deal table with a tasselled cover over it. It was bad to tell the colour of it in the dim light.

My mother told me to go visit Mr Illingworth every day and ask him if he needed anything. Sometimes he would say to me, 'Reach that tea caddy down, lad.' The caddy sat on the mantel shelf and I stood on a stool to reach it.

'Will you go get me some Swan Vestas or Tiger Matches and two ounces of tea, and get yourself some sweets, I know you like humbugs.' Mr Illingworth would take the money from his tea caddy, 'Put the caddy back, my lad. Now away you go.'

I would go to Gill's shop where Jeffery Leak worked. He weighed flour in a little room, and wore a flour bag apron and a flour bag on his head. He put flour into half stone and one stone bags. People bought it to bake bread with.

I went back to Mr Illingworth with his order. 'Sit down a minute, lad. How are you doing with your rat catching?' I would tell him of my trapping the big one by the blacksmith's hearth.

'Do ya know when I was a lad the council used to pay 3d a rat?' said he. He would talk of when he was a young lad. I was told of the Boer War - the pictures on the walls showed soldiers of that time. There was a lovely picture of Queen Victoria, that picture seemed to brighten his little home. He would smoke his pipe and look into the bit of fire in the grate. 'Alright, lad, away you go, come and see me tomorrow.'

I always remember how the homes of older people smelled different. Our house smelled of dogs and cooking or baking. Mother would make Mr Illingworth his Sunday dinner along with ours. I would take it to him.

Then there was Mr Senior. I would say he would be in his sixties and he had very bad legs. They were very bowed because of rickets which was common among people born before the Great War of 1914-18. Mr Senior worked for the Riley Brothers and his domain was in the old barn by our house. The top part of the barn had been floored out at some time. To get up to the work room you had to climb some very rickety stairs. These stairs creaked and groaned so much that the place would have been closed down these days. They looked and felt as though they would collapse at any moment.

The room that Mr Senior occupied was right up under the huge stone flagged roof, among the roof trusses, the pegs of oak sticking down over the batons. A big sewing machine stood rusting at one side and dust was inches thick everywhere. There were wool bale sacks, lay in heaps all about the room and some bundles of sewing string hung from hooks handy to where Mr Senior was working. His job was to repair any of the bale sacks that needed stitching along the seams.

The process was to hang one corner of the sack on the hook, which was about waist high and fastened to a baulk of wood. Then the sack was stretched so that the seams came together and could be sewn up with a large bagging needle and string.

Sometimes when I was mooching about the old barn, Mr Senior would call me to him. There would be a pile of sacks that had been mended that day that needed bagging up. One of the sacks was fastened so that it was held at each end and lay open. The repaired sacks were placed inside and as the sack was being filled up I was lifted inside to trample them down. It was an awful dusty job. When the sack was full I jumped down, Mr Senior would stitch up the bale and it was ready to go away.

Sometimes I would hear a puffing and hissing from the end of our yard. I knew the sound well - a steam locomotive was hauling something along. Maybe it would be a Glossop's steam wagon - they did roadworks. Away I would run, and up the road towards the sound. One day it was not Glossop's but a showman's steam locomotive, a fairground engine. The huge road wheels carried it along, the brass spangles sparkling in the lights generated by the dynamo mounted on a platform just in front of the smoke stack.

Sometimes these monsters were painted a lovely red colour or green. The flywheel if a solid one, spinning the yellow painted line on it, in decreasing circles so it appeared. A fair was coming to town. There were more road engines, a bit smaller and not quite as elegant, each locomotive pulling some sort of trailer, plus caravans, these also brightly painted and gilded. Bowsers were towed as well as much water was used by the engines. I would walk alongside the convoy until it was time to turn for home.

Another of my favourite places in warm, summer weather, were the horse troughs. Close by Bywell Road stood a nice grey granite horse trough. Most of the troughs were donated by people who were wealthy and left them as a memorial to someone or other when they died.

The one I visited most was kept nice and clean. There was one trough for the horses and one at ground level for dogs. These troughs were usually at one mile intervals along a main road. If it was a hot day my boots would come off while I paddled my feet. The Cooperative Society had many heavy horses, as had the railways, plus the local traders, like Rington's Tea Company who had some lovely bay hacks. They were real flyers and pulled vehicles similar to hansom cabs, which were painted green and black with gold lettering advertising the tea.

Tea could be ordered from Rington's and the parcels were delivered by the lovely turned out horses. Brooke Bond had a tea warehouse opposite the cobbler's shop. I watched the cab driver, dressed in smart driving coat, breeches and gaiters and Derby hat, many times as he loaded his cab.

Later on square motor vans started to call at the warehouse and in the end the horse and cab ceased to call. Horse drawn vehicles became a thing of the past, as were the Cooperative horses. Some local traders carried on with horses during the War or just after, because petrol was rationed. By the time I returned from the Army, all were finished and the motor vehicle had taken over.

War and air raids

Lizzy, Shara and Hanna Lumb were sisters. In later years, Lizzy, Shara and Newman, Shara's husband, were all to live together, along with Mary Helen, their mother. Hanna married Harry Oldroyd and lived next door to us. There was always someone coming or going between the two homes. I spent some time at Mary Helen's home. I was made a fuss of, maybe because there were not any children in their families, only Emma and she very much disabled.

I remember when Mary Helen died, I was taken to see her for the last time. The coffin was on trestles in the home, mother lifted me up so as I could see her lying there. I thought that Mary Helen was asleep, she looked just so to me, with powder on her face and she looked nice.

This was a few years before the War started. During the War we would all sit in the air raid shelter. We would sing and talk, us children were put to sleep as best we could. The heaters in the shelters were paraffin, the walls would get wet with condensation which would run down to the floor where pools formed. Later on, duck boards were put down to keep our feet dry. The shelters were very unhealthy; being built of concrete they were cold, but it was all we had.

I remember one night, just before Christmas, there was a bright moon and it was frosty. Mother was baking bread, the air raid siren sounded, that meant everyone to the shelters. My dad was going about to get people out of their homes, some of them old and a bit infirm, I with him knocking on doors and shouting to them.

We had been some while in the shelter when my mother said, 'Herbert, my bread's still in the oven.' Away went our dad to see to the baking. Some time later he came into the shelter and said the bread was done and taken from the oven, and that all was well - and that my terrier, Dinky, had started having pups - what a night.

We could hear the anti-aircraft guns banging away at the Germans. It was bright moonshine, with mist hanging low to the ground. The wall facing the shelter entrance was suddenly lit up by the light of a flare dropped from a German bomber. The light crept down the wall, then disappeared. It was all very exciting to me. The all clear sounded after 6am - that meant no school that day.

People were very proud of their clean steps, flags and window sills. An old woman used to come round with a cart on solid iron wheels, the axle was badly worn, so that the wheels of the cart leaned inwards as the cart passed over joints in the flags, and a clicking sound was heard. In the cart were two kinds of stone - ruddle and scouring stone, usually about the size of a cup. Ruddle was orange colour and scouring was white. The step edges and sill edges were done with these stones - they looked very smart when dry.

The Lodge - Sugar Lane
Uncle John and Aunt Mary lived at the Lodge at the top of Sugar Lane. Mr Lyles, a mill owner, had a large house and a small estate adjoining the twelve acre field. I used to go there at times to play with cousin Arnold. It was a neat place, stone built, a typical lodge of the late 19th century. Some cold frames and a greenhouse were in the gardens behind the Lodge. Uncle John was chauffeur cum gardener to Mr Lyles. I suppose it would be quite a good job in those days.

I remember the war when Uncle John was away in the Army. I stayed with them as company for Arnold. Under the window in the living room there was what looked like a table, in fact it was a table, yet when the top was lifted off it was a bath. Arnold and I were put in it together. It was a real treat for me as we only had a tin bath which we put by the fire at home.

If I remember right, Aunt Mary was a very happy sort of woman, she often laughed at our antics, yet she could be strict. The Lyles' estate was surrounded by a belt of trees which we would climb. We were told to keep off the lawns and not to go near the Big House. Behind the trees on the twelve acre field stood an old wooden railway van. Why it was there I don't know, anyway we called it our headquarters. We had found a long butcher's knife and this we threw from one end of the van to the other, trying to make it stick in the side, pretending to be knife throwers like in the circus.

During the war the twelve acres as it was called, was ploughed out. I cannot recollect what was grown in it. York Road Estate was being built where our old allotment used to be. It was sad to see all those houses being built where we had grown vegetables and had our greenhouse.

Our home and Scott's Yard
Mother said our home had been built around 1900. It was stone faced as was the Oldroyd house next door. The sides and backs

were of red brick and a central chimney with four flues served both homes. The good, strong roof was of Yorkshire flags held on by oak pegs.

George Scott was our landlord. He had a monumental mason's yard behind the outside privies at the back. Mr Scott's home was also in the mason's yard along with his son, George's house. I remember the yard being a busy place. Gravestones were carved there and many a time I sat and watched old Mr Scott at his work. On fine, warm days, he would sit out at his stone dressing. A large, wooden crane stood in the middle of the yard and pieces of sandstone and granite of three different colours were hoisted from lorries that delivered there.

In later years, the Scotts went into the firewood business. A circular saw was installed and a man employed to run the machine. Paraffin could be bought in the yard as well. I used to go for paraffin and always took a pint bottle to put it in. It was pumped from a large, metal tank. On the tank was the Shell advert.

The Scott family were an enterprising lot - they also recharged accumulator batteries. These were made of glass and were of different sizes. I was a regular visitor to the yard with batteries for charging. Our neighbour's sent me; my arms ached, the batteries were heavy to carry and had wire handles. Part of the Mason's building held the large board that was fastened to the wall. On it were the dials and various plugs and connections that charged the batteries with electricity. It took about two days to fully charge the accumulator batteries. I believe it cost sixpence each.

Emma, next door, had a wireless long before us. Their batteries were different - a wooden tray held many small glass vessels which were all connected together and, therefore, held much more electricity and need not be charged as often. A man with a small van used to call at Emma's home every so often to deliver a fully charged accumulator and take away the empty one. The wooden tray of batteries stood on a low shelf under their wireless, which rested on a small table.

As Mr Scott's firewood enterprise got going, some of the sawdust was used to make firelighters. Moulds were obtained - these were almost like chocolate bar moulds to look at, only much bigger. Sawdust was mixed with other ingredients in a large tub, paraffin was poured in as well and the whole mixed together. The paraffin soaked into the sawdust until the mix was quite damp. It was then scooped out of the tub and tamped into the lighter moulds and pressed down solid. Some days later the dry firelighters were tipped out and stacked up ready to be taken to the shops. Kindling wood bundles were made as well. I sometimes helped by clearing the sawdust from under the saw bench.

Mr Scott had a field on the far side of the road. I remember loads of old timber being tipped

Brian and Beryl, 1938

there. Most of the smaller lintels were of oak and about seven or eight feet long. We, our Gang, as we called ourselves, stacked these 'logs' as we called them, into forts and played many a time among the piles of wood.

Mr Heap, the doctor's man

Mr Heap was the doctor's man. In the 1930s he used to call at our home each Saturday around dinnertime. He was an oldish man, quite short but stockily built. He always wore a black bowler hat and had grey hair and moustache to match, a fawn coloured gabardine raincoat and dark striped trousers which covered his grey spats were the rest of his attire along with brightly polished black boots. Mr Heap was a smart gentleman. He had to be for he was the collector for Dr Marney, our doctor.

There would be a short, sharp rap on our door then the call, 'It's the doctor's man,' and he would step inside our home. Mr Heap always raised his hat to my mother as she held out the small book and gave the doctor's man a sixpence. The amount was entered therein and the book handed back. The money was put in a small leather bag. 'Good day,' said Mr Heap and left to call upon our neighbours, but not all of them.

Mother said that care must be taken not to be poorly for we had to pay for medicine and doctors' calls. This was before the National Health Service was introduced. A home where someone was poorly could easily run into debt, particularly where a large family lived. There were many illnesses then that we do not hear of today.

Mother always paid that six pence every week regardless. It was a form of insurance. Mr Heap, the doctor's man, was a familiar figure when I was a young lad. He, like many more characters, has disappeared and is just a memory to old men like me who live alone and dream of a different world of 50 years ago.

Bert Saville - railway truck driver

Twice a week, Bert Saville delivered fresh fish to the Jillings' Fish and Chip shop. His three wheeler articulated railway truck had a special engine note, I knew it well. I was outside as it turned into the yard. Arny Jillings, the fish shop owner, opened a cellar grate and started to hand out empty fish boxes to Bert, the railway truck driver.

Arny then put a short plank of wood through the cellar window and down this the full boxes of fish and ice were slid and stacked up. The delivery done, Bert Saville was given a pint pot of tea and some paper delivery notes were signed.

'Want a ride?' Bert asked me. 'Yes, please.' I was lifted onto the truck seat beside the driver. Off we went as far as Bank Top where I was put off to walk home, a distance of about 100 yards. I looked forwards to the twice weekly rides.

Bert Saville was killed in a fight outside the Scarborough Hotel in Dewsbury. He was struck on the head with a walking stick and fell, hitting his head on the roadside curb. The man that was charged with the offence was called Carrol. I believe he got away with manslaughter. That is many years ago. I was about twelve or thirteen years old. What happened to Carrol I do not remember, I am sure he was gaoled.

BRIAN ASTON

The Penny Shop
Miss Stainley's Penny Shop stood at the top of the yard that led down to the Junior School. Miss Stainley was a big, round woman, always cheerful as she waddled to serve anyone who wanted sweets. Her home and shop were all in one room, the only room in the house. She always wore a flowered pinafore. She was not very old, maybe 40 years. As you entered the Penny Shop, a tall folding screen stood on the left side - screens were much used years ago to stop draughts and give a little privacy. Many kinds of sweets were laid out on a large table by the only window - liquorice sticks and boot laces, pear drops, aniseed balls, bubble gum, sweethearts, humbugs and gob stoppers, and lots more.

Most things could be bought for a penny or maybe a halfpenny. It was a busy shop, with most business done on the way to school. Once the children were in school they must stay there until the bell rang and it was 4pm - time to go home.

When the war started and sweets were rationed, we would buy small tea cakes, sometimes they had some icing on them. Two or three lads would share one between them. The war had much to answer for - our way of life changed completely.

Johnny Turner lived opposite Miss Stainley's. He was a big man. He sat out on his buffet in shirt sleeves. He only had one arm, the sleeve of his shirt pinned back where his arm should have been. My dad worked with Johnny Turner at some time when he lost his arm in a machine.

The Rag and Bone Man
Three or four times a year, a rag and bone man would be waiting by Miss Stainley's shop, always at dinnertime, when we were on our way home from school. The rag man had a pony and cart, a large glass bowl with goldfish swimming around in it and celluloid windmills on sticks all brightly coloured, spinning in the wind.

The rag man held wooden pens in his hand resembling fountain pens, only the nibs were made of glass, all fluted to hold the ink, these too were in different colours. There were some yo-yos in a box on the cart and balsa wood gliders that were made in two parts, the wings could be taken off and put in your pocket - if you had one!

The kids crowded about the cart, asking about the articles he had on display. 'Run home and ask your mother for some rags,' shouted the rag man, 'Bring woollens, no cottons, then you can have your pick, anything you want.'

Every home had a rag bag, I know we had one as it hung in the pantry by the little window. Kids were running in all directions - those that lived close were soon back with bundles of rags. These were sorted out by the rag man. He brought out a hand weight from his pocket and pretended to weigh them, talking all the time and saying that not enough rags had been brought. You needed more for a goldfish. This time he would be kind and let you have something, you must bring more rags in future. The trading went on until 1pm, just before the school started again.

The rag man would go on his way, his cart loaded up with rags, all purchased for a few shillings worth of penny toys. No doubt he visited many schools and had some good days, no shouting along the streets, just sit and wait for the children coming from school at dinnertime.

The Water Main at Bank Top
I would be about six or seven years old at the time when the new water main pipe was being laid along Old Bank Road. Many men worked on the trench digging, how many I could not say, although it seemed more like an army to me, the road was usually quiet.

The trench was dug on the high side of the road, nearest to Lizzy Lumb's house. I spent many hours watching the work. An old man kept a brazier well stoked with coke and a big, black iron kettle was boiling all day long to brew the navvies' tea. It hung on a hook attached to the brazier. A small watchman's cabin stood about halfway along the trench. Around it were cans of paraffin, lots of lamps with red bulls eye glasses in them, spades, picks, crow bars, ropes and all the tools that were needed for pipe-laying.

The watchman's cabin had three sides, the front was open and there stood his brazier. If the wind changed direction the watchman's cabin was turned with the back to the wind and the brazier moved as well, so that the smoke was blown away from his cabin. It wasn't much of a shelter yet the old man seemed happy enough with it.

In the evenings I watched the old man light his lamps and carry them four at a time, two in each hand to iron bars that had been driven into the ground. Each bar had a hook forged into it, on these hooks the lamps were hung. The watchman having all the lamps in place, looked at the ropes that acted as a barrier to stop people stepping into the trench. Once satisfied that everything was in place, he settled himself on his box inside the cabin, a clean shovel was put on the brazier and on it bacon and sausages were soon cooked. The smell was good, I hung about watching it all happen. If it was a cold night, the old man would shift over a bit on his box and let me sit awhile. It was nice and cosy with the red hot coke burning bright in the night wind.

I stayed as long as possible until my mother would shout for me or come and fetch me away to get ready for bed. Next morning out I went - the lamps were all standing about the watchman's cabin, the navvies were busy digging. Behind the diggers another gang of men were laying the new iron pipes. I would say they were twelve inch pipes and shear legs were used to get them into position as they were very heavy. As a new pipe was being pushed into the collar of the previous one, a piece of tow or gaskin like rope, only that it was soaked in something akin to creosote, was passed about around the end as it entered the collar.

Next, the foreman, would inspect them to see if they were straight. If all was well, a man with a bucket of clay stood astride the pipes at the collar and rolled some clay until it was long enough to go round the pipe, like a thick rope. Once the clay was pressed hard to the collar it acted as a seal. Then at the top of the pipe, the soft clay was pulled back about an inch and a small depression made, really it was a funnel. All the while, a crucible of hot lead had been hung above the brazier. Two men with tongs gripped the crucible and carried it to the trench, lowered it down until it was just above the funnel in the clay seal. The lead crucible was tipped slightly until the hot lead flowed into the funnel continuously. Care had to be taken in case the lead splashed back. When the clay seal was full, the men took the crucible back to the brazier.

After a while the joint man in the trench peeled away the clay. Steam would rise from the lead and an inspection was made to make sure the lead had travelled everywhere in the seal. The joint man took a two pound hammer and a three inch wide chisel. The chisel had a blunt front edge. He proceeded to hammer the lead into the joint until it was all very tight. Again it was inspected and hammered again. Eventually everyone concerned was satisfied and the next pipe was laid and the process repeated.

Then there was the pie and peas man, he always seemed to arrive at dusk. He carried two cans on a yoke across his shoulder. In one can were hot peas, grey or green, the peas kept warm by a spirit stove underneath. The second can contained hot pies, these were kept warm the same way. 'Peas all hot, penny a pot,' the pie man shouted as he rang a bell. Anyone who wanted anything from the pie man would take a basin or a large jug for their peas. It was a treat to have a meal from the pie man.

My life almost came to end one day. I had been over the road to the shop and as I was coming from the shop there were some children older than I. They were calling me names. I started calling them names as well. One of the bigger girls was mad, her name was Shires. I was calling her, 'Shires, Shires, like a pair of pliers.' She started after me shouting what she would do to me. I was off, a bit scared of her being so big - I ran into the road right into a lorry.

I never saw it at all. When I woke up I was lying on the sofa. The wagon I had run into was a Pool petrol tanker. It seems the driver was more shaken than I was, poor chap. I made a full recovery but it must have been a close thing. There was not much traffic about in those days and it was much slower.

Brian Keir and his brother, Thomas, lived close to us. We would occasionally go about together. I thought they were rich. Their father, Thomas, a big man, wore in winter a full length leather coat and leather gauntlet gloves. The Keir family had a motor car and a garage too, so to my mind they were rich. My dad only had a bike.

Anyway, Brian Keir had been doing something with his bike. His finger was caught between the crank wheel and the chain, and the finger was taken off at the second joint. There was much talk of the accident. I was told never to play with the chain on any bike - I didn't have a bike.

My Uncle Bill lived along the road by my Aunt Evelyn. Sometimes he would take me with him on the tandem; I enjoyed that. Occasionally we would camp out with a tent at a farm over the other side of Blubberhouses Moor, towards Skipton. My uncle called it 'Old Tom's Place', evidently Old Tom made coffins. We would sit in the farmhouse, the place terribly cold, with a gap under the door a rat could get through.

To get to our camp site we crossed the road and went down some fields to the stream at the valley bottom. Alder trees grew there and there we pitched our tent by the beck. It was all very quiet. It being Sunday morning, the church bells would start to ring away in the distance, at Skipton and Denton. All these years later, I pass Old Tom's Place, standing high above the road that now bypasses it. The place has not changed at all. It is I that have changed, yet my memories of it are still with me as though it were yesterday.

Pilldacre Water Pit

In the 1930s things were pretty bad work wise, plenty of people and not much work, masses of unemployed. Dad told me there were six men to every job vacant. If you told the boss you didn't like what you were doing, he would say, 'Alright don't do it, there are plenty more men that will do it and for less money.' No holidays with pay, either you worked or you starved.

Dad worked at Fittons, and at Whitsuntide he and other men went to the water pit as it was called, as there was some work to be had. This entailed de-scaling the iron pipes that were used in pumping up water from many fathoms underground. The men were lowered down the shaft in a boson's chair, a seat on the end of a long rope, along with the necessary tools to do the job with. After the pipes had been cleaned, they had to be painted with a special sort of paint to stop them rusting. It was cold work in a damp, dark place, hanging in space above the water far below.

Pilldacre Pit had been a coal pit, but like many others about there, it had flooded years before. The water was used by Ossett Council as drinking water and was pumped into a large, ornate water tower that can be seen for miles around.

At Christmas time, a lovely time, being so young and believing in Santa Claus, the days that brought us nearer Christmas were days for making paper chains, yards and yards of them, mainly made of wallpaper and stuck together with flour paste that our mother made by pouring boiling water onto the flour in a bowl and stirring it all the while.

My sister and I would hang these chains of paper all over the house before we went to bed. By next morning some of the chains were hanging from the walls, having come apart with the weight of the wallpaper and so it went on until Christmas Eve. Little did we know that at Christmas in 1937 mother only had 7/6d for the whole of that period. Things were pretty tight money wise. Dad's normal wage was 18/6d a week and with four in the family there were no extras like sweets and fancy things, just the bare necessities.

If we had a chicken, well and good. We once had a goose,

sometimes a rabbit but that Christmas I just mentioned I don't know what we had. But I do remember my sister, Joan, had a chocolate mouse in her stocking and I had a chocolate watch wrapped in silver paper. We also had some nuts, apples and an orange each, and usually some new half pence and odds and ends, that the neighbours had given us. To us it was a great time. People visited each other, we kids went to show our neighbours what we had got, little did we know that they had contributed some of it.

Mother always got up early, long before any of our neighbours. On Mondays our washing was hung out and mother would have been to the butchers and then have got us up and ready for school by 8 o'clock. And all that done, she would set to her baking as all our bread and other food was home made.

The old black iron range was hot all over after the baking. I would come from school and sit on the shelf under the oven door and eat my bread and jam. Sometimes it would be beef dripping with brown jelly on it and a pinch of salt. Over the years I was to enjoy lots of beef dripping.

Once a week mother would set about to clean the range - it was our only way of cooking and heating our home. Out came the wood box with a hoop handle. In it was all the things needed for the work. First of all the flues were cleaned out, all the soot put in a bucket and put in the ash pit. Then black lead from a tin was brushed over all the ironwork. Everywhere was given a good coat of the black stuff, then it was left for a few minutes to dry a bit. Then using another brush, mother would start to polish all the iron until it fair shone, then it was rubbed over again with a cloth.

Three flat irons sat on the top shelf of the range. On the shelf was a plate bearing the maker's name Tate of Leeds. Years later when I came out of the Army, the range had been pulled out and a modern tiled fireplace installed in its place.

Our lavatory was out in the back yard. There were a row of them, five in all and an ash pit in the middle for all the cinders and other waste. We shared our lavatory with the Oldroyds. In the early mornings I could hear Harry Oldroyd coughing as he made his way there. Later Anna would wander there too, with her bucket of slops, nothing indoors to use only the chamber pots, that's all we had. At times I would make a dash for the lav only to find it occupied and then dash back indoors shouting, 'Mother, there's somebody in the lav.' The reply would come, 'Alright then, use the bucket behind the door.'

We only had one sink to wash in and we just had to take our turn. I wasn't bothered about the washing too much, though mother managed to get at me with her flannel and poke about up my nose and in my ears. The towel was sometimes a piece of sacking or a flour sack. They were made of white cotton and if you cut them up and boiled them it wasn't too bad. Hessian sacking was the worst - you just couldn't dry yourself as it is not very absorbent.

The furniture was old yet serviceable: a sofa, two armchairs, three or four other chairs, a Singer treadle sewing machine, a square deal table with very Victorian legs and a tall mahogany sideboard with three mirrors. If I went near the sideboard, I was told, 'Don't you dare put a mark on that, your grandfather will skin you,' and I think he would.

After my father's mother died he was sent to live with an aunt. She lived in Lees Hall, a big Tudor house. Dad told me he slept in a big room upstairs, called the ballroom. Evidently all that was in the room by way of furniture was his single bed. One winter it was so cold that the mouse that shared his room was found frozen to death. I used to say, 'Dad, tell me about when you were a boy.' He told me that one of his jobs on Saturday morning was to drive with a pony and trap to Ravensthorpe for the village laundry and if he was standing about the street corner, his grandfather would come up to him and say, 'Stand up Herbert, here take this penny, now go and clean my boots.' His grandad Steven was quite strict and did not like slovenliness.

Mill Bank
Mother and dad would take my sister and I to Mill Bank. Now our Great Aunt Florrie Hepworth lived there in a tiny cottage by the side of an old wagon way, belonging to Combs Pit. Years earlier most of the coal went on the wagon way to the canal to be loaded on to barges. The cottage stood in a small orchard, all nice and quiet. Aunt Florrie, an old lady, seemed to know all the remedies for ant bites, sprains, bruises and stings. When we went visiting the sun seemed always to be shining. I wandered about looking in to everything, what a wonderful place to live.

About 1938 we had to leave our allotment along with the other people. It was very sad as some nice people had their huts and some had old railway coaches as summer houses, all nice and friendly. There was always a cup of tea going and ice cream when

Rare Birds

Jocky Clegg arrived with his pony and cart. The cart had four poles, one at each corner painted like a barber's pole in red, blue and white, a real smart turnout. Old Paul Senior would send me to tell Jocky that he would give him five shillings for all the ice cream he had left and this was shared out among everyone there.

I enjoyed being among the old folk as they told some good tales. The old men always seemed to have time for me as I was very keen to hear what they had to say. I remember them talking of the Boer War - I suppose some of them had been soldiers then and of course, the Great War was often referred to.

Paradise and Back of the Moon
Some weekends dad and mother would take us up to see our relations at Thornehill. Great Uncle Bill was quite small and bad on his legs. He had been a bit of a lad and done some shooting in his time. He also ran a book, that is for betting on horses and dogs, and he could swear. I heard him a time or two. We would walk up an old track from Thornehill Lees, it was called Paradise, lovely, all fields and hedges, I bird nesting as we went.

The track wound uphill for quite a distance and just over the hill, under a belt of trees, stood three cottages. Some distant relatives of ours lived there. It was called The Back of the Moon. The people were called Broadhead. If we turned to the right and followed the road it brought you to Whitley, past the pub, the Whistling Blackbird and on to Denby Dale. We walked down Dead Man's Lane and looked up at the rocks. Dad said that years before some owls were seen walking up and down a ledge up there and the person had gone home and told everyone that he had seen little people up there. I believe quite a crowd had gathered to look. Then we would go down to Lady Wood where the old iron furnace was beside a pond with plenty of frogs, everything ancient and lovely. Even now I think of those days and how many miles we walked, meeting people, stopping for a chat then away we would go, and all that before the War.

The raft
Whitsuntide was a special time - mother made clothes for my sister and me, short grey flannel pants and grey jacket for me and a dress for our Joan. Mother had got us both ready for the Whitsun Parade, something to do with the church and chapel. I was washed and

dressed ready. One of my mates called at our house and said there was a raft being made on a pond, Pit Dams, and it would be ready any time, and would I come with them. Well, mother had told me to stay about the house and keep clean.

I didn't need much persuading. It was a lovely hot afternoon, just the kind of weather for raft sailing. 'Come on, let's get away quick.' Where the pond was there were a lot of pit ponies turned out for the holidays. Some more lads were there with the raft, not much of a raft for a lad was already on it and water was washing all round his feet. A long pole was used to propel the raft.

'Go on, have a go, kid,' someone said to me. The sailor before me jumped off and the raft returned to the surface. On I jumped and immediately black water came into my shoes. I pushed off with the pole and managed to get out about the middle of our pond and there I stuck. Shoving and pushing made things worse, I just stirred up the thick, black mud.

By now I looked like a Dalmatian dog with black spots on the light grey pants and jacket. My white ankle socks had taken on a very dark grey shade. I knew what Robinson Crusoe must have felt like. I was marooned. It was only a small pond but at that moment the bank seemed to be a mile wide.

'Brian, Brian,' I knew that voice. I looked towards the way we had come to the pond. I could make out my mother's head and shoulders above the tall grass. 'Brian, Brian,' she could see the lads standing about the pond edge. I was lower down, being on the water. 'Have you boys seen our Brian?' she asked as she pulled herself out of the tall grass and on to the pond side.

'You bugger, you buggeroo Ranter. Wait till your dad sees you. Come here, come here.' 'I can't move it' I said. 'Come here,' shouted mum.

I did a lot of pushing and shoving. I was doomed, I was trapped, there was nothing for it. I stepped off the so-called raft, which came to the surface immediately and waded ashore, almost to my waist in black mud. I was marched home, watched by my mates. It hurts me to think of what happened after that. I do know I spoiled the day for mother, it seems as though I was trouble to her all my life!

Saturdays in winter, my father went to watch the rugby league. He loved it and when he arrived home it would be nearly dark. Mother would sometimes have some kippers for his tea. I sat by the black iron range with the kippers held in a wire fish toaster, the oil from them dripping on to the fire and flaring up and lighting the room as the fish was blackened by the smoke. We usually had celery in a jug of water and a small bowl of salt to dip it in. Toasting the pikelets was my job too, sometimes there was a pile on the plate in the hearth, it all being done by the cosy light of the fire.

Dad would let Joey the budgie out. He was caught flying outside by my dad, someone must have lost him, he was never claimed. I have seen Joey paddle about on the table and then walk on dad's dinner plate and wade in the gravy. Dad never seemed to mind.

We didn't have a wireless at that time. Father had to borrow a paper from someone to see if he had won anything on the football pools. Sometimes we would all sit by the fire, the light out and mother would say she could see strangers coming by staring at the fire!

Sister Beryl

In the year 1938, my sister Beryl Ann was born. I was packed off to Thornhill Lees to my Aunt Mary's, and sister Joan was placed closer to home at Aunt Evelyn's at Bank Top. I remember my dad taking me on the bus with a carrier bag in which were the few clothes I had. It was evening when we arrived as dad had been at work and then had his dinner, washed and changed his clothes, so it was quite late. My Uncle John was very severe, my Aunt Mary lovely and very kind. My cousin Arnold, who was just a few weeks younger than me, and I, were to sleep together in the back bedroom. We were put to bed directly. I was a bit uneasy as it was my first time away from home and Dinky, my dog.

How I slept I don't know but I was awakened early by the noise of the milking machine next door at the farm. I was up before everyone else. This early rising did not please Uncle John as it was Saturday and he was not working. We were sent to Mather Broadhead's farm for the milk. The Broadheads were some relation to my uncle. I liked the farm and would have stayed there. Cousin Arnold said we had best get back or we would be in trouble with his dad. Next day, Sunday, we all got ready and away we went to Ossett, to a tiny little chapel. We travelled by bus and there was a fine old walk at the end of the ride. Before the service began I was given a pencil and a bit of paper and told to draw on it and to keep quiet by Uncle John. There were so few people in the place and it was all very queer to me.

After the service all the people left except us. We sat there with some sandwiches. In the afternoon there was another service. I was fair fed up with all the sitting. I was used to being out and about with Dinky. Uncle John was not pleased with me. I had soon tired of drawing and was fidgeting about. He very soon told me what to expect when we got home. I was pulled and pushed and got to thinking Uncle John didn't like me, and I did not like him.

Tea was some sort of fish which I said I didn't like. 'You will eat that fish, or else.' 'No, I don't like fish.' Uncle John grabbed me, tied my hands behind my back and stood me on a stool in the kitchen and forced the fish down my neck. So, taking it all in all, it was not a very good start of my stay at Thornhill Lees.

On Monday morning Uncle John was away, he was chauffeur to a wealthy mill owner somewhere. Cousin Arnold and myself were packed off to Arnold's school. We both carried a brown paper carrier bag with some slippers inside, we had a fair walk to the school.

The day went well. It was a nice school, everything new to me, and time passed quickly. After school, Arnold and I walked towards home. We were supposed to be going to Mather Broadhead's farm for tea. As we got to the canal I said to Cousin Arnold, 'I'm going home.' I just left him there and set off the five or six miles to Bank Top, my home. I was seven years old.

When dad got home from work I was sitting on the doorstep waiting for him. By God, he wasn't pleased to see me. He gave me a few good clouts and a bit of strong language. I curled up with Dinky in the chair and had to be awakened up as dad was taking me back to Uncle John at Thornhill. As soon as I landed there I was put to bed. I could hear dad and Mary talking downstairs, I suppose it was about me. On Friday night I was in bed asleep, when I awoke suddenly to hear dad's voice saying, 'Do you want to come home?' Home? I was out of that bed and out of that house fast, it was too much a prison for the likes of me.

The next day dad told me that the day I had run away from Thornhill, sister Joan and Aunt Evelyn had seen me walking home. They had been on the bus coming to see me. Dad said we had a baby sister and we would go and bring mother home with the baby and so I landed home. The neighbours never let me forget the day I ran away.

Shortly after that we went on holiday for the first time to Bridlington. It was September and I remember the warm and sunny tune *South of the Border down Mexico Way* being played. I developed earache, my dad was not pleased with me. Our accommodation was a small caravan. It was made of plywood and was very primitive with a canvas lean-to that was the cooking place.

We were very cramped in that caravan. I opened the door next morning and a shoal of earwigs dropped out - they were everywhere. The plywood was coming apart and the earwigs found it a good spot to live.

Because I wasn't well, dad said he would take me out to sea fishing at six the next morning. I was told if it made me sick I would feel better. So, fishing we went and I enjoyed it and caught some whiting and saw how the fishermen cut up the small fish to use as bait and how to open mussels, which they also used as bait.

Well, I wasn't sick but a few of the others were. When we docked dad took me into a cafe on the dock where we had Bovril and biscuits to warm us up. It seems that I bucked up after the cruise, I made pals with another lad and had a good time.

Dinky had a litter of pups. When they got to waddling about I would get them all to follow me. I loved to play with them and even when they were asleep I would put my face among them - I thought their breath smelled of onions. I was very happy with them. One by one the pups were sold. I cried many a time, and always asked the people who bought them where they lived and could I come and visit the pups. I had names for them all - Inky, Pinky, Blacky, Browny, were some of the names. Over the years Dinky had more pups, (her nest was in the corner by the oven, it was nice and warm there).

While we were on holiday War had been declared. Little did I know how it would affect our lives; everything seemed to change. At first I thought it was a game, but I soon changed my mind.

School

I don't think I was doing too well at school. My elder sister was about two classes ahead of me and the teacher would say to me, 'You are not as bright as Joan.' I am sure I wasn't.

I wasn't really interested in school, only when there was a party or something else. We used to collect jam jars and if they were dirty, we would wash them out. Two pound jars were worth one penny, and one pound jars were worth a halfpenny. All the jars were stacked up in the school cloakroom, hundreds of them by the time we had finished collecting. Then a man came and bought them all. I am sure they went to the pickle factory in Earlsheaton.

Us lads went on the tips and rummaged about among all the rubbish. Most of what we found was dirty, so we took them to the beck and washed them. We had two wheeled carts, old pram wheels and a wooden box and two shafts nailed on. Most lads had a cart in those days.

School parties were fun, but the best part was the time when we each received a small bottle of pop and a French bun. The bun was a tea cake with icing on it. The money for the party came from all the jam jars we collected. You didn't get owt for nowt them days.

Winter days at school we would sit on the hot water pipes that ran along the wall in the classrooms. Chilblains were very common as we got more snow in them days, much more.

Charley Jackson's stall (1940-41)

I remember it was winter and early morning. The light from the acetylene lamp threw yellow light over the tin bath where I worked behind Charley Jackson's grocery stall.

My job was scrubbing celery, and I had a heap of the stuff beside me. My ganzie sleeves rolled up, I was up to my elbows in water, cold water. The stiff scrubbing brush I held with difficulty - my hand was so cold that I held it without feeling it. Any outer stems that were slug damaged I dressed off with a knife. When Charley had inspected the celery and was satisfied it was clean, it was laid on the stall. There was a demand for it in those days.

I would be nine years old when Charley put me to work. It happened like this. Charley Jackson's greengrocery boxes, crates and sacks that were going to his market stall were loaded on to one of the Riley brother's lorries the afternoon before. I sometimes helped and was usually given an apple or whatever there was. The lorry loaded, it was sheeted up and ready for the early start next morning and driven into the old barn by our home.

I had watched Charley dressing lettuce and cabbages, taking the outer leaves off, the ones that were yellow or eaten by slugs. He must have thought me useful because he asked me, 'Do you want to go work on the market stall on Saturdays?'

At 7am the lorry with Harry Ripley, Charley and me set off. The rows of stalls were all lit with lamps, and the market men were still bringing more of them from a building close by. The lamps were large, only two at a time could be carried. Heaps of dirty snow had been shovelled into any spare space. Some snow lay between the close packed stalls, trampled upon and dangerous to walk over. A council wagon was moving away loaded with it. I had seen the drivers at times open up a grate in the road, tip the snow into the sewer below, shovel in what was left, replace the grating and away for another load. Gangs of men, many of them building workers, were paid by the council for clearing the footpaths and roads, the building work being at a standstill owing to the weather.

Charley threw some green matting which looked like grass over his stall, and then placed the vegetables and fruit on top - heaps of potatoes and cabbages, sprouts and a place left for my celery.

Two weighing machines were put out, one at each end of the staff, the weights besides them. Various sizes of brown paper bags hung from nails. Below them were paper carrier bags with Chas. Jackson stamped on them, hanging at each end of the stall. These were only used for people who purchased several items.

It would be 8 o'clock when Harry Riley drove the lorry away. There were still vehicles arriving as they had been held up by the bad roads on which snow had lain for weeks. Snow chains were fitted to many vehicles, that had to be about in the bad weather. As they went along the wheel chains cut the snow which was hard-packed into squares and made patterns.

Back at the stall my tin bath which was called a semi-bungalow bath, because of its size. Each size had a name and was set up on two empty crates. It was too high for me to work in comfort. I was given an iron bucket and told to fetch water, 'The tap's over there by the lavatories.' I had to pick my way amongst the stalls and I found it exciting. I knew one stall holder, Sheila Jackson, who had two stalls, selling bacon and cheese. A queue was forming, rationing had start and ration books were used. The stall holder was only allowed to sell you food such as meat and eggs if you had the necessary coupons.

I found the water tap but it wasn't a tap like ours at home. The iron pipe the thing sat upon was very thick and a large iron plate about as big as a dinner plate with some lettering on it was fixed to the wall. In the centre of the plate an iron handle stuck out something like the handle on a butcher's steel.

Setting my bucket beneath the thing I turned the handle. It turned and turned, but no water came out, so I tried the opposite way, but still no water. Men were coming and going to the lavatory. Eventually a chap stopped on his way out and asked, 'What's up lad?' 'I want some water mister.' 'Come here, I'll show yer. Look just pull it towards yer then turn it, alright?' 'Yes.'

'Where yer been?' asked Charley when I got back. It was starting to get light and he was busy serving customers. 'Get three more, look sharp.'

I scrubbed celery and dressed it. I could have cried - my arms were blue with the cold. 'Here, dry yourself on that potato sack. Come and have a drink.'

Charley's wife had arrived to help him serve. She had a basket with a packet of sandwiches and a Thermos flask of tea. 'Put yer coat on lad.' She helped me with it. The tea was good, the sandwiches I ate though the pasty stuff in them wasn't to my liking.

It was now properly light. It was December and the snow was coming down again. It was starting to get busy with people doing the weekend shopping.

'Do some more sticks will ya?' Charley was busy and my celery, wrapped in newspaper, was selling well. Charley's apron pockets were heavy with change. He went to a small wooden box and started to empty them, copper into one compartment, silver the other. His wife was small and had to stand on a box to serve the customers. She had a tin box for her change. She sometimes threw the money into it and now and then a coin missed and I was told to pick it up. First I had to find the coin among the snow and ice.

The water in my bath was muddy, with about one inch of sludge on the bottom. 'Get some clean water will yer lad? Just tip that out. Be careful, not all at once.'

I struggled through the throng of folks to the tap. There I had to wait. Other chaps were there. They had two buckets each. 'Come on lad, get yer bucket filled. Look sharp.'

I made three journeys and it warmed me up a bit. Back at my bath I had to rinse some of the previous sticks as Charley said they were too mucky. I was given tea and bite now and then. Quite a pile of celery lay on the stall. I watched Charley and his wife weighing vegetables and pouring them into bags. Later in the afternoon trade slackened and by 3pm the celery trade went quiet. It was quite dark under the stall roof. We started getting things ready to go home as the lorry arrived at 5pm. The stall was finally empty. The un-sold vegetables were put in crates, the fruit into boxes, eventually the grass mats were folded, and all was ready.

I was frozen. Ice lay all about our stall, the water that I tipped from my tin bath had frozen and was dangerous. The cabbage leaves and other green things that had fallen during the day made moving around worse. A chap with a barrow full of sand passed us, 'Hi,' Charley called, 'chuck us a shovel of sand behind the stall, mate. Here you are two shillings.' We got a double shovel full and he got his two bob.

The lorry was late. 'There's hold-ups - Wakefield cutting is an ice sheet. Daren't go down it, had to go via Earlsheaton,' Harry said, 'and we'll have to go that way home.' Everything was loaded and a sheet thrown over it and well fastened down. We all crowded in the cab. It wasn't much warmer in there. I snuggled between Charley and his wife. We were moving, only just, the wheels were spinning. Finally we were on the main road, where the going was better as cinders and sand had been thrown down. It was snowing again. We were all very quiet, no doubt wondering would we get home.

We did eventually get there. Charley gave me two half crowns and said he wanted me on the market next Saturday.

'I was worried sick,' our mother said, 'look at you - what a state you're in. Come on, let's give you a wash. Stand by the hearth.' It felt good to have my backside against the high fender - it was the first time that day I had felt any heat on my body.

Later, my tea over, my two half crowns lay beside my plate. I was rich. I turned them over many times. I would go with Charley Jackson next week.

Fred Thornes, the coal man

At the beginning of the War, dad had to go on directed labour as he was not fit for soldiering owing to him having a bad arm. He was sent to the wire works at Ravensthorpe where barbed wire was made for the troops. How long he was there I don't know. Later on in the war, dad was at Burton Wood, Warrington, attached to the Americans as that was their base. Dad said it was a really big aerodrome. He stayed there until after the war ended. We didn't see much of him at that time.

I went a little wild at that period having no dad to keep me right. I had started to work with the coal man. We went for the coal to the Manor Haig Pit at Wakefield. It was a good ride out for me. I liked the old battered wagon, all tied up with wire and string. It was always overloaded when we left the pit.

In the pit yard we backed the lorry up to the coal chutes and while Fred was filling the bags, I was away to look around. Up above the coal chutes were the screens down which the coal came. The small coal dropped through the holes in the iron screen, all the dust and slack dropped through as well so that only good coal went into the sacks. Up above the screens there was a large building made of iron sheeting and in there a conveyor belt worked. As the tubs of coal came from the pit head, the tubs were tipped over, the coal fell on the conveyor belt and was carried to the screens. Young boys stood on each side of the conveyor belt and their job was to pick out all the slate and pieces of shale from the coal and drop the stone down a chute at their side.

I liked the pit. I liked the muck and I loved delivering the bags of coal. My job was to go on ahead of Fred and get people to unlock the coal house or as maybe the iron grate that was set in the footpath. These grates had a long chain attached to them to stop people opening the chute and entering the premises. Wherever we delivered coal my job was to shovel any coal that was left at the side into the chute and clean up before we moved on.

Sometimes Fred would go for the money and have a cup of tea. I was left in the lorry and in winter it was freezing. When at the end of the day I got home, mother said, 'Where have you been? Look at you. Black as black. Did he pay you??' 'No, he didn't.' 'Well, get yourself washed and get your tea.' The price you pay for learning - I was young and daft.

There were some water troughs outside the stables. Sometimes on hot days I would sit with bare feet in the water. If Tebby saw me he would shout at me and chase me away. He was old and I suppose not at all well. Then the coal man, Fred Thornes, he lived up there with his mother and father and a sister who I never met.

Their house was a gaunt sort of place, stone built. You hardly ever saw it without a light on. It was called Breeze Lee House. They kept an old grey parrot and in summer on warm days they hung the cage with the bird in it on the wall. It sometimes squawked and climbed about the bars of its prison. Its name was

Polly, all parrots are called Polly, or so it appears!

The coal man, Fred, as everyone called him, brought our coal and later as I grew older I was his mate in the old two ton Ford wagon. I caught rats about his place too. In winter when Fred, the coal man, came home at night. He would park his old lorry under the lean-to at the back of his house. When the engine had stopped, he lifted the bonnet up and opened two taps on the engine side and let all the water out so that it would not freeze at night and crack the engine block. Next morning the taps were turned off, hot water was poured in the radiator and the engine started with a handle. There was no anti-freeze then.

The Goats and the Small holding
The coal man had a small holding - a long, narrow field. It would be about ten acres and was quite steep. It ran from the village, just behind Butterfields, the plumbers' shop, almost to Earlsheaton Railway Station goods yard. At one time he had six goats and these had to be milked twice a day. He had some North Holland blue hens too, some pigs and a goose or two.

I started my visits there when I was about ten years old. He would only take me now and then. Time went by and I used to go on my own and look about the place. Anyway, the coal man let me have a go at milking. I started off on Old Nanny as he called her. I soon got the hang of that job. Each goat had its own standing in the goat house and its own trough for the cake that was given to each animal just before it was milked. When we had milked them all, the milk, about two buckets full, was carried down the hill to a small cabin where a table with some bottles and tops for them were kept. We poured out the milk into bottles through a strainer with a wad inside it. The wad collected the hairs and any small bits that had fallen into the bucket while the milking was going on.

I started feeding and watering the hens, yes, and a few ducks too. The water for the goats had to be carried from a spring at the far side of the field, up the path to the goat house, about 150 yards away. My arms got very tired.

The pigs were kept inside a building made of bricks and blocks. They were really big pigs, sometimes they knocked a wall down inside the building. I used to pour the swill over the wall into their trough. I daren't go inside the sty, they would have eaten me!

As time went by, I spent most of my spare time at the small holding and less time on the coal round. I could hunt rats there as well and now and then a rabbit would appear. Then I would have a right tally ho after it. It was a busy time. I was now more or less in charge of the farm as I called it. The docks were to cut and we started to plough some of the land.

Fred, the coal man, had another old Ford wagon made in about 1925. We took the whole of the back off the chassis and took the tyres off. The metal wheels were holed drilled in different places and cleats were bolted onto the wheels. This gave the lorry plenty of grip on the soil. Then a short chain of about fifteen feet was fastened to the chassis of the lorry as far back as we could and the old single furrow horse plough was fastened to the chain. So now it had been made as good as we could, we set out to try our tractor-cum-wagon out!

I was only ten and not very big and was put behind the plough. It was no good putting me in the wagon as I couldn't drive it. So I took hold of the handles of the plough. Fred let in the wagon clutch and we moved off. I should say I was dragged off. A horse plough is no small tool. To start to plough, the handles must be lifted up to get the nose or share into the ground. The plough was dragged along on its side. I couldn't shout, I had nowt to shout with. My clogs full of soil and stones I was out of wind very soon. Fred's face appeared at the back window of the wagon. He stopped and walked back to me and looked at the trail the plough had made. It didn't look much like ploughing to me either and I wasn't an expert on that.

'We'll try it uphill, it might go better,' said the coal man. He went back to the cab and away we went. We made a mark a bit deeper this time as the plough and me went from side to side. 'Keep it straight,' shouted Fred. I was just managing to hang on to that plough. It went where it wanted and just looked as if a drunken snail had been up the field. How long we kept at it I don't know but it was a long time before we tried it again.

If I remember correctly, the coal man got a man with a tractor and plough to do the job right. I wasn't at all sorry as I was fair bruised about by the coal man's invention.

Harry Bloggs' petrol
And so time went by. By the time I was eleven I was quite a farmer. I was more or less looking after the holding on my own. Fred, the

coal man was spending much time at Harry Bloggs' place at Flushdyke where we got our petrol.

The petrol pump was old. It was a tall metal cylinder with a glass bowl on the top of it from which a rubber hose hung down. Halfway down the pump was a handle which you had to turn. It lifted the petrol from the underground tank up to the glass bowl on top. When the bowl was full it held one gallon. At the lower end of the hose there was a heavy brass tap with a short pipe on it. This was inserted into the vehicle's petrol tank. The tap was turned on and the petrol ran out of the glass bowl by gravity. The process was repeated until you had the amount of petrol required. It could take quite a while and on a wet day it was a miserable job.

Harry Bloggs' wife Jane worked the pump and took the money and petrol coupons, for petrol was rationed. I spent many hours in the old lorry waiting for the coal man. On winter's days, motors did not have heaters like today.

Fred the coal man, spent a lot of time in the house with Jane Bloggs!! Sometimes, on our way home, we would stop at another coal man's house. He was called Jimmy Dibbs. Why we stopped there I never knew. He had a daughter that helped him. The Dibbs didn't keep goats or hens as did the Bloggs family. Maybe Fred was just being friendly to the other coal man?

Another journey we made about once a fortnight was to Brighouse. We went there for animal feed - cattle cake for the six goats and meal to make mash for the hens and pigs. Brighouse was a long way off or so it seemed to me. I loved the ride out there. It took us about half a day for the journey. Then something happened, what I never knew. The coal man told me that he had finished with the holding, that I was to stay away from the place as it did not belong to him anymore. I was devastated - I had lost my farm and my shooting too, as for a while I had an air rifle that Fred gave me as he never gave me any pay, only milk and eggs. So that was the end of my farming life for a while anyway.

Some weeks after the coal man gave up the small holding I sneaked there again. I was wondering what had happened to all the stock. The place was very quiet, not a hen or duck to be seen. The pig sty was empty, grass and weeds had started to grow about the cabins. The place was very sad to see and the path to the spring from which I carried all the water was starting to grow over.

I took myself up to the goat house, it was so still. I expected to hear a chain rattle or a goat bleat at my approach, but there was nothing, just stillness. The door was just a little bit open - I shoved it wide. I thought they were asleep. All the goats were in their stalls, laying as though resting. They all were dead and had been for a few weeks, the bodies mummified. I turned one over, the maggots had eaten everything apart from the bones and upper skin. I was out of that place like a shot and into the sunshine.

Wondering what awful thing had done that to my goats, I told my mother what I had seen. She said I should keep away from the place and keep away from the coal man too. I was very sad at what I had experienced; I could never understand it.

Alan Quincey and the air rifle battle
Air rifles were quite popular among some of the older lads. Alan Quincey had one, so had Golly Tempest and Alan Scott. I would at times be bird nesting about their territory. I had to be on the lookout at all times as they would open fire on me. A small beck with bushes overhanging it passed through the Quincey Tempest Territory. Being shallow I could with luck pick my way along the beck bottom, looking for nests on my way and keep out of sight at the same time.

On my rounds I did sometimes travel along the track that led to some allotments belonging to the Stocks family. Turning the corner it brought me into view from the Stocks' back door. One day I thought I had passed unseen, until I heard, 'Where are you going, Aston?' 'I'm going home, Colin.' He was a big lad, was Colin Stocks and could be a nasty bugger into the bargain. Colin raised his air rifle and fired - the pellet hit my leg beside the knee. 'Bugger off then,' he said as he loaded the rifle again. My knee hurt and blood was on my hand from holding it. I was wounded. I ran home. Mother was there, I showed her my wound and told her who had caused it. 'Well, keep away from Colin Stocks, then.' Not much sympathy in those days.

I had gone one day to see Alan Quincey. His mother said he was out in front of the house. As I approached the front of the house, I found myself caught in an air rifle battle. A balcony was cantilevered out with a low wall built upon it. Behind the wall, kneeling down, were Alan and Alan Scott. Both had rifles and kept peeping over the wall only to duck down when a pellet was fired at them. 'Get down, Asty,' they shouted.

Golly Tempest and his older brother were behind a wall about twenty yards away. They too were armed with rifles. A lot of shots were fired. I don't know if anyone was hit. I crawled away and went home. I had been shot once and didn't like it.

Mr Quincey was the engineer for Porritts, the cabinetmakers. His job was to look after the huge horizontal engine that made all the power needed to drive the machines and make electricity as well. It was painted a nice, dark green and shone all over. Mr Quincey was hardly ever without a bit of rag in his hand.

Occasionally we were allowed to enter the engine house and watch the piston going in and out and the cylinder, the big flywheel whizzing round and round. What the governors were for, I was later to understand more about it.

Colin Scott's father was a builder and had a large yard where all sorts of materials lay in heaps. There was a building too where stone was dressed into gravestones. I watched the old man cut in the letters with a sharp chisel and a wooden mallet. He was never in a hurry. Sometimes rifle practice took place there but Mr Scott would say, 'Right, you lot, go on home,' and lock the yard gate on us. Eventually I got an old rifle from the coal man. The spring was weak but I thought the world of it. I was armed at last.

One day mother was out shopping. I went upstairs, the front bedroom window was open a little. We had lace curtains, long ones that covered the whole window. I fired a pellet at the door of one of the cottages opposite. Nothing happened and so more shots followed. The door was flung open and Clifford stood glaring at my window. He was shouting at me. I had ducked down quick. He had seen the curtain move. He was mad and I was scared. I took my rifle and hid it, fearing someone would smash it. I had been threatened before with that.

Harry Benn and the bike
The war was almost over. Bicycles were in demand as very few, if any, were manufactured at that period owing to the War Effort, as it was called. I had been saving my money in an old cocoa tin. I had been to a small holding not far from my home, it was owned by a butcher called Harry Benn.

He had some goats and as I was interested in goats, I would go now and then to have a look at them. In an old shed I saw a bicycle. I took it outside to have a good look at it, not much of it really. The frame, wheels, chain and the saddle were not much good and it needed brakes, mudguards and new handle bars.

The wheel size was twenty-four by one and three eighths. I sat on the bike, it was just my size. Putting it back where I found it, I waited until Harry Benn came out of his house. 'Mr Benn, that old bike in yon shed, is it for sale?' 'I don't know, we'd best have a look at it.' We got the bike out again. 'It's a good bike,' said Harry Benn, 'it would fetch a few pounds in the right place.'

My heart sank, a few pounds. I didn't have a few pounds. 'Does it fit you?' 'Aye, it's my size alright. Can I buy it?' 'I'll think about it, lad. Put it back will you. I'll see you later.'

My mind was on that old bike all week and on Saturday afternoon I was at Harry Benn's holding again. He was usually at his butcher's shop until late Saturday night. Today he was at home. I hung about waiting to see if he would mention the bike. He was making a tractor from an old car. It was much smaller than the one that the coal man and I made some time before.

'Have you thought about that bike, Mr Benn?' 'Oh, aye, the bike, you can have it for fifty bob.' I walked back home. I knew that I was a lot short of fifty bob. I went back later that evening and asked Harry Benn if he would keep the bike until I had enough money. He said the bike was mine when the money arrived.

I remember paying Harry Benn a ten shilling note and the rest in all sorts of coins. I wheeled my bike onto the road - was I pleased with my purchase. Much more money was needed for repairs and parts. Uncle Bill did a lot of the work and helped with the spare parts, he being a keen cyclist himself.

I later acquired an old dynamo, it was worn and if the tyres were wet, the drive wheel wouldn't grip - no grip - no light! I was working for the cobbler at that time. My 3/3d wages were much reduced as I had to give mother 2/6d out of it. The 9d I had left plus a few pence in tips didn't go far. Eventually I bought a cycle cap and some gauntlets and a pair of waterproof leggings. It took years to save the money. I eventually grew out of the bike and it was sold and a bigger one bought.

The old toll gate at the top of Old Bank was not used when I was young, like many things it was obsolete. The house was used as a Penny Shop and there were three or four more cottages in the row. I remember the Manor Croft Dairy that lay directly behind these houses being on fire. Furniture was piled out on the road and there was much running about, people carrying whatever was to be saved. The dairy was gutted, cans of cream were exploding in the heat, flames were high in the sky and huge clouds of smoke hung over the area. The cottages were saved. Later I wondered how could a dairy catch fire, milk doesn't burn, or does it?

When snow was on the ground lots of lads and girls would sledge down Old Bank and Sugar Lane. Motor vehicles avoided these places as they were too steep for the old motors of the day.

The cobbler man
Albert Exley, the cobbler at Bank Top, had had his eyes on me for some time. I was hovering about Tebby Gibson's stable yard, Tebby not being about. The cobbler had a shop at the entrance to the yard and the window where he worked looked out that way. One day the cobbler called to me from his shop door. Oh, hell, what had he seen me do? People only called to me to say that they would tell my mother that I done so and so. Or why didn't I go away and play elsewhere?

I was surprised when the cobbler asked me into the shop. Inside were two rooms, and as you went in a kind of counter with some advertisements for shoe polish and a few laces and odds and ends. Through a black curtain you went down a step and into the work room. I had never been in there before but had jumped up to have a look inside when the place was locked up at weekends. There was a machine for polishing soles and heels when the boots and shoes had been repaired. There was also a small iron stove on legs, raised up on bricks, a bucket of old soles and other bits of leather that were to be burned. On the work bench there was a thing like a small mangle but with concave rollers for rolling the soaked soles before they were nailed onto the welts of boots and shoes.

The cobbler sat himself down on a low bench. It had a place at the side to put the things he needed for his work. He was sewing soles on a pair of men's shoes. As he worked he said he was looking for a lad to help him as his lad had finished school and started work on the railway. Was I interested? Well, the cobbler's shop was handy for my home and right next door to Breeze Lee House where the coal man lived. Mr Exley, the cobbler, said I should think about it. I did think about it and decided I would work for the cobbler and at the same time keep an eye on the coal man, just in case he decided to start farming again.

And so began another chapter in my life. Dad was away at the war. I still set my traps in the old barn and I still went out with Dinky to the Tenter fields and Scott's field which by now had had a lot of old timber dumped upon it and was ideal for stacking up to make forts and dens. Sometimes I was called upon to take Dinky to the allotments as a rabbit was under one of the huts there. It was a busy time for us both. I was growing up, the cobbling job was my second job and I was only eleven years old.

I started after school on a Monday night. First I went home for a wash and tidy up. Mother said I must be smart on my first day. I parked my bike against the shop wall and went in. The bell rang, it was on a spring, all shops seem to have those bells that made you jump when the door opened.

My Exley looked me up and down. 'Go under the counter, you will find a shoe brush and a tin of polish. Give your clogs a clean.' That done, the cobbler had a black cloth bag in his hand. He showed me some shoes with a name on the sole done with black heel ball and the price as well and told me where to take them to. Did I know the place? No, he described the place, altogether there were three pairs to deliver and the cobbler said it was easy night for me.

So that was my job, after school, delivering shoe repairs. Some nights I would be busy, another nothing to take out and I just helping out in the workshop, taking off soles, sweeping up and making myself useful.

I should say that I quite enjoyed my cobbling days. I was paid 3/3d a week for five nights and Saturday morning. The cobbler was good to me and tried to teach me to be smart and polite to people and not to be conceited and call myself 'Mr'!

On Saturday morning I had to go to the bakers, Sam Rhodes, at Chickenly, to collect tea cakes and sponge cake for the Exley's weekend tea. Mr Exley was a very tall man. Sometimes I had to call at his home. He lived in a terraced house overlooking the cemetery where my grandmother lay buried. His wife was very pale looking, almost white. They had a son called Malcolm who was a bit of a mammy darling. Why he didn't work for his father I don't know?

And so now I had acquired a fair bit of knowledge. I could catch rats and rabbits. I could milk goats, feed hens and pigs. I had learned about delivering coal, how to work the petrol pump and done a bit of cobbling. Then I heard of a chap who wanted someone to deliver early morning papers. Laurence Day, he was called and he had a tiny shop at the Toll Bar. I wandered down and applied for the job. He seemed pleased to take me on. The wages were 6/6d per week for six mornings. He said he knew my mother - she must have been quite a lass in her day.

I had to be at the paper shop for 6.30am. A bag of papers were ready for me, every one with the address written on it. What a weight to carry. Well, the first morning was hard as I had to find my way down yards and not all the letter boxes were easy to find. Some boxes were so high I stood on my toes to reach, some boxes at the door bottom, some doors no boxes at all and I put the paper through the handle.

I improved as time went by. Being up early was no trouble to me but going to school after finishing my round was. Some weeks later one of the school teachers told me that I would be getting myself into trouble by doing two jobs. Evidently young children can only work so many hours in a day and I was doing too many. I was told I must give up one of them. I gave up the paper round and stayed with the cobbler as he gave me more time for my rat catching.

Fishing at Syke Mill Dam

Some of the lads at school used to go fishing in Syke Mill Dam, where there were a lot of bronze carp - so I turned my attention to fishing. I soon found that the fish were daft, least ways, in that dam. All that was needed to catch them was a bent pin, some bread, a length of thread and half a matchstick and you were in business.

That summer I spent a lot of my time catching fish and some men would come and fish with us. They were real fishermen and the fish they caught in our dam were bait for the pike fish that they were after on another water at a place called Wintersett. Us lads soon found we could sell the fish we caught to these chaps. I think we got 6d for four fish. Well, the weather being warm, some bigger lads got to swimming in the dam and so afore long we young ones joined them. The water wasn't too clean and many a time we came out of it dirtier than when we went in.

One of the lads said he knew of a pond with some big fish in it. The pond was in some private grounds. We arranged that one night at dusk we would go there. It was a warm summer's night, starting to get dark and lots of frogs were croaking. We could see the frogs' heads out of the water. Using the same tackle that we used at our dam, we got started. They were big fish and they were eager to be caught. I had one directly but it was too big for my jam jar. I couldn't get its head in the jar, never mind its body, so back the fish went. We had some good sport - now I had started poaching!

Conker time

It was a normal day in the school playground until some enterprising lad produced some conkers which were sold for half a penny each - they were soon gone.

As soon as school finished the great conker hunt was on. It was always the same - during October the lads began to take an interest in the horse chestnut trees and could be seen craning their necks and wandering about below, a piece of wood or stone in hand to throw at any fruit that looked ripe. Groups of boys spent hours with a piece of rope or a long pole, even climbing among the branches to get at the precious conkers. All the known chestnut trees were visited. Lads walked miles up hedgerows, even private gardens were not safe - it was a kind of madness among the young male population.

Where could the largest conkers be found? A lad showed a handful of beautiful chestnuts. 'Where did yer find 'em, kid?' We were told all sorts of lies, anything to keep the other boys away from the prized trees.

Days later, everyone had some in his pocket and conker battles were taking place on the way to school, in the playground, anywhere at all. All kinds of remedies were tried to make the conkers hard. It was thought the harder they were, the more lasting they became, therefore more victories could be won. Some were put in the oven, others soaked in vinegar and left until the following year. Drawers were turned out in the hope one of last year's conkers lay there.

A hole was made through the conker, as small as possible, just large enough to take the length of string. Several knots were tied at one end to prevent the string being pulled through. The two contestants took turns at striking each other's conkers. Sometimes the knuckles of the contestants were struck causing them to let go the conker while they nursed their bruised fingers. Arguments started, the person striking had not conformed to the rules and struck from the side not from above and had caused the two strings to become entwined.

After a few arguments one of the contestants would leave, stating that he had had enough of the cheating and would do battle elsewhere. When a fight was won a knot was tied on the string. The conker of the opponent must be broken to win. If the defeated had, say, six knots on his string they were claimed by the victor as his own. Eventually the conker fever died down but something else was soon to start another hunting fever.

Chumping
In mid-October, heaps of wood would appear on waste land, usually placed where an eye could be kept upon it. Each evening gangs of lads and girls foraged about the fields. Dead branches and old wood, anything that would burn, was dragged or carried to the ever-growing heap. 'Chumping' had started. November would soon be here and until then the various gangs would be out every night, ranging further afield, entering onto the territory of a resident gang. Now and then they met, fights took place and the older and stronger gang took away the branches or whatever the losers possessed.

Guards were mounted on the bonfires and raids were made on each other's heaps. Sometimes the raids were made late into the night when the younger gangs had gone home to bed. It was on the following morning that it was discovered - the bonfire had been pulled apart and the best chumps had been taken. How did it get the name chumping? I never knew, even today the word sticks. I have never heard of it anywhere else.

As it got nearer the 5 November, the fever grew more intense. Older people became involved, sides were taken and men were about the bonfires heaping the stuff that was brought, ever higher. Visits were made onto rival territory but at a distance to see how big their heap was and what were the chances of a raid being made. The best time would be on a rainy, windy night, when there would be hardly anyone about.

The York Road estate had been built on our old allotments, just after the war. Many rough families had been moved there and they united in the building of their fire. They could recruit many older and stronger lads and lasses.

After the war most things were in short supply and fireworks were one of these, but they could be obtained at Lepton, near Huddersfield. One lad I knew went there and bought direct from the Standard Fireworks Company. He stayed away from school to do so. Good profits were made by anyone willing to make the journey to Lepton, the fireworks were sold on again to lads such as me.

More rubbish was sent to our bonfire - old chairs, linoleum, mouldy rugs. We knocked on doors asking, 'Have you anything for our fire?' It was surprising what came from cellars and outhouses.

November 5th dawned and we went for a final look at our bonfire before setting off to school, the topic of conversation being fireworks. A banger was lit and thrown over the wall by the girls' lavatories. After the explosion and screaming died down the teacher took all our fireworks from us until it was time for home. Tea was bolted down and the gang assembled by the bonfire. Just after dark we started to get excited, fathers turned up and more and more people arrived. A couple of trestle tables were put up and brandy snaps, parkin pigs and ginger pop were set on them. There were apples and spuds in buckets to roast later.

The men started placing old sacks soaked in paraffin beneath the heap of wood and torches were made with rags soaked in paraffin tied to long sticks. The great moment arrived and the torches were lit then pushed among the old motor tyres. If it was a still, damp night the fire was slow and more paraffin was thrown upon the flames which rose high, starting to crackle and roar. Sparklers were held by the young ones, fathers let off the rockets, Roman candles and the rest. The brandy snap, slices of parkin and parkin pigs were handed round.

Some of the older people turned up, no doubt to remember their younger days. A while later as the fire died down a great heap of glowing ash remained. Potatoes were placed to roast and men with rakes and shovels tended them. Now and then there was a 'bang' as someone had discovered a firework, kept for the finale, among the string in a pocket. The crowd about the fire dispersed when it started to rain. I hung on a long time, looking for empty firework cases.

Back home and smelling of smoke I was given a wash. Small holes were burned in my pullover, mother said it was a good job I had the old one on. Lying in my bed, my mind full of the day's events and fireworks, fireworks, what a bonfire it had been. All the effort had been worthwhile.

Early next morning I was at the fire again, finding more empty cases. The rockets had not gone far, their sticks were standing up among the grass. I found rocket remains for a long time, well into the summer in fact. The bonfire fever was over, it had been a great time but when the snow came another fever would start - the sledging fever.

Scar End dam
Suicides were at times reported. Evidently the Scar End dam was the scene of a few of these. The dam was round and the sides were sheer. I believe it tapered towards the middle. I always thought it had a sinister look about it and kept away, an unusual thing for me to do. Now and then bodies were caught up on the dam stakes and would be talked about, as it was usually someone local.

Old Annie's
The old manor house in Earlsheaton was haunted. The place had been empty a long while. After school, lads went there and the door was open, across the passage was the cellar door. We dared each other to go down the dark, damp place. Some lad said, 'I'll go down!' We crowded in the doorway, he opened the door at the top of the steps and put a foot out. 'Go on, kid!' we urged. The dank smell of Old Annie's cellar was enough to scare anyone. I know my imagination conjured up skeletons hanging in chains, with huge bats clinging to the rib bones, rats as big as cats, great spiders with webs big enough to catch birds, secret passages that led to the church and the Park Mansion.

Highwaymen had frequented Old Annie's, as we called the place. Who Annie was I don't know. I suppose she was a witch. She could still be down there brewing evil potions and casting spells on lads like we. Maybe she slept in a coffin during the day, her broomstick at her side. Maybe she never slept and waited for a victim to enter her den. Shadows were seen to flit about the manor house at dusk - it had a sinister look about it. I know we lads kept clear of it.

The daredevil was frozen on the cellar steps, his mind, like mine, would have visions of the horrors below. We at the door, urged the victim on, 'Go on, kid, go on!' 'I'm going, I'm going!' he would say as he moved. Hardly had his foot touched the second step when there was something on the stairs. Someone said, 'It's the ghost!' The sound echoed loud then a crash, that was enough! A great shout came from us, everyone dashed out into the yard, the last one banging the door shut. We pulled up on the street and looked at the manor door. There was shouting, the door shook, more shouting.

What was the ghost doing? The door was thrown open, Woody, the daredevil emerged pale and tears down his cheeks. In our panic Woody had been shut in with Old Annie.

What was down in the cellar? Eventually one of our mates admitted to rolling a few small stones down the stairs, followed by a large one which made the crash. Later we visited Old Annie's, and armed with stones, we stood in the passage and pelted the gloomy vault below, daring anything to attack us.

The Blazing Rag Pit

It was called the Old Pit Road and just an old dirt track. No doubt it had been a tramway from the Blazing Rag Pit years before. The track was badly rutted where it passed between spoil heaps. Earlsheaton Cemetery lay on the right hand upon the high ground. Ghosts were seen there among the tall gravestones and trees.

At dusk I always walked quickly by, whistling or shouting, being brave and keeping a sharp lookout. I had been told of skeletons there, skulls resting upon their boney arms, leaning over the wall and beckoning travellers to enter their domain. I had heard that late on warm summer nights, the ghosts moved about the cemetery alone or in pairs and that several had been seen at one time.

Derek Collier, a cousin of mine played jokes on people. He was forever telling of places and buildings to keep clear of, because they were haunted by one thing or another. Later, as I grew up I discovered why more ghosts were seen in the cemetery on warm summer nights. Relatives visited graves and courting couples strolled there late on.

Two cottages stood alone, we stopped at these when mother took us walking. They were just beyond the cemetery and some old people we knew lived there. Close by, a red brick air shaft stood. It was circular and had been filled in years before. Some brickwork had been knocked down to make a narrow entrance at ground level. The filling had settled leaving a drop of about fifteen feet.

Dad often used the Pit Road, coming and going to work. Early one morning, about 6am, dad heard cries coming from the old air shaft. A tramp had evidently been looking for somewhere to spend the night and had fallen down. Rescuers arrived and the tramp was soon on his way again, none the worse for his fall. Many tramps passed that way and used the old Winding House as a resting place.

Later the same building had many barrels of tar stored in it and was kept locked. I was mooching about by the building one day when I saw that the door was open and went in.

'Now I got ya!' A man came from behind the door and got hold of me. 'It's you, you bugger isn't it? I know it's you, I have been watching you looking about.' 'I was looking for rabbits, mister.' 'Have you been in here before?' 'No, it's always locked, mister.' 'So you have been here before then?' the chap said. He was fair mad. 'I only looked through a crack in the door, mister,' I said. 'What about all this then?' He pointed to the far end of the building. Some of the wooden tar barrels were overturned, the thick, black tar spread over the dirt floor and among the remaining barrels.

'What's yer name?' he asked, still holding on to me. I told him my name and where I lived. I was threatened with the police. He would tell them he had caught me in his building where all the damage was done. I was pushed from the building and went home. I expected the police to come by they didn't. Eventually I forgot about it but I was a wary lad when passing that way again.

An old bridge built of sleepers carried the Pit Road out to the fields. The stream below was stained with iron oxide and tasted of salt and was quite warm having been pumped from far underground at the Shaw Cross pit. Sister Joan and I went paddling there with our mother nearby, our shoes and socks in a heap. I remember coming out onto the bank and our shoes and socks were covered in ants, hundreds of them.

Later, the area I mentioned was used as a council tip. We scrounged among the rubbish and brought away many jam jars which were sold to the pickle factory in Earlsheaton. Many gulls and other vermin lived on the rubbish and rats were plentiful. Donald and I bought a short-barrelled 12 bore shotgun. It was our first gun and we shot at gulls and owt else. The gun was dangerous and later we got rid of it. The next weapon was a double-barrelled hammer gun. Our shooting days started in earnest then and at times caused trouble too!

The Rhodes Family

What with school and the cobbling job at nights, fishing and spending much time about the farm, and exploring further afield, my time was taken up. I was now thirteen years old and was mixing with older lads and, of course, sometimes I called at their homes and was asked to come in. Most of them knew mother or father and so I was called 'young Aston'.

One family that I used to call on were the Rhodes family as their son George was one of my mates. The lad was a bit untidy, many lads were not too fussy how they looked then. The Rhodes family lived in a big, old stone house and it was old, and it had a stable and some outbuildings, all set on a hillside. A footpath went right past their door and on up the yard were two more cottages on Mill Lane.

Mr Rhodes, or Simon as he was always called, kept a pony, a dark brown one. She was called Dolly and was about thirteen hands at the shoulders. Dolly was used in a tub cart and sometimes pulled a flat cart. She was a bit of a flier when touched with the whip and she would go bareback for the lads.

There were three boys in the Rhodes family - Lionel, the eldest, Francis, second eldest and George or Plonk as he was called at school, and a girl, Sara. Mr Rhodes was a big man as was his wife. Simon Rhodes always seemed pleased to see us lads about the place.

Mr Rhodes' business was cleaning mills and mistels as they are called and then spraying the walls and roof with lime wash. The lower part of the byre walls was actually painted with Stockholm tar. These jobs were usually undertaken at the weekends when the lads were at home to help him.

Dolly, the pony, was yoked in the tub cart, then a big barrel of lime loaded in it, along with pumps, sprayers, brushes and a small barrel of Stockholm tar and a few buckets. Then how Simon got himself in was worth seeing. As he put his weight on the step at the back of the cart, the shafts tilted up and it looked as though Dolly would be lifted off the ground. The Rhodes lads grabbed hold of the shafts and helped hold the cart till Simon managed to wedge himself in. The three lads perched anywhere they could.

The springs of the cart were flat with all the weight on them. Simon would touch Dolly with the whip and all the lads on board would shout for her to get on, and away they would go along Jim Sheards and up the old pit road to some farm where they had work to do. The road was badly rutted and almost washed out in places.

I remember the Rhodes family, all of them, setting off in an old car, it fairly bulging with them. Later, one of the lads came back for the pony and a rope. The car was towed back home still crowded with the whole family, poor Dolly.

Close by the Rhodes family home, behind the house, was a small orchard and behind that, a shop quite newly built, the owner being Ivy Clare and her husband, Walter. They had two sons, Norman and Peter and a daughter called Barbara. She was infirm from something or other. Mr Clare kept a fine horse, a big, strong bay and a small well painted flat cart with a high driving seat upon it.

If we had any money we would probably get a bottle of pop and share it around. Some days Mr Clare sold ice cream and if we happened to be there, he would ask if we wanted to go for a ride. We lads would sit on the cart, our feet sticking out as we went. That horse could really go. The dairy where the ice cream came from was about three miles away and the round trip and nice ride. I liked horses and it was my ambition to be a horseman.

Willy Lumb's farm

The lads would hang about the farm during hay time and harvest when the men brought the horses back. It was quite late some nights, maybe nine o'clock. They were fed and watered and cooled down. Colin Pinder, the horseman, would say, 'Right, lads, get 'em away to the field.' Lads would each get a horse, walk it to the mounting steps, get on its back and, if too many lads, they would ride two to a horse.

The door was opened and down the lane they would go, the horses keen to be turned out for the night. Once the head collar was taken off, they would gallop and roll about in sheer joy at being free. We sometimes stayed awhile, leaning on the gate and just doing nowt. By the time we had got home it was quite late, a wash and to bed if you could manage it. I to bed without a wash! I wonder why young lads seem to be allergic to water with soap in it, yet they will play all day in a pond or a beck?

I slept well and I seemed to have outgrown my earache and other ailments and was enjoying life. Dad, when I saw him, would say, 'What are you doing with yourself?' When I said I spent a lot of time at the farm he would say, 'You'll never make owt on the farm.'

I was spreading my wings more and more. The lads I was at school with were going to the farms at Chickenly and to Willy Lumb's farm. The latter was a big old place, like Willy Lumb himself, a great big fellow. He spent most of his days and I believe the nights as well, in a building called The Light House. It was a long room above the cart sheds, with two large windows overlooking Water Lane, opposite Chickenly Hall.

Some of the old men gathered there during the day to smoke their pipes and talk, some chairs, piles of sacks, old harnesses and tools lay about the place. There was a big, open fireplace and the fire was lit on cold days. I thought it very cosy to get in there and listen and watch the old men.

A year or two before I had come to the farm with Herbert Exley, the butcher. We were there on a pig killing one Sunday morning. The butcher travelled the countryside with his humane killer, killing pigs on licence - you had to have a licence from the ministry. My job was to get the copper going and keep it going, as lots of boiling water was needed to scald the pig after it was killed. These Sunday morning outings usually took place just before Christmas and the bigger the pig, the better, as you were only allowed to kill one per year for yourself.

Peter Ratcliffe
Racker, we called him, but his real name was Peter Ratcliffe. He lived in the new steel houses, as we called them, built at Chickenly just after the war. He was a mate of ours, and was a few years younger. Peter appeared as though he had been running, always panting and a bit short of wind. We all went fishing together, some days when it was hot we gave up fishing and took to the water instead. Poor Racker wouldn't come in and swim, it knocked too much out of him. He would sit and watch and maybe carry on fishing.

The Ratcliffe family hailed from Kettleage, to give it the proper name, Providence Street. Peter Ratcliffe's grandparents lived there as well, almost at the bottom of the steep street. They were called Izaacs. Jim Izaacs worked in the mines with his son, Fred. I delivered milk to their home when at Grove Farm and knew them well.

The Izaac family were good shots and attended the clay pigeon shoots or anything else to do with shooting. Peter was taught to shoot but I never remember him being out with our posse. He was a good mate and on the days when he was well enough he was good fun to be with. I don't think we lads realised how Peter felt on his bad days. He was a little shorter than normal, with pale ginger hair and a white face heavily freckled. He was a likeable lad.

When Peter Ratcliffe left school he managed to get himself a trainee game keeper's situation somewhere in Kent. How long he stayed there I don't know. Anyway, Peter arrived home and said he would not be going back again. We all carried on more or less as before he had gone away. When I heard the news I wouldn't believe it, but it turned out to be true. Peter had killed himself. Evidently he had a bad day or two with bronchitis and had taken the gun he had into the kitchen. He said it was to clean it and then shot himself in the head.

He was found behind the kitchen door and a right bloody mess he made. He was buried along with his gun. It was a very sad occasion indeed. As I said before, us, his mates never realised how poorly poor Peter was. I know his grandparents took it very badly. Mrs Izaacs went very quiet and I don't think Jim, the grandfather, ever shot again. I know that over the years, I have thought of Peter. He will always be young in my mind. He just didn't live long enough to get old like us!

Wakefield and a body drowned

I must have been in my early teens and had acquired a bigger bike. I called it my racing bike because it had drop handlebars and a light frame. Anyway, it was different to what I possessed before and it had toe clips to stop my feet from slipping off the pedals, celluloid mudguards and cable brakes. So, to me, it was a racing bike. I once took off the free wheel cog and put a fixed gear sprocket in its place. I soon changed it back to the way it had been before as my legs had to keep pedalling when going downhill, I found it hard work.

I started to ride as far afield as Wakefield. I had seen a fishing tackle shop there, just below the Bull Ring. Many times I stood looking into that shop window; everything a man needed when going fishing was displayed therein. As time went by, I bought a rod from that shop. It was a plain, coarse fishing rod - I reckon it was the colour of it that I liked the best - it was a deep red mahogany colour. I saved up my pocket money and bought it. It was my pride and joy for a while.

One day I was riding to Wintersett Reservoir on a fishing trip. As I was passing Chantry Bridge, a crowd of people were gathered at a wall alongside the river. I, being nosey, got off my bike and joined the crowd at a weir across the river upstream of the bridge. Some men were carrying the body of a woman from it. She was wearing a pinafore and was quite small and looked fairly old. People did drown themselves in those days; now I had seen someone.

I made my journeys to Wintersett fishing to the two reservoirs which supplied water to the canals in that area. I was on another of my fishing trips alone and was at about the same place where the woman's body was found. Above the weir was a large stretch of water lined on one side by warehouses. Barges were often moored beneath these buildings, unloading their cargoes.

Today there was a lot of activity as the whole side of a warehouse had collapsed, letting tons of corn cascade into the river. Some of the lighter corn was floating in a yellow scum mixed with lime dust. It was a real mess, the fish would have plenty of food for a long time.

At Wintersett Reservoir good pike fishing could be had as well as roach and perch. The lower reservoir had a huge pump house - a beam engine was used to pump the water into the canals. As soon as the pumping commenced and the water started to flow, shoals of fish came to feed - the water being fairly shallow, one could see them plainly. When the pumping stopped, the fish went off the feed. I decided to have a walk about to see how the other fishermen had done. There was a water bailiff on duty - a ticket was needed before you started to fish. I spent many a day at Wintersett, some lovely summer days. I got to know how to fish for pike, live baiting. Some of the older men gave me bits of tackle now and then. I wished I lived much closer to that fishing paradise!

Clay pigeon shooting

The old men used to talk of live pigeon shooting when the pigeon was put in a wire fall trap. The trap was worked when a man pulled a string and the trap sprung apart releasing the bird. The man with the gun stood 25 yards behind the trap in which the bird was. When he shouted 'Pull', the cord to the trap was jerked, the trap sprung apart and the pigeon flew away. If the bird did not fly, the man with the gun could shoot it on the ground.

Sometimes the men would catch sparrows. A small trap was used for them, the shooter standing fifteen yards behind the trap. Live pigeon shooting was stopped, when, I don't know. The shoots were held on the field behind the Crown Hotel. They would have a sweep for so many birds, maybe 2s 6d for six birds. The man that killed the most birds, with the least shots, won the sweep. They would adjourn to the Crown and drink the winner's health.

With the shooting of live pigeons being stopped, clay pigeons were used. These small, solid targets were thrown from a mechanical trap worked by a man hidden away behind bales of hay or straw. The 'pigeons' as they were called, were not made of clay, it was a black substance and quite brittle. When the shot struck, it would shatter in bits. The clay trap, as it was called, could throw two birds at once - what was called a double rise.

I watched the older men playing 'potty' - evidently it's quite an old game. A thin stick like a driving whip is stuck in the ground in a grass field that is close cropped down. What would be the lash of a whip hanging from the top of the stick has a sling like on a catapult. A potty - being a round, hard, white ball about as big as a shilling piece - is placed in the sling. Each person playing the game has in his hands a long, thin stick about three and a half feet long. At the opposite end to the handle, a wooden block of hard wood is fixed to the stick. Now the idea is to strike the potty in the sling as hard as you can. The one who drives it farthest wins. The men would give us boys one penny when we found them. They were often driven a long way. Care had to be taken to keep out of the line of flight - you could be seriously injured if hit by a potty.

Pitch and toss was another game. It was a gambling game and illegal. You could be fined heavily if caught. Some of the men who took part were miners. I have watched them at one of their favourite places down the Pit Road, below the cemetery. A level bit of ground was cleared and the group of men that were to play stood around the 'ring' as it was called. Two coins were used - these were placed on the hand and tossed into the air. The people playing would bet heads or tails, one had heads, the other must have tails. The betting was sometimes heavy - £5 or more, sometimes only a few shillings.

These gambling men would offer us boys a shilling to keep a look out for the police. We were stationed a field or so away, and had to let the gamblers know when anyone suspicious was about. I have known the gambling men clear the snow from the tossing ring, they were so keen on the game. I have also seen the police trying to catch these men, as they ran in all directions to get away. I have found several tossing rings - gambling was more widespread than people thought and some of the men I knew well!

Rats at the lagoon

Shortly after I got my BSA air rifle, my mate Donald Auty and I set off to look for rats. Now the place where the rats lived was the lagoon at Mitchel Laithes Sewerage Farm. It was a bitterly cold, cloudy, winter's day, I think it was a Sunday.

The lagoon had been made years before - the sides were raised up to about fifteen feet high. The lagoon had been there so long grass and all kinds of vegetation covered it. What the lagoon had been made for was to pump into it sludge from the filter house - all the nasty black stuff you could imagine. Over the years this area of lagoon, about ten acres, was almost full, maybe to about three feet from the top of the embankment and all grown over with grasses of all kinds, even small bushes and trees grew there. It was an ideal place for wildlife as no one ever went on it. We often saw barn owls hunting in the daytime over it.

I heard that Jim Izaacs had lost a spaniel dog there one time. It had gone after a wounded partridge and gone through the soft crust and was sucked down. As me and my mate Donald walked along the top of the bank, we saw several rats run through the rough grass just below us.

I was ready with my air rifle and fired at them time after time to no effect, they were too fast for me. There were plenty of rats if only they would sit still, I could get a shot. After a while I started to get mad. Right, I thought, the next bloody rat that runs through the grass below me gets it. I hadn't long to wait. When the rat was just below me I jumped on it, forgot the grass was only a crust on the sludge and went straight through and was up to my armpits in a second. I was so surprised I didn't know what had happened. I was stuck, bloody stuck. There was no bottom to stand on. Donald, my mate, tried to reach me and could not. He looked about and by the grace of God found a rusty piece of iron pipe long enough to reach me. I managed to get hold of the pipe somehow and was pulled from the stinking mud. I scraped the awful stuff from my clothes and we set off home.

The rifle had been in my hand when I had jumped on the rat and through all the process of me being pulled free, I had kept my hold on it and it was still in my left hand. Home was some two miles at least and with the weather being so cold, I was severely chilled. I got home to our back door and shouted to mother. She came out and when she saw my state she couldn't believe it. 'Get into the coal house and get all them clothes off. I'll get the bath ready.' I could hardly move I was so frozen. Mother gave me a coat to put on. The bath, an old tin one, was in front of the fire but it took some time to get enough hot water for me. I bathed myself, how mother managed I don't know. All she kept saying was, 'I hope your father doesn't come in while you are muck up.' He didn't come. As soon as possible I got cleaned and dried, then I went upstairs with a hot water bottle to my bed.

Mother put my clothes in the bath to soak, she tried several times to clean them, yet the smell was still on them, nor would the black stain come out. In the end the clothes were thrown away. Even today, all these years later, I still think of what could have happened but for the quick thinking of my mate, Donald and a rusty bit of iron pipe. That was the second time I had been close to meeting my end. First being hit by a motor lorry then nearly smothered in the lagoon. What next?

Shooting with Norman Clare

Mr Clare's eldest son, Norman, was a tall lad of about twenty-three. He was a good looking lad, his hair black and wavy, he wore long side whiskers and was very much gypsy-looking, not at all like his father or mother. Maybe I thought they had got him from some gypsy when a baby? Norman had a double-barrelled gun, an old type of gun, one with hammers for striking the cartridges. He also had a golden retriever bitch that went with him when shooting.

Several people had guns and did a bit of shooting. Norman would always talk to us lads and we would watch him set off, the dog at his heels, away down Mill Lane towards the Bullcroft and Mitchel Laithes Farm.

Some time when I was about thirteen years old, Norman said I could go with him shooting partridges. The corn had been cut and was all stooked ready for carting away. We walked up and down the stubble fields, about thirty yards apart. When the partridges are just in season, 1st September being the start of the season, they are not too wild and you could sometimes be almost on them before they got up to fly. When they did get up, making a hell of a noise, it was enough to make me jump.

The chap with the gun would let the birds fly about thirty-five yards and then fire at them. A good man will shoot at one bird and not into the middle of the covey. To shoot right into the middle of them wounds birds that die later and there's not much sport in that. So we walked up and down the fields. There were lots of partridges, lovely birds, brown in colour, quite plump and about as big as a pigeon. If Norman shot a bird he sent his dog to fetch it. If it were not quite dead, they were knocked on the head and put into his game bag.

The smell of the fired cartridges filled my nostrils. It was a smell that I would be familiar with for the rest of my life. It meant excitement and the hunt for game, be it rabbit, duck or pheasant; I will never forget it.

Duck shooting

I was asked if I wanted to go duck shooting and of course said yes. I had to be at Norman's by 3pm on Saturday afternoon. People worked until 12 midday on Saturdays. I was early, Norman with his gun and dog came from the house and off we went for two and a half miles. We crossed the river, walking over the weir, water up to my knees and the river about a hundred yards wide at that point. At the far side were council filter beds, lots of them.

Now filter beds are used to filter the water in the sewage that comes from the pump house through pipes. It is then turned into pond-like areas called beds. When a bed is full, the water is blocked off and turned into the next bed and so on. Water filters through the soil and into the river again, leaving a kind of fine sludge which is good manure. These filter beds were ideal places for all kinds of birds. There were plenty of insects and bugs about and plenty of weed that ducks like.

We arrived just as it was getting dark on a cold November night. Norman said that the ducks followed the river then circled before landing on the beds and starting to feed. We had to keep very still and not move one inch and keep our faces down so that they did not show white - the ducks were wary.

We were just in time. I heard a faint quack, quack and the whistle of wings. I looked out of the corner of my eye but could not see anything, but could hear them again circling round. Norman stood up. Crack! Crack!. I saw the two flashes as he fired, all was still, then a splash. Norman was loading the gun. 'Get down!' 'What about the duck?' 'We'll get it later. Look out! Some more coming.' More wings whistling. 'Keep your face down.' Ducks were everywhere in the sky. I couldn't see them. Norman shot again, reloading as fast as he could. The dog was excited and wanted to be away for the ducks. I heard a few splashes after the shots.

All went quiet. It was dark now, really dark. The dog was sent out to fetch the ducks that were shot. She was back very quickly.

We got to our feet, I was frozen and walked about a bit. After about twenty minutes we set off home with four ducks in the bag. It was a bit frightening crossing the weir in the dark, the stones were slippery, my boots full of water and I very cold. I arrived home in a mess. How mother put up with it I don't know. It seemed to get worse as time went by - farm muck, sewage, water, mud, and the rest - poor mother!

Finding out about guns
Now that I had got to know a bit about partridge and duck shooting, my thoughts were on acquiring a gun. I didn't know much about them, so asked the men who did have them about what I needed. I found that you could have a gun in your house and you did not need any licence for it but to take a gun onto any public highway, you had to have a ten shilling (50p) licence and if you were going to kill game, such as partridge and pheasant, you also needed a game licence which I think was £2.

Cartridges were ten shillings for 25 - it was a lot of money before you even bought a gun. Well, I could not see my parents letting me have a shotgun. I was only thirteen and too young to be about with a firearm of that sort. The BSA Cadet Air Rifle was newly on the market. It came in two calibres .22 and .177. Well, seeing as I would not be allowed a shotgun, I managed somehow to acquire a BSA .177. At first I was useless with it but after a bit of tuition from someone older and wiser, I started to hit my targets in the middle.

What was wrong, was the two bolts that hold the wooden stock to the rifle barrel would come loose after the rifle had been fired a few times, causing the rifle to be inaccurate because of the movement of the loose bolts. And so my air rifle was the beginning of my lifetime of being involved with firearms.

I tried it out on all sorts of things and looking back, boys are cruel. I shot sparrows plus starlings and other birds, pigeons, rabbits, and hares. I didn't know that the rifle was not powerful enough for larger animals.

We older lads were taken on as potato pickers at 5/- per day. We were given time off school to do this work, the farmers being short of men, because of the war. I was coming in contact with more men who were hunting rabbits, anything for the pot, as meat was rationed and a rabbit fetched two shillings. The trouble was, cartridges. These were very scarce owing to the war and there was a black market in cartridges. People who killed something like partridges, pheasants or rabbits, usually got cartridges from the ironmonger who sold them.

Mrs Hirst and Schofield Raynor

Mrs Hirst kept a shop, a low-built house-cum-shop, just an old, stone bungalow as we would now call it. It must have been built when Jack was a lad! Its outer walls were weathered, with odd stones had dropped out at times, some pulled out by children as they lounged about the place. Mrs Hirst's Penny Shop stood at the corner of Mill Lane. Inside the place was quite dark, the high counters ran along the right hand side. It was filled with jars, some full, all with a little something in them.

Right at the back of the shop there appeared to be boxes piled up. The light was so dim I never really knew what they held or what else was there. Mrs Hirst would appear through a heavy curtain on the left side of the shop. 'What do ya want? I'm not weighing any mushrooms.' Occasionally lads would have been out for mushrooms and called at the shop to get them weighed so as to split them between them equally. The bell behind the door rang - someone pushed the door trying to get in - the place was small, if three people were being served the spot was full.

'Move yer bloody selves, you lads.' The door was opened wide enough for a large head to be poked inside, a checked cap on top of a red and heavily lined face with a big strawberry nose stuck in the middle of it. It was Schofield Raynor, 'Mrs Hirst's boyfriend', we called him. He finally managed to get himself into the shop. He was a big man, well built and would be about 65 years old.

He wore a fawn coloured suit cut in the old style of 80 years ago - his jacket like a short frock coat, a waistcoat, watch and chain, his trousers flared at the bottom and a gusset almost to the knees with buttons stitched in them, like gypsies wore.

Schofield disappeared through the hanging curtain into the living quarters. 'Now you lads, who hasn't been served? Right get your selves away then.'

I was in the shop one day, my mates were on the corner waiting for me. I started to sniff the air - there was a very strong smell of billy goat. 'What are you sniffing at?' snapped Mrs Hirst. She always snapped at us lads. 'Nothing,' I said. 'What do you want?' I was soon outside with my mates. I said, 'Bloody hell, she stinks of goat does Mrs Hirst.' They looked at me and started laughing. 'What's up wi ya?' I asked. By now they were howling with laughter. Evidently Plonk Rhodes had passed by the shop with his billy goat. Male goats piss on themselves and believe me they do stink!

In summertime on hot days, I would sit under the hawthorn bushes that overhung one of the three dams that held water for the Syke Mill. Snails were plentiful and great crested newts came up for air - these if within reach could be caught easily. The male newts were black on their backs, underneath pinky orange with black spots. I have handled many of these lovely creatures and returned them to the water. The female newts were brown and much smaller. The smell of the hawthorn blossom, even today, brings memories of warm, summer days, fishing, bird nesting, a wonderful time, wandering about, getting to know the world about me.

Walter and I were working in a field over towards Mitchel Laithe. There was a magpie nest in a big thorn bush. Walter said that magpies were thieves and maybe there could be some trinkets in the nest. I climbed the bush, Walter pushing me from behind. By the time I reached the nest, thorns were sticking in me all over. There was nothing in the nest. On the way down the tree a branch broke and as I fell a thorn stuck in my nose. All these years later, the black mark is still to be seen under my nose - it reminds me of Walter.

Just after the war, Donald and myself visited Syke Mill which had been burned down by incendiary bombs. It had been a weaving mill where woollen blankets were made. Only the walls remained standing and a few huge wooden beams spanning the engine house.

It was a dark, winter's night and we had an electric torch with us. We entered the stoke house - four boilers were side by side, all rusty, the fire doors open. A variety of large tools lay about the floor - part of the boiler room had been a smithy as well. We shone our torch through the fire door of a boiler, it was a long ways to the back of it.

'Let's look inside,' we both climbed through the opening. It was quite roomy inside. We crawled to the back of the boiler and came to an upright steel door on pivots. A chain was attached at the top of it and it was open. I pushed it and it swung shut. We shoved it open again and went through into a large chamber, a mound of soot lay like a pyramid in the centre. Looking up we realised that we were standing in the chimney bottom. It was draughty so having seen all there was we went back to the boiler room.

The steeplejacks had a ladder up the stack so we climbed to a scaffold of boards, the same height as the engine house roof or where the roof had been. I climbed over the wall and onto a big wooden beam that was charred when the mill burned. I worked my way out on the beam by sitting astride it and moving myself along with my arms. Someone shouted, 'What are you doing up there?' I froze. We should not be there, we were trespassing. I waited a long time before making my way down the ladder and met Donald. We had done no damage yet we were scared to be caught. Later, in daylight, I saw how high I had been perched on the beam - it would be thirty feet or more. I had been lucky again!

Coal scratting
During the war, fuel was always in short supply and anything to stoke the home fire was collected and burned. We had the old iron range for all our cooking, baking and heating. Father was away on directed labour to do with the government and mother needed all the help she could get.

Some of my mates and myself turned our attention to the pit stacks where all the waste from the mines was tipped. The one belonging to Shaw Cross Pit would be about one mile away across the fields from our house. In fact there were several stacks belonging to that pit. Light gauge wagon ways led from the pit top all the way to the tipping area. Some of the older pit stacks were on fire. Small ponies, of Welsh or Galloway breed, were used to draw the tubs of stone that was to be tipped.

Evidently, the smouldering stacks had hollow places where the fire had eaten deep down inside them and could be dangerous and collapse at any time. We were warned to keep away from them. I remember hearing that a fatal accident occurred - a workman and his pony taking tubs to be tipped were swallowed up - they disappeared tubs, pony, man, the lot.

When the work was ended each day, we would root about the sides of the stacks for pieces of coal. We called it 'coal scratting.'

It could be quite dangerous as the stack sides were very steep, everything was loose. Large pieces of stone would start to roll down, taking others with them. There could be as many as ten people scratting for coal, each one shifting the rubbish about.

If we found a place with several bits of coal, a hole was excavated in case more lay there. I had been scratting a while and there was someone who had climbed higher above me. That was time to move away, find a safer place. There would be some strong words between us - I have learned how to swear. Crushed and broken wooden props were tipped as well, although these should not have been sent to the tip, because they helped to set the stacks alight.

I have carried many bags of coal home and props as well. We had to take care on reaching the road and watch for the police as we were breaking the law. The police were not so sympathetic in those days. I enjoyed coal scratting days. We were doing a useful job, it got us away from home and did no-one any harm.

Later on I went after rabbits on an old, burned out pit stack, down below the Earlsheaton Cemetery, called the Blazing Rag Pit. That stack was just like a huge cinder, completely burned out. There were lots of holes and crevasses - it was an ideal place for rabbits. It was a lunar landscape, with humps and bumps, holes and cracks - the heat from these burning pit stacks must have been very great - the sulphur smoke enough to make you ill and take your breath away. Now all the pit stacks are gone as if they had never been at all.

Briquettes from Shaw Cross Pit

As well as scratting for coal, we had the pleasure of queuing for briquettes at Shaw Cross Pit head. On cold winter days, women and children, and a few old people, made their way to the pit for a few briquettes. These so-called briquettes were made of compressed coal dust and a bit of cement, so I was told. They measured five inches square by two inches thick and were steaming hot when you got them.

You were allowed a dozen each - two wheeled hand carts, prams, wheelbarrows were all used to cart them home in. I have seen people with old carpet bags, one in each hand, carrying them home. If I remember right, they were one and a half pence each or 1/6d a dozen. I made that journey many times as a lad.

The briquettes burned dull but with a bit of coal they were better; we were glad of anything in those days. There were some things called 'duck eggs', these too were made of coal dust, the same as the briquettes. All kinds of things were tried, even jam jars filled with coal dust were put on the fire while it was red hot, these were said to last a long time.

Firelighters were made of compressed sawdust and paraffin - Scotts the masons, made them. They were made in a mould with a heavy weight put to press out excess paraffin. Some people made their own briquettes from a mould of their own making.

The soldiers

Convoys of arm wagons, all sorts of vehicles were on the move - the war was in its last year. We played war games. The news was about war, at nights the sky was full of bombers going out on raids to Germany. Things were fairly buzzing.

One day some Army Bren carriers arrived in our park. As soon as we could get loose, lots of boys and girls gathered about the machines and the soldiers. The troops were very friendly to us. We were almost allowed to climb into the Bren carriers and lorries. They gave out sweets and chewing gum. One chap took out a revolver, unloaded it and let me see how many times I could pull the trigger - not many, the Enfield Service Revolver had a stiff trigger pull. It was exciting while the soldiers were there.

Boys used to collect badges of different regiments. If they got two of the same they were swapped for something else. Bullets were also exchanged. I once got a Mills Bomb with the explosives had been removed. Army caps were worn by some boys. All sorts of paraphernalia was about and later lots of pistols that the troops brought home.

Tatie harvest

We were picked up by the lorry and taken to various farms that grew potatoes. October and November was the spud harvest. It was a cold job too, with an 8 o'clock start and 4.30pm finish. The spuds were spun out with a tractor and spinner. It was far better than the old plough way of getting them up, but we still had to scratch for some of them.

There were large gangs of thirty people in some of the fields. We picked the spuds into wire baskets or swills then went and tipped them into sacks when the swills were full. The bags were set out about ten yards apart and each person picked between the bags.

That was your stint for the day. We worked Saturday morning till noon, and received 27s 6d for five and a half days work in wet, cold weather. There was no rest till dinnertime. If you wanted a piss you did it where you were, you dare not hold up the tractor. As for the women, and there were plenty of them, the other women stood around the one who wanted to make water. If you wanted to shit, then you went to the side of the field into the ditch or the hedge.

Charlie Pickles and sledging
As I remember Charlie Pickles, the thick spectacles he wore seemed to make his eyes deeper sunk into his head and he appeared to have difficulty seeing. He craned his head forwards almost to unbalance himself when standing. He was of average height and build and about 50 years old. What Charlie's job was I don't really know, something to do with mill work.

Several children were in his family, most of them grown up. A daughter, Sheila, was in the Land Army and was away on farm work a lot. Lawrence, a year or two older than me was a mill worker too. Another youth was in our class at school, I do not remember his name. They seemed a healthy family, rosy cheeked and quite well built, evidently their mother fed them well. They were typically dressed as most working class families of that period, the war being just over and most things in short supply. Any coat or trousers had to do, people were not fussy, they couldn't afford to be. Wages were low, coupons were needed when buying clothes or shoes, rationing was still on.

Charlie and his son, Lawrence, were sometimes teased, they both being a little slow at thinking. It was a good job they were good natured. I remember in the warm, summer weather many lads gathered at the Syke Dam where we used to cool off in the water. The Pickles' lads were there, a lot of horseplay developed and of course they came in for it. We would surround them and grab a hold of one and throw him as high into the air as possible to land with a great splash far out into the water which was none too clean, being churned up by all the activity.

We would eventually have all the Pickles' lads in the water and stop them climbing out for a while. How anyone was not injured in the dam I just do not know. Years later I paid a visit there and the dam had been drained. I was surprised how shallow it was, with many pieces of iron bar and wood embedded in the muddy bottom.

We had been swimming and diving among it all - the water was so dirty it could not be seen.

I remember one winter there was deep snow on the ground. In those days the roads were quiet and any place was used for sledging. Being hilly where we lived, we had only a short way to go. One of the favourite places was Syke Lane down to the Syke Mill. It was possible to sledge right into the yard, a distance of several hundred yards. I have seen crowds of lads and girls going up and down the run on a winter's night, especially if there was moonshine.

Providence Street was used too, it was very steep and good speeds were to be had there. I would say it would be all of 500 yards to the Syke Beck where it ended. Sugar Lane was a very fast sledge run, from the top at Crown Flatts to Wakefield Road would be a similar distance. It was possible to turn to the left about halfway down on to Crackenhedge Lane which was on old unpaved way. The old pit hills between our home and Frances Road were a favourite sledge run, only a very short run compared to the others I have mentioned. Pilldacre Hill was used at times, as were Ossett Lane from Earlsheaton to the railway yard. These were only used before the council workers salted and gritted them.

The winters in the 1930s and 1940s always had snow and it stayed for weeks, the stuff got packed solid. Night after night we visited various sledge runs. One run from the top of Old Bank was a dangerous one, steep and quite straight, it was possible to go all the way to the old Toll Bar and Crackenhedge Lane. If you overshot the Toll Bar you would land on the Wakefield Road. If there was snow enough it would be possible to sledge into the town centre.

Most lads made their own sledges or their fathers' would make them. My dad was away a long time, therefore, I had to make my own. I remember asking Mam for the rockers off our rocking chair. I got them, leaving a very short-legged chair. The sledge turned out to be failure and I made another one which had iron straps nailed on the runners. The older lads had joiner made sledges which could reach very fast speeds. Care had to be taken on the runs with many people travelling up and down. Collisions were common, most of them caused bruises although I have known of broken arms and fingers. I have myself run into a wall now and then, while trying to avoid a collision.

Tin trays and pieces of sheet iron were also used. I have used a strip of oiled cloth or plywood. I used to get home at nine or ten at night, wet through, tired out and after a hot drink, gone to my bed and slept soundly. We would sledge night after night - there was no television in those days.

But to go back to Charlie Pickles - it was winter, we were out sledging and had been at Kettleage Street. We were on our way to Chickenly Lane, there being a good run there. Knowing we would pass the Pickles' cottage, we had stopped and loaded one sledge with snow balls. Stopping on the lane in front of the Pickles' cottage, someone knocked on the kitchen door. Charlie stood framed in the opening, 'What yer want?' he asked. A volley of snowballs hit him. Again and again we let fly, some missed him and landed among the family seated about the fireside. About fifty snowballs had been made and every one was thrown. It took less than a minute, then the attack was over. We charged along the lane feeling pleased with what we had one. Looking back I wish I had not been there, but what is done is done.

The Park Mansion School
I was growing up and was at the senior school. It was an old mansion in the big park as the old senior school was used in the war as a first aid post, with sandbags stacked up about the doors and windows - it was like a fortress. So there we stayed until we were old enough to leave school. At that time everyone that had a bit of ground that could be used to grow vegetables, was asked to put it in cultivation - Digging for Victory.

Our school, being in a large park, had plenty of land available and so tools were issued, forks, spades, rakes and barrows. The boys were given time off lessons to do the digging and to get the land ready for planting. All the sods were taken off and stacked around the piece of land we were working, just like a wall. Once that was done, the digging started, soon some lads got tired of the work and started playing about. Sometimes the fooling got out of hand. I remember one lad had a fork stuck in his foot - that caused some trouble. After that the chap in charge of us kept a close watch on us and if anyone was caught playing the fool, he was sent to Mr Denham, the headmaster. He soon put things right with his 'strap'.

The gardening went ahead quite well. Loads of sewage manure arrived, all to be dug in to enrich the soil. Now among the sewage manure there were lots of rubber condoms. The older lads told us what they were used for, we were laughing and thinking it all very funny.

As we loaded our barrows with the stuff, all the condoms were picked out. Quite a pile of the French letters, as they were called then, had grown. Somebody said, 'Let's hang them on the barbed wire.' Soon we were all busy hanging the things up - the bloke in charge had gone somewhere. It was quite a display to be sure and when he saw it all hell was to pay for that little joke. We got one hour extra to do that night.

I enjoyed being out on the allotments. All our tools were kept in the cellars beneath the school. There was always a scramble to put them away, all the tools were cleaned first, it was a bit of good training for later life. So, now I was learning to be a gardener, what a life!

Camping at Coxley Valley

Donald Auty and I had bought a secondhand Army bivouac tent and a few tin plates and a billy can-cum-frying plan. We were going camping to Coxley Valley. The war was about over and Coxley Valley was a nice place to camp. We went by bus, then had a fair walk from Horbury Bridge. The path followed the stream to the ruins of an old watermill, it must have had a fair old wheel, the flume from where the water came was still running, though the wheel long gone. A dam held back the water that at one time served the mill, it was a fair sized mill pond with a few cottages overlooking it.

We walked past the pond, still following the feeder stream. The woodland started to improve, and it was now looking more like the wilderness we imagined it would be. Eventually a place was found for our tent. Afore long it was erected, we put all our bedding inside and set about making a fire. It being summer, some dry wood was soon set alight. We had bread and butter for tea - I was starting to enjoy myself. I had with me a big butcher's knife and this was used for the firewood and any other job.

Later we wandered back downstream. Just before the mill pond a lad of about our age was tickling trout and had caught about four that lay beside him. We had no idea that fish of that size were in a small stream like this one.

On we went and explored the pond - there were plenty of sticklebacks and bull heads - what a place it was and enjoy it we did. It was getting dusk and we were beginning to feel a bit lonely out in the wilderness and we soon got into our sleeping blanket, but not to sleep. We talked about what we would do next day. The only light we had was from our fire and that had died down to the odd flicker or two. I dozed off a while, all was quiet apart for the trickling of the beck water. Then something moved against my back which was turned towards the tent wall.

I kept still. Thoughts flashed through my mind - was it a snake, a rat, what else? The movement went along the underside of my back and travelled towards my feet. I'd had enough - I put my hand out feeling for whatever it was, 'Bloody Hell!' I shouted, as I had got hold of a hand which was pulled away. 'What's up?' Donald asked. 'There's somebody out there!' We both crawled out of the tent. We could see a figure disappearing through the trees, as it was much lighter out of the tent.

The fire was stoked up again and we sat with blankets about us and talked a long while. I was very alert in case the robber came back. I told Don what I had felt while we lay in our tent and of the hand feeling about. Someone was trying to rob us. We didn't have much and what few pence we had lay in our pockets and we slept in our clothes, so all was safe. It was a long night. I did sleep a little, very little. I was on my guard, this time and I faced the tent wall.

We were up before the birds next day. It was a Sunday and people were out walking and it soon got fairly busy. We tried tickling trout without success and made a meal but our minds were made up, we were going home. We packed our belongings and set off for home; we were still thinking of our first night camping and the creeping hand. We told our mates at school of our adventure in the wilderness of Coxley Valley and how we had fought off the raider in the night.

Later we spent more nights in the wilderness, with more lads and more tents - we had reinforcements. This time we would be ready for the thief in the night. In our armoury we had an air pistol and an axe so we were prepared for war!

The day hole, Clough Wood

When I was about thirteen years old, some more lads and myself happened to be in Clough Wood on our rambles and came across the entrance of an old 'day hole' or drift mine. The wood was in a shallow valley where a seam of coal outcropped. I believe the seam was about two feet thick and had been worked some years before. The entrance had been blocked by a fall of soil. We set about clearing away the fall and soon had an opening big enough to crawl through. Someone had matches and by the light of these we could make out what the coal face was like. It was a fair sized place and about four feet high from floor to the roof and fifty feet to the coal.

Donald Auty and I returned a day or so later. Some rusty rail lines with a few wooden tubs lay about at the front of the mine. I had heard dad talk of the day hole, evidently it had been worked for a while and then abandoned. We had brought a small collier's pick, a shovel and some sand bags. We were soon busy by the light of an electric torch. It was hard work getting the coal loose but we managed to get two bags filled. We hid the tools and set off home with our coal, very pleased with ourselves.

The coal was fairly soft and had traces of iron oxide in it and burned poorly. I cannot remember how long we worked the day hole, but looking back, I think we were lucky not to have had an accident as there were no props to hold the roof. Little did I know that a few years later I was to work in a deep mine and nearly come to grief there at Inghams, Thornhill.

II
LIFE ON THE FARM

Leaving school and Ned Ramsden's

It was time for me to leave school. I knew what I wanted to do though my dad had different ideas. I had always wanted to be out in the fields, it was where I spent most of my young life. I was interested in wildlife, farms had been a magnet, I was drawn to them. At school, lads that were to leave as I was, were talking of what they were going to do. Jeff Simpson was going to the railways. He would start as engine cleaner, later he would be promoted to fireman and eventually he became a train driver. Donald Hirstal went to Fred Lumb's Grove Farm. My mate Donald Auty was going to his brother James' firewood business. All the lads had some sort of work to go to - there was no shortage in 1946.

My dad told me one evening that he had got me a job. I was to start at Ned Ramsden's, the painters and decorators. Fred Croft worked there, he was a mate of dad's. They met at the Globe Pub where my future had been arranged. I remonstrated with dad I was to be on the farms. 'Its a dead end job, low wages and no future,' he told me 'and don't argue with me lad.' It was final. 'Listen,' he told me, 'as long as you live under my roof, you shall do as I say and if you don't like it, you can find somewhere else to live, that's the end of it.'

Herbert Exley, lived close to us and was a master butcher. He had hinted that it was a good job and could perhaps find work for me. The following evening I dared to bring up the subject of work to my dad while we were having our meal. 'Dad, Mr Exley said he could find me a job butchering with him. I would sooner be a butcher than a painter.' Dad looked across the table at me, his knife and fork were put down. He leaned towards me, 'I've told you tha's starting at Ned Ramsden's whether tha likes it or not, now get on with thi tea, let me hear no more of it.'

Ned Ramsden's was halfway up a steep hill. His house and paint shop were together. From the side door of his home, a long flight of stone steps led down to the paint shop. A side street brought you to a large door through which ladders, trestles, planks, barrels, etc., were taken in and out of the workshop. I propped my bike against the wall and looked in. Men in white overalls were standing about; some younger men, a bit older than me were among them. Teddy Bird, I knew him, Fred Croft, my dad's mate stood there craning his neck to listen to a chap talking to him. Fred was quite deaf as I later found out.

A man of about sixty appeared among the crowd. Some of the men were given bits of paper, they were the ones in charge of the jobs. The man handing out the slips was the boss, Albert Ramsden, now his father Ned was dead. I was sent with two men who were working at a big house some way off. We loaded cans of paint and a keg of lime and an assortment of brushes into an ex-army Bedford 15cwt truck. The two men squeezed in with Nelson Hargreaves, the driver. I was in the back sat upon the lime keg. At the house which was among more big houses in a wealthy area, the tackle was unloaded and I was told to carry it all in.

I was told how much lime to mix with some blue powder to kill the white glare and to stir it well and keep it stirred. A whitening brush was shoved into my hand and I was led down to a big cellar. Stone slabs were around the walls and flags on the floor. It was cold and smelled damp. 'Right, lad, start with the ceiling. Scrape any loose lime off then brush it down with that dry brush, put the dust sheets down first. Do the same with the walls. Have you done any of this work before?' 'No, I haven't.' 'You will soon learn.'

The one light bulb was dim and there were shadows. I scraped and brushed the ceiling which was low enough to reach without steps. I was shouted, 'Come on, lad. Get thy tea.' The other two were already at theirs. 'What's ta got, lad?' I was asked. 'Onions, onion sandwich.' I could have done with summat to warm me up, it was cold down that cellar. Vacuum Thermos flasks stood by their seats. I had a bottle of cold tea. 'Tha must get thyself a flask lad.' 'I cannot afford one,' I said. 'After this week you will be able to afford one,' the old man said. 'How much are you starting on, lad?' '27/6d.' 'Nearly as much as we get,' China replied. China was his nickname, he signed his betting slips with China.

In the afternoon I was busy slapping the lime wash on the cellar walls. Two wires were hanging close to the wall and a lead pipe ran on a slant close to these wires. My brush caught one of the wires and there was a bright flash accompanied by a crackle and a bang and I was sent flying across the cellar. Water jetted from the lead pipe. I could see it starting to flood my cellar. Upstairs I told old

China, 'Me cellar's flooding.' 'What's ta talking about, lad?' 'Come on, come on, have a look.' All three of us looked at the pipe and at the water spreading across the flags. 'What's ta being doing, lad?' 'Them two wires, they did it,' I said and told them of the flash and bang and of me being knocked across the cellar. The two old chaps did a bit of mumbling and China said to me that I'd have to be more careful with other folks' property. A search was made and the stop tap found. I was told to stay with them for the rest of the day.

At home, mother said, 'By lad, look at you and the new, white overalls, lime everywhere.' My eyes were sore from wiping them clear of the burning lime. It had been my first day at work, what would tomorrow bring?

The house was large, so were the grounds about it and there was a tennis court with a high wire fence around it. Old Albert Wardle was in charge, 'Come on, you two.' We were walked round the court. 'Now, you lads, this here fence is to creosote, get yerself a wire brush apiece and some steps. Start at the top, brush the rust off, make a good job of it.' We followed Albert back to the house. We had a big wooden box with a top that could be locked at night with shafts, where tools, brushes and many cans of paint were stored when the men went home. 'Here you are.' We were given a stiff wire brush apiece. 'Take them steps over there. Away you go, no slaking now, you will be in full view of the house. Everyone can see you.'

It was a grand, warm summer's day. I would enjoy being away from the ladder work when we had cleared out the house roof gutters, brushed them clean, then tarred them all. It was a mucky job and hard on the legs being on the ladder all day. This was a nice change.

'Which side do you want, Sharpie?' My mate's name was Barry Sharpe. 'Inside.' I found out why he preferred being there later, the steps were always on level ground, mine sank at times and bushes, grass and other stuff got in my way. Two days later we had brushed all the netting about the tennis court. Albert came now and then to inspect our work. The weather was still good, sunny and warm.

We were all gathered in the paint shop and Albert Ramsden was going among the older men handing out the usual bits of paper. Mr Ramsden stopped before me, 'How are you getting on Brian?' 'Alright, Mr Ramsden.' 'What do you think of the painting job?'

'Alright, Mr Ramsden,' I said. 'How's yer mam and dad?' 'Alright Mr Ramsden.' Albert Ramsden had been a neighbour of ours when I was very young. I had been a regular visitor at their home, where I used to ask for pop and was given a glass of water. Years later mother said I always called water 'Yamsden's Pop.'

Albert Ramsden, our boss, did not look a happy man. His thick glasses made it hard to look into his eyes. There was little colour in his face, he looked an old man though he wasn't. 'Have you lads got that creosote loaded?' Albert Wardle wanted us away out of the paint shop.

Five men were on our job. The tackle box was unlocked and cans of paint mixed and brushes dried to get the water from them. The men went to their work, some on the window painting, another doing doors.

'Today's the day, lads,' said Albert as he led us to the tennis court. 'Lay them old dust sheets down and move em along as you go. A word of warning, be careful with the creosote. Don't splash it about, do you hear?' 'Aye, Albert, alright.'

We used four inch brushes instead of the normal, long-handled brushes, with a round head. They were called a Turk's head brush. Sharpie and I talked as we creosoted the wire, 'Thin stuff this creosote, Sharpie.' It ran down the wire in streams. 'Don't put so much on yer brush,' he said. Our talk ran dry. We had given ourselves room so as not to splash each other. It was impossible not to splash, the creosote came back at us at each stroke, our faces were soon splattered. The stuff burned and the hot sun made it worse. It had to happen - I got some in my eye, it burned, the pain was awful. I shouted to Sharpie, I couldn't see and my good eye was watering as well. Holding my bit of rag against the eye made it worse. I was led to the water tap and held my head down to sluice the place. That helped. After a while the water started to numb my face. There I stood, blinking, tears streamed down my face, the pain was severe, what could I do? Some of the older men knew what it was like. They had experience of creosote. Old Albert Wardle decided I should go to the hospital. I was taken and immediately the nurse set about the job and soon cleaned me up and it was a great relief.

It was some days before I could see properly. I was taken off the tennis court work and given a good little number in the paint shop. I was to strain paint. I was given a tin drum which held six gallons when full. I sat the strainer on top of the empty drum and any tins of paint that came from jobs and were only part full were tipped into the strainer, first having the skin taken off. With a stick and a brush I pushed the paint through the sieve then used a little turps to wash the tin out. Many different colours of paint were strained and it all finished up a khaki shade. It was used as undercoat on rough jobs such as gutters, downspouts and coal hole doors.

'There's a big job starting in the town,' Nelson Hargreaves said. 'You are going, Brian.' We started loading ladders and planks, many dust sheets and buckets, all ready for the morning. 'What's ta like at heights young un?' Cloghead Harrop asked me. 'I don't know, I haven't done any roof work,' I said. 'There will be loads of shit in them gutters, thow's in for some graft, young un.' Cloghead Harrop was older than me and bigger. He was a clever sod and a bit of a bully.

Six or seven men arrived, the ladders were put up with treble extensions. It was a long way to the top where the gutters were. The tackle was hoisted up to the chaps on the roof who set about making walkways and laying short ladders over the glass of the arcade roof which we would have to cross. The gutters were over a foot wide and six inches deep. They were almost full. I set about cleaning them with a pothole shovel and two buckets as my tools. My buckets were full in short time. I had to carry them about 30 yards to where the ladders were for going up and down. A rope and pulley were fixed for me to lower the muck down and another lad below emptied them. It took a day to clean that gutter. It had to be washed down and brushed before drying and tarring could be done.

One short ladder rested in the gutter that I had cleaned, the top rested on the ridge above the glass arcade. Another ladder went down to the gutter on the opposite side and they were tied together. I set about mucking out the gutter, it was hard work carrying two iron buckets full of dirt. Coming to where I must cross the arcade roof, I stopped and set my buckets down. It was tricky crossing over even empty handed. I looked at where Cloghead Harrop was sitting watching me. 'Go on, young un, go on,' he was laughing and pointing at me, the other chaps were watching.

I took a hold of my buckets and stepped on to the ladder. I managed but was sweating, I would be more confident next load. I stood by my roof ladders, my buckets filled. 'Go on, go on, shift yerself young un.' Cloghead Harrop was coming towards me. 'Shut yer gob, Cloghead.' 'Don't call me Cloghead, I'll bray ya.'

'Tother lads call yer Cloghead,' I said. 'I've told yer, don't call me that.' He held me by the neck of the overalls, his pasty face glaring into mine. 'Get them buckets emptied,' he said giving me a shove. 'I'll attend to you later,' he added.

I steadied myself, my buckets heavy in my hands. Once on the ladder I had to keep going, the momentum was essential. I made that journey many times that morning and by early afternoon I was very tired. As I turned, my buckets in my hands, my heel caught the long glass light. There was a loud crack. A big piece of glass broke away and fell into the arcade where people were shopping. The sound the glass made striking the floor below I shall never forget. I came down from the roof quickly and stood beside the Bedford truck. I was sure the falling glass must have hurt or killed someone. I had a glimpse of them as the glass fell.

Later I was told it was alright, nobody was hurt, though a woman had her coat slashed at the back. For days after I refused to go on that arcade, someone else finished my gutter job. I had had enough of the painting trade. I was going to get another job and started looking elsewhere.

Chickenly of old

Looking back over the years of plenty in the mid 1940s, we shot green plover, lapwings or peewits, as some called them. These could be sold for six pence each. The game dealers hung them in bunches of six and they good to eat. Little did we think that the day would come when they must be protected because they became an endangered species.

Peewits used the cornfields to nest in, the corn in spring being only a few inches high. The horseman with his roller would roll the field and would keep an eye out for the nests. When seen the eggs were moved and when the roller had passed over the empty nest, the eggs were replaced. Most farm men had a soft spot for peewits.

People gathered the peewits' eggs for eating; they fetched 21/- a dozen in large cities. If a nest had three eggs they could be taken, if four eggs we left them as they could have been sat on. Because the eggs were cool the mother could have been off them for a long while. It is surprising how much cold eggs will stand and still hatch.

The land we young lads and men shot over was not keepered. Foxes were killed whenever we got a chance as well as crows, hawks and owls too, though not barn owls, there were plenty of those about. Despite the number of people shooting the partridge stock was good. We had some good days walking the fields. We thought it was sport to wait behind a wall or in a ditch at evening time and call to the partridges as they were going to jug, or to bed. At times the coveys were shot into as they sat upon the ground, any way was used to secure birds. Looking back I wonder how this small game bird survived at all. Little was in its favour - farm dogs ranged the fields while the men worked looking for rabbits or just hunting anything that moved, they no doubt disturbed many sitting birds. Game was sold in the pubs and clubs, some to regular customers and some for Saturday night raffles which were held in the Crown Hotel and Providence Pub. None of the shooting men held a game licence. It was unthinkable, why buy a licence when we could kill partridges just as well without one!

Moorhens or waterhens were fair game and these too were eaten. They abounded wherever water lay. Canals were always worth walking up. The moorhens would dive and lie there a long while,

just part of the beak above the surface. A dog that is used for flushing game will soon start catching these birds as they hide among grass and weeds. We never plucked moorhens - the feathers will not come away as with most game. I skinned them which is far easier. The flesh is quite dark and good to eat.

Pigeons were shot at all times of the year and on a windy day they would fly low. I have sat hidden on the riverside where the banks were high as the birds would follow the water, keeping between the banks. Some good sport was had at times. Now and then a flock of racing pigeons would come along - they too came in for a few shots.

One recipe we used to make was to put a moorhen, a pigeon and a young rabbit in an earthenware jar. Add a large onion and carrots chopped up and some sage. Fill the jar with boiling water and put it in the oven. When the baking is finished the oven will be very hot, leave the jar overnight, look to see that the juice has not boiled away and top up if necessary. The flesh will have dropped from the bones, a plate full of the stew is a great meal. This delicious meal is best served with bread. We ate this food just after the war. I would still have it if I have the chance.

Foxes would lie up in drains, one of these situated on a fairly steep embankment. One chap with a gun waited by the lower end of the pipe, the other chap at the higher end rolled stones down the drain. Foxes would bolt quite often. The old pit stacks at the Blazing Rag Pit were a favourite place for foxes to lie up. Old Jim Isaacs waited there and shot them.

An old cottage stood where the Smallpox Hospital had stood. It was quite isolated and a kestrel hawk lived there. It was a wary bird and flew out on being approached. A short distance away there was a shallow quarry, long grown over, which sheltered a fox at times. One evening I watched a fox mousing.

I had a passion for ducks. The mere sight of one would send me rushing for a gun. While working in the harvest field late one night I saw ducks land on the river. It would be 10pm and the last load had been stacked. I got my gun and went after those ducks though they were all of a mile away. I don't recollect what happened, whether I had a shot or not, I just had to have a go at 'em ducks!

George Cody
What a place it was! It was ancient. The low stone cottage was mouldering away, the chimney stack leaned over, some of the roof flags were broken and the gutters sprouted grass and various weeds.

We stood before the door, the paint long gone, that too had a tilt. There was a heap of straw and muck next to the remains of a yard brush in a corner by the step. China knocked on the door, it fairly shook. 'Don't knock it down, China.' I heard a noise that sounded like a creaking and a groan, then 'Who is it?' 'It's young Aston and China Winterbottom,' I shouted. More creaking and groaning,

'Come in, come in.'

I shoved the door open - it stuck halfway. 'Yer have to lift it a bit,' the voice said. In we went. I could hardly see owt in the gloomy place. 'What yer want then, you two?' 'Don't yer want yer chimney swept?' More creaking and groaning. It was the bed that made the strange noise. 'Ho, have yer come to do that, good lads.'

Our eyes were now used to the gloom and could make out the big iron bedstead that took up most of the room space. They were in bed the pair of them. George was sat up, his cap on and smoking a pipe. Joe Sugar appeared to be asleep, he too wore his cap. What a state they were in. On a small table by the only window stood an old wireless, the glass accumulator batteries below it. The fireplace was full of cinders, empty bottles, sardine tins, a pair of boots with the toes kicked out. A bucket held God knows what - they were not at all house proud. The oil lamp sat on a chair by the bed, no shade and the glass chimney almost black. How any light came from it I don't know.

There was a bit of a back house, sort of a lean-to with a water tap above the slop stone sink and a few bits of china lay there. The old pair seemed happy enough with their accommodation, the flagged floor could have done with a swill out, horse shit was the most prevalent among the straw and hay and other farmyard debris.

I would say George Cody, or as he called himself, Mr Norfolk, would be about 65 years old. He hailed from that part of the world. I believe he had originally worked with threshing and steam ploughing teams. How he came to Chickenly I never knew. He was a big chap and had a patch over his left eye. He always wore a dark suit much dribbled down and he used his coat sleeve to wipe the snot from his nose. George's old cap was rouen, it had seen better days. It was always pulled down just about covering his one eye - hair and whiskers stuck out everywhere, he was a right scruffy bugger.

George Cody kept a Galloway pony, it stood about eleven hands. I could never make up my mind as to its colour, a sort of brown mixed with grey, and was just as scruffy as he was. There was a flat cart to match the pony, the paint had peeled from the woodwork long ago, in fact the cart matched the firewood it carried.

George was in the firewood business or I should say kindling wood trade. When on his rounds George would drive up on the flags as close as he could get to the customer's door, then rattle it with the butt end of his whip. If the woman of the house wanted kindling, she held out her apron. George would fill a small bucket with sticks from the heap on his cart, then tip them into the woman's apron, get his few pence and drive to the next door. He would not leave his seat at all. That was Mr George Cody.

Joe Sugar had lived with George for years. His proper name was Joseph Swithenbank. He was as different again as his mate, Cody. Joe Sugar was small made and more tidy. He too wore very old clothes and a cap. He never seemed to do much at all apart from sitting with Willy Lumb in the lighthouse across the lane.

Old men smoked pipes and never appeared to be in a hurry. They sat about and talked now and then. 'Now then, young Aston, how's thy dad these days?' and that would be it. It was nice in the lighthouse, a long room above some cart sheds with windows overlooking the lane and Cody's home. There were piles of sacks, old harness and tools and some armchairs by the fire. Willy Lumb kept it well stocked with coal. There were clouds of pipe smoke and they would sit for ages and never speak. Probably they had nowt to talk about anymore - it had all been said years ago.

'You will find the tackle out the back in the far corner,' George said. What we found was a length of rope tied to a sack and a round weight at the other end. 'It won't take yer long, just get on the roof, its low. Go into the hall yard, there's a wall, you can get off that.' 'What about the soot?' I asked. 'There won't be much, it was swept two years ago.' 'When yerv done that you can have a go at the wireless.'

China went up on the roof. 'Bump,' the weight landed on the hearth. 'I've got it China,' I said as I pulled on the rope. A cloud of soot flew out into the room. I couldn't see it but knew as I could taste it. 'I could do with some light, George, open the door.' Ay, that was better, soot was everywhere, the pair of 'em in bed didn't mind, they were getting their chimney swept.

I pulled the rope more slowly and the soot cascaded into the range and about my feet. I had the sack now. 'Done it, George,' I said. 'Good, do it again will ya.' 'China,' I shouted up the chimney, 'we have to do it again.' Out in the lane I was dazzled. He was sat on the roof ridge smiling and singing Al Jolson's *Mammy*. We finally got the job done and the soot bagged up. 'Put it in the back house,' said George. 'If yer know anybody wants it, they can fetch this lot.'

The wireless had stopped during the news. 'I don't know owt

about wirelesses,' I said. I had seen my dad larkin about with our old set at times. 'Yer batteries are flat, George.' 'No,' he said, 'only charged last week, needs a good clean. You can do it, my eyes aint any good now.' 'Turn the wireless round, there's a couple of screws holding the back on, they're loose yer don't need a screwdriver.' It came off alright. Dad used to fiddle with the valves and condensers and God knows what. In a corner of the wireless there was a small heap of hay and straw, I poked about, bloody hell, a mouse jumped out and ran off. 'There's a bloody mouse nest in the wireless, George!' 'Well, clean it out, give it a good muck out, we'll try it afore yer put the back on again.'

Out came the nest and plenty of dust too. 'Make sure the wires are connected,' George said. 'The light's come on, George.' 'Good, turn the big knob in the centre,' a bit of crackling. 'Now, turn the small knob on the right.' We could hear a faint voice. 'It's working, George, it's working.' 'OK lads, turn it off, I'll attend to it when I get up. Do you lads want a cup of tea?' 'No thanks,' we said. 'How the heck can you make tea, you haven't a fire, George?' 'I was going to send you to Colin Pinder's across the road. You could have got us one an all. Here's yer two bob you have done a good job you lads. Don't forget if you hear of anybody wants some soot for the garden, they can have this lot.'

George Cody and Joe Sugar liked a pint or two and their watering hole was the Crown Hotel where Percy Womersly was the landlord. Joe got so bad on his legs that George had to push him to the Crown in a pram. So much for old age - it's hard work growing old as I now know.

What happened to that fine pair of men I know not. I went away into the Army and never saw then again. The old village was pulled down, gone like the characters that lived there, nowt but memories are left. What we now have is what is called progress - what a price to pay!

Charley Thornes

Charley Thornes' face shone. He was always clean shaven and had the appearance of a wax doll. His hair was shaved close to his skull - he just had a tuft at the front and he would be in his fifties. He was a small man, about five feet five inches, and skinny. His clothes were old but clean - many patches held Charley's trousers together - in fact patches were sewn upon patches. He always had cycle clips about his ankles, holding his old Army denim trousers tight. I seldom saw Charley without his bike. He could appear almost anywhere in town or in the countryside; he seemed to travel about a lot.

When I first met him I don't know, for sure. We were young lads starting to spread our wings and Chickenly was our favourite place. Charley was very interested in firearms so we had something in common, he and I. I have seen us walking up partridges, several of us walking in line across the stubble. Charley would appear, lay down his bike and join the line and spend the rest of the day with us.

Sometimes we would meet Charley along the river with a haversack on his back. 'Want a few shots?' he would ask. 'How much?' I asked. 'Six shots a shilling.' 'OK let's have a go.' We made our way to a shallow quarry, overgrown with grass and a few bushes, close by the river. The quarry had been abandoned years ago and was an ideal site for rifle shooting.

'Let's see your money,' Charley said. We showed him our money. He took his haversack off and started to put his rifle together. It was a Winchester .22 slide action rifle, exactly like the ones at the fairgrounds in those days. We walked to the quarry face, Charley produced some targets and set them up.

Walking back some fifty yards, Charley stopped and pulled out the tubular magazine from under his rifle and dropped six cartridges into it. 'Right,' said Charley 'who's first?' 'Go on,' I said to Donald 'you go.' 'Let's have your money,' said Charley. The money in his pocket, Charley loaded the rifle. 'It's ready to fire,' he said as he handed it to Donald. After the shots we all walked forwards to see the results. Now it was my turn. Charley pocketed the shilling and I was handed the rifle and fired my shots. I think Charley Thornes worked in a mill, he never said much of work - a deep bugger he was.

I had a few guns at Grove Farm - all muzzled loaders which I used often. One Saturday afternoon I was in the stable where the guns lay in a trough in front of an empty stall.

'Now what are yer doing?' Charley was in the doorway, gleaming as usual, his clogs shone too. 'What yer got there?' I showed him a short steel barrelled Blunderbuss. 'Let's have a look at it.' Charley took the gun, stroking it and examining the gun carefully. 'Unusual,' he said 'it's rifled, and a spring bayonet. It's a conversion from flintlock to percussion. Made for the East India Company.'

Later Charley asked if I wanted to sell the Blunderbuss, or would I do a swop for another gun. So it was arranged and I went with Charley to his home. The house was very big, red brick built in Oxford Road, a quiet street. I followed him down a path to the side to the kitchen door which was below street level. We entered a room which was dimly lit with a bare electric bulb. A small woman appeared. Charley introduced me to his mother. 'Sit down, I'll go get the gun.' It was a single barrelled ten bore and we did the swop.

Rabbit poaching

We heard that a farmer and some of his friends had a lot of rabbits on their land. Evidently these rabbits had been left to breed as they intended to have a day's shooting. Anyway, four of us, three lads and Norman, who was grown up by then, set off to have a go at these rabbits. It was a long walk. We crossed the river by way of the weir - the water was quite strong and just below our knees. The stones were very slippery.

We then had to cross the railway. There were several small tunnels through the embankment for the cattle to go from field to field. We crossed a field and next was the canal. There were two bridges about one and a half miles apart. The only way for us was the one on our left, close to Healey village, that carried the railway over a loop in the river.

I would say by the time we arrived at the quarry where some of the rabbits were, we had covered about four miles. We soon set about those rabbits. We had three guns, but the shots must have been heard. One of the lads spotted a man approaching fast, then another bloke appeared. By the look of them they meant business and could be Saville estate keepers.

It was a quiet Sunday and the noise of our shooting had carried far so as we were poaching, we beat a retreat back the way we had come. We made good time across the canal and over the railway. It was a long way along the track by the railway side, about three quarters of a mile. We were all blowing a bit, particularly the big lad. He was a bit younger than us, Bentley he was called and he weighed sixteen stones.

By now, away back, a vehicle had joined the chase. Also someone else was coming at us from the front. We were close to the river and once across the weir we would be safe, back on our own ground. We all charged down the bank to the water and out onto the weir, Norman in front, the rest of us after him. Bentley, the big lad, was last.

By now we realised that the police had joined the chase. It was their vehicle we had seen coming at us and they were giving us a good run. I had been chased many times before and didn't panic. All thoughts of danger had gone from me. The stones were bad to get a foothold on, you just had to slip and slide, fall down, get up and get going, and all carrying a gun at the same time.

The police were shouting at us to stop. They were now on to the weir as well. Knee deep water is very strong and if you slip then you are pushed down the weir. Norman was now on the bank shouting for us to hurry.

Three of us made it up the bank and stood a minute to look back. The big lad, Bentley, was stuck in the middle of the weir and had lost his nerve. A police sergeant got to him first and two of them managed to get him back to the bank. The rest gave up on us. We had a good start on them now.

We made our way back and I left my gun at the farm. We all went separate ways home, hoping Bentley would keep his mouth shut and not name us to the law. We knew that we would be in real trouble as it was Saville estates' land where we had been. Fortunately we had escaped and no rabbits were found, so killing ground game on a Sunday did not apply. We all had a visit from the police. We were all given a warning and that was the end of it, at least for a while.

I did have another encounter with a farmer. I was on his land and had shot four partridges. I was walking along a beck side, a rabbit got up just in front of me so I shot it. It rolled into the water. I had just retrieved it and was shaking the water from it. I looked up to see Edmund Lister, the farmer, running down the field. Well, I soon left him behind as I was on someone else's land.

My Aunt Evelyn had said she would have any partridges or a rabbit and so I made my way to where she lived. I said to my aunt, 'I got you some partridges and a rabbit if you want them,' thinking to make myself a few bob. 'You've been running haven't you?' I must admit I was a bit bedraggled and scratched. My gun was in two pieces, barrels in one hand, the stock in the other. The four partridges and the rabbit stuffed inside my Army blouse and water still dripping out from the sodden rabbit. 'You've been poaching?'

Brian and friend Norman with flintlock guns.

'No.' 'Where did you get them? Don't bring them here, go on, take 'em away.' Edmund Lister, the farmer who chased me was my aunty's milkman. The partridges were raffled in the Crown Hotel that night. Pubs were places where most things could be sold at a price.

I almost shot a farmer one evening. I was on a field overlooking a small wood. I was about a dozen yards from the hedge looking towards the wood. I heard a scrambling noise from the other side of the hedge. Thinking it was maybe a rabbit, I put the gun to my shoulder ready to shoot. A man's head popped up. He had a trilby hat on. I don't know who was more scared, Leonard Hetherington, the farmer, or me. It was a close shave for both of us. It takes a fraction of a second to squeeze the trigger and a lifetime to regret it.

Donald Auty and the firewood business

Donald Auty, my mate, had an older brother called James who lived a few miles away at Ossett. James was in the firewood trade, or kindling wood business. Any old wood that was suitable for kindling would be begged or bought cheap from building contractors, sometimes it was delivered and sometimes brought back on the pony cart.

The small, black pony of about ten hands and a flat cart were the pride and joy of James Auty's business. It was the only transport the business had and was used whenever possible. The headquarters of the Auty Firewood Company was a very old, stone built shop, a tiny place underneath the railway arches that spanned the road. It had one window and a door where lengths of wood were pulled inside to be cut into seven inch lengths.

If the wood was too big to go through the doorway, it was sawn into shorter pieces outside on the road. Once inside, a small circular saw was used to speed up operations. I went there at nights when my mate was working overtime. We sat at either end of a baulk of heavy timber and with a short handled axe cut the wood into kindling. When we had a pile cut, it was put into buckets and tipped onto a bench by the window. Two bundling machines were fastened on the bench. Two handfuls of sticks was placed in the machine, upright, then a pedal under the bench was pressed down with the right leg. This caused the jaws to close around the sticks and held them tight. A wire was then passed around the bundle and twisted, the pedal released and the kindling was ready for sale.

We spent many winter nights in the Auty firewood shop. The only light came from a gas bracket on the wall by the saw and if you were on the bundling machine your back was to the light. We managed and must have had eyes like owls! James would say, 'Look quick, lads. I have orders for so many bundles tomorrow.' And so we bundled on well into the night.

Donald travelled by bus to Ossett and had a short walk to the firewood shop. Dolly the pony was fed and got ready for the day's work, driven to the shop and tied up outside. Bundles of kindling were loaded on the cart. When all was ready, James, a tall, usually unshaven chap, untied the pony and sat on one side of the cart, his feet about touching the road. Away he would go, shouting for Dolly to get on, the cart canted over with his weight. Small shops about the area bought the kindling. Most people had open fires in their homes and it was quite a good business in those days. Once James had gone, Donald would be back to the sawing and bundling all day long in the dark little shop. In winter I would say it could be miserable.

Donald sometimes delivered the kindling. On these days he was dressed in an old jacket and a cap of black corduroy, a bit like a seaman's cap. Sometimes riding breeches and long boots, but always a red handkerchief about his neck, tied in a dog knot.

His father worked at a place where uniforms were brought back from the battlefields. My mate and I both received a pair of German riding breeches, the wings at the sides stuck out a long ways as stiff wire was sewn into them to give them a smart appearance. I had an English officer's Air Force jacket. It too was smart apart for a few bullet holes in the skirt of it. We went about at weekends dressed in breeches, white long socks turned over the top of dispatch rider boots and usually a smart tweed jacket and the crowning glory, a pork pie hat. Boy were we smart, least way we thought we were!

Wanted - British Boys for British Farms
I saw the advert for farm hands just before Christmas in 1947, wrote off and was accepted. I was to report to Hull, from there I would be met and taken to the headquarters at a place called Mapleton.

I said goodbye to my mother and with a brown paper parcel I was away to Hull. I was picked up by a chap in an old van and taken to Mapleton. There was some sort of camp there, with wooden Army huts, very bare and cold. The wife of the chap who had collected me was a sort of matron at the place.

I was told which bed I was to sleep in and had a locker to keep things in. The hut was empty, the other lads that slept there had not come back from work yet. It was dark when the lads started to arrive, not all together. They all wore canvas leggings, thick trousers and jackets. When they had washed themselves, we all sat down to a good dinner. There was a recreation room where we all went after we had washed all the plates and stuff.

Bedtime was 9pm and I was glad to get to bed as it was cold in the hut. I don't think I slept much, so much had happened to me that day and I was away from home.

At 6am we were called out of our beds, 'Get washed and dressed,' shouted a chap. Another chap said, 'Breakfast's ready.' Long tables were laid out for us, with porridge, bacon and eggs, bread and tea. 'I want you away at 6.30am.' Evidently the lads all worked on different farms scattered about the countryside. From what I had seen the day I arrived, most of the land was arable, growing corn, spuds, beet, beans, mangolds, turnips, etc.

My horse Pilot

It was dark and a very cold morning with frost everywhere on the hedges and trees. I was taken into a farmyard and into a byre where some men were milking cows. The chap who led me there said, 'Here's your lad, Mr Spite.' Mr Spite looked at me and said, 'Right come with me, lad.' We went into a stable, some horses were there eating hay. 'That black yan yonder is yours and that cart out by the midden is yours as well. Get him yoked, they call him Pilot.'

That was it. He left me and went back to the byre, milking. The light in the stable was not too good. I don't think the lamp had been cleaned since it was new. I looked at the horse, at its great big arse and thought, how the bloody hell am I going to get the gear on him?

The harness hanging on the wall was big, very big. The horse, he too was very big. Pilot was a Clydesdale and at a guess he was all of seventeen hands tall. I was about five feet three inches. I got into the standing in front of the horse, thinking to make myself known to him. He was a quite lovely animal, black with white feathers on all his feet and a blaze of white down between his eyes, aye, a lovely horse.

So, having made myself known to the horse, how was I to get the collar on him? It was all I could do to lift the collar off the wall. I went into the standing in front of Pilot. I was talking to him all the time and put the collar in his trough. Then I climbed into the trough. I thought, what if he throws his head back, some horses do that. I was lucky, the tether rope was short and the horse quiet. He stood as still as could be. Maybe he knew I was struggling - it was one thing to get the collar on, but another to turn it round the way it must be when working. I was sweating by the time I did it and that was just the start.

Gathering myself up I struggled to get the breechings off the wall - three straps of heavy leather and two tug chains in my arms. I had yoked horses before but Pilot was like harnessing two horses at once, hell, he was big! Well, I was still talking to him and he was watching me perform. I swung the breeching up as high as I could but it only went halfway. Pilot never moved. I was able to scramble around his arse end and reach the tug chain and pull the gears onto his withers. Buggered again, it was daylight outside the stable and I was still not ready. The saddle and breechings are fastened together by two straps and buckles. These would have to wait till I was out in the yard and found some steps or whatever to stand on.

The saddle and belly band were heavy. I had it over my right arm, and was looking about the stable for something to stand on but there wasn't even a bucket. I looked up at the horse's back and said to myself, I shall never get it up there. Pilot was looking at me as though I was something new. I was new alright. Right, I'll have a go. I swung the saddle up as far as I could. It was nearly in place. I stood on my toes and pushed it and it slid into place. I was knackered.

I went back to the front of the horse, still talking to him. I put the blinkers in the trough and climbed up as well. Now would he let me put the bit in his mouth? It was off with the head collar, I was holding him by his forelock and struggling with the blinkers. The bit rattled on Pilot's teeth. 'Come on, open your mouth.' More rattling of teeth and in a second I had the blinkers over his ears. I had done it. Outside I stood on some steps and fastened breechings and saddle straps.

'Right, my lad,' I said as I led the horse into the yard and, as the granary steps were handy, I led Pilot up to them and leaned on his back and fastened the breeching straps. The cart wheels were much taller than I - they were six feet or more. The shafts were up in the air, almost straight up. A rope was hanging down from them and the back band was in place. The whole cart was huge.

I looked about everywhere, were they watching me? No, I couldn't see anyone, no-one was bothered about me so it seemed. Walking the horse to the cart I turned him and backed him to where I thought the shafts would be when I pulled them down with the rope. It had to be right as I couldn't hold the horse and pull down that shaft at the same time, I would need all my strength and weight to do that.

I was still talking to Pilot and told him to stand 'whoa.' Right, I grabbed the rope and pulled as hard as I could. The cart was well balanced, the shafts started to come down. I darn't let go of the rope or the shafts would go back up, down they came, but not into the groove in the saddle but onto the saddle leather. Pilot moved a bit, 'Whoa, whoa,' the cart weight was all on the saddle but the back band must be in the groove, so by lifting one shaft a couple of inches, I managed. The rest was easy. I hitched the tugs and breeching chains and fastened the belly band and then there was just the driving reins to buckle on and I was ready.

Leading Muck

'Leave him there, he'll be alright, come and have a drink but don't hang about,' said Mr Sprite, 'I want you to put a load of muck on, then take it to the field, just follow the wheel marks. Tip it and bring a load of kale back.'

The snow lay thick on the ground, and it wasn't a hard task to follow the ruts. I managed to load the muck, a nice warm job, the load steaming in the frosty air. Away I went, walking at the head of my own horse. The wheel marks were easy to follow and it was about half a mile to the field. Muck had been tipped there before, heaps of it evenly spaced out. It would be spread by hand, later towards spring. I stopped Pilot where the load was to be tipped, took out the bar holding the cart top to the body of the cart, up it went. The muck came out easily, as I'd taken off the tailgate. Drawing Pilot forwards a bit, I put the tailgate on again, pulled down the cart top and put it in the holding pins.

The kale was at the far end of the field. I stopped Pilot nice and handy, not too near. It was marrow stem kale, tall, thick stuff like young trees, about six feet high and maybe ten inches around it. It was frozen. I looked at the slasher, it too was frozen, the wooden shaft white with frost crystals. Bloody hell, I thought, now I'm for it. I had done this sort of work at Willy Lumb's farm at home.

I let fly with the slasher, hitting the kale hard with a downward stroke. The slasher almost shot out of my hands with the frost on its handle. The piece of kale had shattered and flew in pieces of different sizes, mostly about a foot long. I hit at it again, a shower of ice flew everywhere, it seemed most of it over me.

The handle was thawing out now, but my hands were getting colder by the minute. I kept on striking at the kale until I was blown. I had brought a muck fork with me - it was no good going without a fork into unknown territory. I started to gather up the kale, but because it was frozen it wouldn't stay on the fork. There was nothing for it - I loaded it with my bare hands.

I had helped do this work before and knew I was in for a soaking. I had to reach up so high to get the broken stems into my cart, that any water or ice that was on the leaves ran down my arms, my ganzi was wet in good time, and I couldn't feel my hands. How long it took me to cut and load the cart I don't know, I lost all sense of time.

At the end of the day I had managed one load of muck out of the yard and one load of kale back to the yard. I was tired out, all the food I had was the few sandwiches in my bag and a flask of tea. I was helped to unharness the horse and put him up in the stable. Back at the camp our dinner was ready, it was about 6pm. Later that night I got into my bed wearied out.

It snowed that night and was still snowing when we turned out to work. I worked in the yard and buildings that day so that wasn't too bad. It snowed all day and was still at it at night.

The camp and village were right on the cliff top and there was nothing between us and the sea. It was bitterly cold. My next day at Spites Farm, I was back with my horse, Pilot, same as before. I took a load of muck out of the yard, but by now there was three feet of snow on the ground. Every bit of work was that much harder, and I had to dig through the snow to get at the muck, but at least it kept me warm.

I had to make a new track to the kale field. I kept stumbling into holes and ruts with the snow so deep. What a sight as I entered the field where the kale stood. It looked as though a wall had been built and there was no kale to be seen, just a bank of snow. I tipped my load of muck and led Pilot to what looked like the wall. 'Bloody hell,' I said to Pilot, 'how the hell do I get at it?'

I knew whereabouts I had stuck the slasher the time before and with the fork soon found it. I started slashing at where the kale should be, the snow flew about me. Cutting the stuff was one thing, finding it after was another. I had to rake about with the fork to find it and so it went on. I got a load at last, little did I know it was to be my last!

Next day at the Spite farm, I was called to help with some young bullocks in the yard. An old windmill was used to house these animals. The mill had long ceased to work as such, only the bottom or ground level was used.

The door was narrow, very narrow for a beast to get through. Earlier, Mr Spite had been in to the mill with feed and somehow left the door open and the bullocks had escaped out to the yard. We had most of them back in but two were very difficult and would not go in again. Without more ado, one beast was cornered and a head stall put on its head so it could be led and pushed into the mill. Now for the last one. We cornered it and, the head stall put on, it led alright but only to the door. I had hold of the rope and was in front of it. I opened the door and started to pull at the bullock's head. It came a bit then stopped, half in and half out of the building. I pulled, they shoved, shouted, cracked it with a stick, but no, it wouldn't ga.

I heard a voice say, 'Look out!' Like a shot out of a gun the beast leapt forwards, knocked me over and landed on my legs. I managed to roll under a tumbril, out of the way, as the other beasts were dashing about the place. My leg hurt and the men came and lifted me up. 'You'll be OK in a minute, my lad.' I was carried into the house kitchen and sat on a chair. 'Tha's just bruised, lad.'

My leggings and boot were taken off, then my stockings. The right foot was swollen up. Someone came in with a bucket of cold water with bits of ice floating on top of it. 'Put yer foot in there, lad, it'll bring down the swelling.' Somebody lifted my leg and stuck my foot into the water. I almost jumped off the chair, the shock was so great. I was wrapped up and put in the van and driven to our camp.

They put me and my bed in a small room on my own and gave me some aspirins for the pain. And there I stayed for five or six days, my leg propped up on pillows. I was given loads of aspirin but I could not sleep, it hurt me so much.

The matron that was looking after me had a look at my leg which was a yellow and purple mank to the top of the leg, something was wrong. She got the wind up, 'Poison.' The old van was fetched and I was carried to it and placed on blankets in the back. It was an awful journey to Hull Infirmary. I was operated upon straightaway, and a metal plate and screws were used as the malleolus bone was broken. I stayed in the hospital all Christmas 1947 with my leg in plaster. Later, I was sent home, the snow still lay deep everywhere.

Grove Farm

With my foot in plaster I got an old Wellington boot, one that was a lot too big for me and cut the leg from it, leaving only the length of an ordinary boot. This I cut from the toe to the front top and then I could get my plastered foot into the boot and the wet didn't bother me. The hospital people told me to keep it dry.

So, I was back with my mates again and when I had healed and could walk again, I started to look for a job. There wasn't much in my line of work. Then a mate of mine left Grove Farm where he had been working. I knew Fred and Benny Lumb - they were nephews to old Willy Lumb at Grange Farm. I went to see them and got the job. It was only a small farm, maybe sixty acres.

Mrs Lumb was a widow and lived in the farmhouse alone, Fred and Benny having their own homes a short way off. We milked twelve cows by hand and did a milk round later until dinnertime. After our dinner we started doing all the jobs that belong to farming.

An old man worked there in the afternoons. He was called Uncle Walter and his surname was Sheard. He was a small man, Uncle Walter, always had a stubble beard as he only shaved once a week as did most men at that time. A leather jerkin and cord leggings and an old cap were Walter's garments. He was about 80 years old and still very strong and was a man of all trades.

Over the years I worked with him I heard a lot. He was a very quiet man not given to much talk, but he took an interest in me and I in him. I liked to hear about the Mary Pit and how quickly it flooded. He remembered the railway being put through the farm fields. Walter lived on Station Road, it was not really a road, just a dirt track and quite near where the coal man used to have his holding.

I started at Grove Farm and found Fred and Benny easy to get on with. I started at 7am in the dairy to get the four milking buckets then set up the cooler and syle, a strainer with a wire gauze in the bottom and a cotton wade to catch the hairs and other stuff. The syle was placed on top of a churn and the churn set under the cooler. Water was run through this cooler, it was made of thin copper and tinned over. Two pipes, one at the top and one at the bottom were connected to the water tap and the tap turned on when in use.

We went into the byre or mistel, as they were sometimes called, and any muck on the step where the cows stood was cleaned off before the milking started and the cows' tits wiped over with warm water. Now we got our buckets and stools and commenced the milking - most of the cows were old and very quiet. I would tuck my head into the cow's side and talk to her. I found the smell of cake that they each received before being milked, and of hay, muck and the cow's breath comforting.

Cuss Alert, a lad from a fairly large family was supposed to help. Cuss had a problem, or I should say problems. He couldn't get up in the mornings. If he was late Fred would say, 'How's my country cusin this morning?' Cuss would answer, 'Alright,' get his stool and start to milk his cows. You could tell when he was using both hands by the sound of the milk hitting the bucket bottom. Another of Cuss' problems was he sucked his thumb. After a while the sound of milk hitting the bucket would change, Cuss would be thumb sucking and milking one handed.

Cuss' family lived in a pokey little yard with two cottages. His father, a very small man, worked at a mill and his mother, was a big woman, I would say about sixteen stones. The house was very untidy. I think there were three lads, their legs were bitten by bed bugs to red sores. The Alerts were a poor family. I felt sorry for our Country Cusin. Mrs Lumb gave Cuss eggs and milk. You couldn't send him on the milk round, he was too scruffy. No-one would have bought our milk. He smelled a bit too!

The milking was usually done by 8.30am. We all had scones and tea that Mrs Lumb had brought out to the dairy. We washed our hands and put on the grey smocks with side pockets for the money. We loaded four churns of milk into the old Morris 8 van, plus three hand cans with the measures in them, a pint and half pint. The van, which was only small, was full. I climbed in and sat on the hand can, then Shep, Fred's dog got in as well, what a crowd. In got Fred and Benny and so we chugged away to start the round at the top of Chickenly.

Fred opened the rear doors and out fell Shep - Fred grabbed me to stop me doing the same. Out came the hand cans, they were oval shaped and held three gallons of milk. The hand cans were filled up and away we went, each to our own customers. When the hand cans were empty, we would wait until Benny brought the van to us and our cans were filled again and so it went on until we had completed the round.

By this time it was dinnertime and we all went home. Once dinner was over we all went back to the farm, Benny to wash all the churns, cans and dairy utensils. If I was to go ploughing, Uncle Walter would have both horses already cleaned and polished and geared up ready for me. If it was warm and there were flies about, Walter would wipe the horses over with a rag with paraffin on it.

I was now about sixteen years old. My two horses were Royal and Bob. Royal was half hunter and half shire and a bay. As he was half hunter, he was lighter legged than a shire and had been used in the milk float before the van arrived. Royal stood about sixteen hands at the shoulder. He was a quiet and a useful horse, good to work with and about eight years old. Bob was shire bred and almost black with a white blaze down his face. Bob was about five years old, had white feathered feet and stood about sixteen hands two inches. He was a bit more frisky but a useful type of horse.

The plough was made of wood and was quite old, made by Yates. It was a proper plough, not a semi-digger as a lot of ploughs at that time were. Uncle Walt would come along with me and put me right. Then Walter would go on with his own work. These were happy days for me.

Buying guns

I used to see Norman Clare and the Isaacs out shooting when I was working out in the fields. I was thinking about getting another gun. There was a policeman I knew and at that time there was a fire arms amnesty - you could hand in any firearms that were illegal or ones you didn't want. This was because as men came home from the war they were bringing a lot of firearms with them. A lot of these guns were not illegal - there were good quality muzzle loaders and very nice guns even though they were from an age gone by.

The policeman used to visit Grove Farm and sometimes firearms were handed to him on his rounds and as time went by I bought some good old guns from him. It was wrong of the policeman to sell me these weapons but he was happy and I know I was. Fifteen shillings was the most I paid for any gun. I once acquired a double barrelled muzzle loader, a very nice gun, complete with powder flask, shot bag, wads and caps. No.1, No. 2 and No. 3 garden guns were plentiful - these fired a bullet or a shot cartridge. A Blunderbuss also came my way. I used this weapon but was never keen on it as it had too short a barrel. It had a bayonet laid upon the barrel top which could be brought forwards by pressing a button releasing a spring. I was shown how to load them, how much powder and shot to put in and what cap to use to fire them.

My mate Donald and I were offered a gun for £2/10s. It was a single barrelled gun - one barrel had been sawn off. It was a semi-hammerless gun and now I look back it could have very easily killed one of us. It was very unsafe but we didn't know that. I did buy a double barrelled 12 bore at Greenwood's Pawn Shop for £5. It was only proofed for black powder and we were using smokeless diamond cartridges. It was all very dangerous as I now know.

While I worked at Grove Farm, shooting was my sport and I spent as much time as possible out with my double barrelled 12 bore gun, an old hammer gun. I remember one Saturday afternoon I was over on the Bull Croft and had not had a shot - the partridges were too wild and were on the wing well out of range.

I made my way towards John Ackes as it was called, a lot of rough grass, ideal for a rabbit or hare to sit in. I had covered most of the ground and stopped, leaning my gun against the wall. Down below I could see the railway station and goods yard lay as well as the field where I used to work when I was with the coal man. It was all grown up with docks. I was thinking of when I had the shooting over that land. I could see a man was on the station platform.

Just then I heard a noise, it sounded a bit like a goose calling. Looking up I saw it. If it kept the line it was flying it would come directly over me. I grabbed my gun and cocked both hammers, click, click. Ducking down behind the wall, the goose came at me, bloody hell I thought, it's too high, well out of shot. It must have been eighty or ninety yards up and the effective round of No. 5 shot was only about 45 yards.

The goose was right above me. I stood up giving it plenty of lead and it seemed to falter. I shot again. By God, it started to lose height and swung in a half circle. The goose finally dropped behind the station waiting room and the bloke on the platform ran across the lines and picked it up.

I had run about 400 yards and when I got to the station the man was walking away with the goose under his coat. 'That's my goose you've got,' I said. He opened his coat, it was a Canada Goose. 'I'll give yer five bob for it.' I grabbed it, a thousand pounds would not have bought my first goose. Boy, was I proud - I showed it about, I wanted everybody to see it.

While I was on the farm I had the right to shoot over the land which I did. I used all kinds of guns, rifles and also some pistols. And so time went by. Walter and I worked together and I was keen to learn from him. Some days in winter we would sort spuds. Three swills were used. We would kneel at the heap of spuds on a sack each, the big spuds were put in one swill, the seed spuds in another and the very small chats, as they were called, in another swill. As the swills became full we emptied them into sacks and repeated the process until they were all sorted.

I was shown the proper way to sweep up the haycocks and take them to the stack and to ride the horse rake, a big clumsy machine. I learned how to mow the grass with a Bamford horse mower, and at harvest to build corn stacks - the square ended one and the 'tatie pie stack' and the 'round' or 'Scotch' stack. I learned how the courses of sheaves were laid and tied in to hold the stack solid. There were three different ways to do that. Walter let me mow when opening out a field before the self-binder went in to start cutting the corn and he showed me how to make the straw bands to tie the corn that we cut with the scythe.

The horses needed shoes when working to protect their hooves and had to be taken to the blacksmiths. It usually took half a day for that job. When you arrived at the smithy there could be more people waiting with their horses so sometimes we could have a good crack, or have a look about after tying up the horse. Old Oliver, the smith, would start coughing when burning on the shoes as a cloud of acrid smoke came from the burned hoof. He would swear between his coughing.

When loading sheaves in the field, different methods were used. Barley was very short in the stalk, wheat longer, rye very long and slippery, oats too were fairly long so a way had been worked out how best to load each type of corn. Once a wagon was loaded we had to look at it to make sure which way to rope it down. This was very important as, if the loads were not secured properly, it could come off. The tracks were very rough and much jolting about could occur before the load reached the yard where it was stacked and thatched down with wheat straw and a net put over it until it was threshed. When all the corn was harvested and if the field was to be sown with winter corn, ploughing would start. Sometimes the field would need to be cleaned as twitch, bindweed, convolvulus and other weeds are detrimental to growing crops.

If, after ploughing was done the weather was dry, a set of harrows would be taken to the field. Corn harrows, what was called a set, were enough for one horse to pull. The harrows were fastened to what was called a baulk. This was a long piece of strong wood or iron pipe with short chains about one foot long attached to it at intervals. These were fixed to harrows, the chains were fastened, each section of harrow having two hooks.

When the corn harrows were ready, a swingletree with an eye in the middle was fastened to the long baulk. The swingletree had a hook at each end and was about three feet long. The long chains for pulling the harrows were fastened to the collar of the horse and the other end to the swingletree. This sounds complicated but had to be done to give the horse room to move and not to get tangled up with the harrows. This could be hard work on warm autumn days as many miles would be walked. We put dock leaves in our boots or clogs to keep our feet cool.

Hoeing at Jim Sheard's

Jim Sheard's Field, as we called it was at the far side of the village, I would say about a mile or so from Grove Farm. When we ploughed it the soil would not turn over because it was too light, it just ran in front of the mould board of the plough. Walter said that for years the field had been used for tipping night soil - night soil is the stuff shovelled out of the old earth closets or outside privies.

After Jim Sheard's field had been prepared and sown with turnips, Walter and I set about singling the plants out. This is done with a hoe with an eight inch wide - that is the width we left between the plants. Walter's old leather jerkin had a big pocket sewn into the skirt, as we went up and down the rows, pieces of coal and coke were picked up and put in this pocket then, having reached the headland his pocket was emptied into a sack. Some days half a sack of fuel was picked up and taken home. It had to be carried home on Walter's back but he didn't complain, it was all for nowt.

I once found an old medal in the same field. It was bent and I cannot recollect what was on the face of it. Occasionally a coin would be found that had dropped from a pocket when someone visited the privy. When the turnips had been pulled during the winter we used a horse and cart. It was a long way to the field and I only managed one load in the afternoon. I believe Jim Sheard's field is now covered in houses as are many more of the fields that I used to work in. It makes me sad to see everything gone - roads, houses and buses everywhere where we used to shoot partridges and rabbits. All for the sake of people who are spreading like a plague over everything.

The Cow Chase

While I worked at Grove Farm a cattle wagon arrived early one afternoon. The back of the wagon was let down and the driver got into the back among the cows. A while later he shouted for someone to open the tailgate, out came the driver holding the rope but the cow stood still in the wagon not wanting to leave its mates. After some shoving and stick waving the cow finally got out and immediately made a dash for the open gate. It got out on the road trailing the rope behind it. I managed to grab it before the cow had gone far. Sticking my heels in I did all I could to stop it.

I might as well have tried to stop a train. Luckily, the rope was a long one. I had to run with the cow as it passed the hall entrance and Mill Lane cottages, down the hill towards the railway station then up the hill past the station. Almost at the top of the hill there was a row of houses and in front of them a piece of grass where some washing was hung to dry. By now the cow was tired and so was I. I had fallen along the way and had been dragged along the road. My breeches were roven at the knees and so were my hands.

The cow turned in by the cottages on to the drying ground. I saw my chance. I wrapped the rope around the washing post, 'There, you bugger, that'll hold you!' The van pulled up, Fred and Benny got out, 'Good lad,' Fred said. All of a sudden the cow set off again. As soon as the rope tightened on the clothes post it snapped, down came the washing, the bloody cow took off again. This time I had some help, Benny and Fred held the rope with me and at last we bossed the cow. It was almost a mile back to the farm, some cow! Who was to milk her? She turned out to be a very quiet old thing, but what a start we had.

Mitchel Laithes farm
Mitchel Laithes farm was owned by the council and was a big farm. It was built as a model farm in the 1880s. Two brothers farmed it - George and Ernest Tebb. I knew the men that worked on the farm and was told they wanted a tractor/horse man. I had been thinking about spreading my wings for a while. I went to see George Tebb and he said he didn't like to take me away from the Lumbs and Grove Farm. I said I would go elsewhere even if he, George, didn't take me on. So George took me on. 'You're a useful lad, we'll give you a start.'

So I went back and told Fred and Benny I would be leaving them. I worked my time out with them. I would see them every day as I had to travel across their land to get to Mitchel Laithes farm.

One Monday morning I was biking along the lane to work and Don Jowett, the head cowman, was just in front of me. He got off his bike to get through the stile. I caught up with him so we went together over the fields. It was still dark - our bike lights were not much good, the footpath slippery and the ruts in the gateways deep. We had to cross five fields to the farmstead. There were a few lights on when we got there.

I went into the cow house, where forty cows were tied up, with Don. The building was divided into four sections with ten cows in each. I felt proud - this was a proper byre, no hand milking here, the Alfa Laval machine had just started up.

I knew the farm well as I had been there to help with threshing and taking cows from Grove Farm to the bull at Mitchel Laithes. George walked into the byre, 'Right Brian, you can have the Major,' the Major being the tractor, a Fordson Major. It was a big, dark blue machine with huge orange wheels as big as me.

'See Ike, he'll show you what to do with it.' Ike Tebb was Ernest Tebb's son, George's nephew. I met Ike by the tractor shed. The Major was standing beside the fuel tank that held the TVO, that was the stuff used in the tractors in those days. 'Sa you thought you would come and wak with us?' 'Yes, I thought the Major was your tractor Ike?' 'No, I've got a David Brown now that Jowett's in t'cow house.' 'Ho.' 'You want some petrol in that small tank nearest steering wheel, about a gallon will do, doesn't hold much more. She will warm up on two pints, then turn her over on TVO, keep the blind up till the marker is on green. She will need some TVO,' said Ike.

The Fordson Major had two fuel tanks - a large one for TVO or Tractor Vapourising Oil and the smaller tank for petrol. You had to start the tractor on petrol until the engine was warmed enough to run on TVO, which took about ten minutes. On top of the radiator was a gauge with glass with a red and green background. A pointer moved from red to green when the engine was warm enough, then you turned a tap below the fuel tank and turned on the TVO. Sometimes clouds of white smoke belched from the exhaust pipe that stuck up in the air along with the air cleaner. The white smoke meant the engine was not hot enough to vapourise the TVO so you just turned the tractor back onto petrol a while longer.

So started another page in my life. I was seventeen years old. My work at Mitchel Laithes was quite different from what I had grown used to at Grove Farm with the Lumbs. I helped with milking but not often. We worked at weekends, one on and one off, with the milking, to give the stockmen a rest. Apart from the forty milk cows, there were calves, forty stirks and a fold yard with about forty bullocks. The bullocks were about three years old when they went to market for killing. We had many horses, before the tractors were bought, and four horses were still kept on the farm. Across the green were the old farm buildings where about two hundred pigs were housed. Behind the barn at the top of the yard was a round house where the horse gin or horse engine stood. It was now used as a yard for stock.

A herd of sheep came to the farm to be fattened over the winter on turnips, rolled barley and hay. The sheep were folded, that means an area of the turnip field was fenced in with stakes and wire netting, usually about half an acre. Sheep were let into the fold where they stayed until all the turnips were eaten off. Troughs and hay racks were put in the fold with them and they were well looked after. Sheep do the ground much good, their droppings enrich the soil and make it very fertile. When the fold was eaten out, another fold was erected and the sheep moved on to fresh ground.

I travelled to work on my bike in all weathers and many a morning I was wet before I started work. Tractors did not have cabs on them, the driver was open to the weather. In wet weather we would wrap sacks around us and an Army overcoat and always a cap. We were out in all weathers and just got on with whatever we were doing.

Turnips and feed had to be brought into the yard for all the stock regardless. Turnips were pulled and carted, then tipped in a building close to the turnip chopper which cut the root to about a good sized chip. They were then mixed with barley, rolled barley or rolled oats and fed to the fat stock. Turnips were loaded by sticking a fork in them. Mangolds were pulled but care was taken not to cut the root as they bleed and go bad. We left about two inches of the leaves on them.

Mangolds have to be picked up and loaded by hand. Two types were grown at that time - yellow globes, a round mangold, they could grow very big and gate posts, they were longer and narrower and a red colour. Mangolds had to be covered with straw to keep the frost from them.

Kale was also grown at Mitchel Laithes Farm. It was nearly always a marrow stem, the same as they grew at Mapleton which I shall never forget. One year my boss said we would make silage with the kale. The stuff had to be chopped up, so we mounted a hay chopper on an old horse wagon and fastened it down to the floor boards and pulled it to the kale field. We had put a pulley wheel on the chopper so that it could be driven from the power take off behind the David Brown tractor seat.

The side boards were put on the wagon, and the pulley belt fixed so all was now ready, so we thought! Four men were to do the job, so we all went at the kale with slashers. As soon as we had a good lot cut the tractor was started, the chopper gathered speed. Before long the chopper and the wagon were shaking. It was a bit frightening at first, all that vibration. The hay chopper was very old, it had a wheel somewhere about three and a half feet across and two sharp blades fastened inside it. It was meant for a man to turn it by a handle and was meant for a slow speed, just as fast as one man could turn it.

I stood back from the contraption, the tractor engine was running just about tick over speed. I couldn't see the two blades in the wheel it was turning that fast. 'Right, lads,' George climbed on the wagon, 'Let's have it.' Albert Taylor threw an armful of kale onto the wagon. George gathered some of it up and put it in the wooden trough that fed the cutting blades. Crunch, crunch, crunch. Now George Tebb was a very strong man, short built but broad. When George said it had to go, it had to go. He was ramming the kale down the trough too hard. 'Ike, give her a bit more juice.' The throttle was shoved down and the engine revved faster. 'That's better,' shouted George. Bits of kale about as big as a crab apple came showering down the chopper chute. The wagon started to fill up with chopped kale.

The Major was brought alongside with a trailer and I started to shovel the chopped kale in. It was loaded and was away with it to the stack yard where we had made a place for it. Then I tipped it and away for another load. Don Spurr kept at the kale with a slasher, he was just about able to keep Albert Taylor going who loaded for George.

And so it went on, day after day. There were four acres of kale in the field and we moved the chopper nearer every time we cut further into the standing kale. The pile of chopped kale in the yard got longer and longer. It had been quite high when we started but had sunk to about three feet high and was spreading. We looked at the heap, it was more like a muck midden and still spreading.

One day the boss said, 'That's enough. We shall cut if for the stock when we want it.' Well, the heap in the yard sank lower and lower and spread further out, the smell was awful and I wasn't much bothered by smells. Later on the heap was so offensive that we had to cart it away and spread it on a field a long way off.

The old Albion self-binder had been converted to be pulled by a tractor, previous to that two horses were needed to draw it. The pole was shortened and two plates of steel bolted on with a hole through the steel plates so that a steel pin could fasten it to the tractor. The Albion binder was heavier than the old Macomac binder. Uncle Walter told me when he was a lad, before the self-binder came on the market, a man stood on the bed when the corn was cut and he pushed the corn off with a rake. Walter called it a 'putting off machine', the sheaves were then tied by hand by women.

Seven men worked the farm - George, Ernest, Albert Taylor and Ike, they lived on the farm, Don Spur, Don Jowett, Albert Richardson and myself, who lived away.

A place had been specially built for the workmen - it was a decent sized room, the walls white washed with brown tiles on the lower half, a black iron range and an oven to make meals on. There was also a deal table and some chairs and a copper in one corner for boiling water at pig killing time. We called it 'The Shant'.

Four of us had our bait in the Shant along with Shep, the cow dog. He always managed to get in there with us. A few pictures hung about the place and some of my muzzled loading guns. Old Albert would come out of the byre when about halfway through the milking and get the Shant fire going ready for us. By the way, we called Albert 'Meat' behind his back as he had been a butcher in his early days.

One morning Meat had lit the fire and I had been up on the roof and put a sack down the chimney. I was in the smithy and could keep an eye on things - smoke was coming out the Shant door, you couldn't see in the place. Meat was poking the fire and swearing, then he came out for some air, then he went back again to do battle with the fire. I was almost in tears with Meat's antics!

Later he got onto the roof and pulled the sack down from the flue - our bait tasted of smoke, Shep did well that day. Later that day Meat let my bike tyres down - he must have known who did the mischief.

Brian Aston

Threshing at Mitchel Laithes

On threshing days the engine usually arrived in the late afternoon. It would have been on the move a few hours as their speed was only about fifteen miles an hour. The contractors' base was at Kirk Burton, near Huddersfield, but they would have been at work on a farm not too far away from Mitchel Laithes. The old Fowler steam locomotive had been put in retirement years ago and in its place was a David Brown Industrial tractor. David Brown's were painted red - the Industrial was a fair sized machine. Three men could sit side by side on the driving seat. Ike Tebb thought it was marvellous.

It was a good mile and a half from Earlsheaton to the farm and a stiff climb up the lane to the stack yard. The yard had been cleared of all tackle and anything that would have been in the way the day before. The David Brown pulled the threshing tackle up to the Dutch barn - six bays all full of barley, wheat and oats. It was a good barn with twelve brick piers carrying the domed galvanised iron roof.

The tractor was unhitched from the threshing box and yoked to the bailer and towed into position. The foreman set out levelling up the thresher with a spirit level. That done the tractor was set and the belts put on to drive the machine. The tractor would be slowly run to make sure that the belts were true on the pulleys. If all was ready the machine was run at threshing speed for five minutes. After all that was done the tackle was stopped and sheeted up for the night.

Days before we were due to thresh the granary was swept clean. Many sacks were needed and these were rented from the railway yards and were good, strong sacks which came in ten stone, twelve stone, fourteen stone, sixteen stone, eighteen stone, which were very big. Forks were put ready, bundles of baling wires all nice and handy and some four wheeled wagons were put about on which the sacks of corn could be loaded. A place was made ready for the wheat chaff which was used with the horse feed.

Early in the morning of the first day, sheets were put down at the corn end of the thresher to catch any corn that over-spilled the sacks and the barrow cart was put beside the weighing machine. A pile of sacks were all nice and handy - it could get a bit hectic at the corn end! If we were going to thresh out, or thresh everything in the yard, it would be over a week's work and some very tired men would make their way home each night, wishing it was the last night.

The lights of the tractor were on and at first light we were started. Eight men were the norm - two on the corn end, two on the stack, two on the bales, one on the chaff and the engineer. Everyone was kept busy. The men on the corn end were weighing and bagging, lifting onto the barrow cart, winding up the cart, then carrying the sacks to trailers and then back for another. Still at the corn end, bags of seconds and bags of small seeds were all to be tied up and moved and more sacks to be hung on.

Two men on the stack had it easy for a while as the sheaves were slid down to the man feeding the sheaves into the drum and cutting the bands at the same time. Later the stack men had to work harder as they got closer to the ground, as all the sheaves had to be picked upwards onto the machine. The chap on the baler had the job of shoving the needles into the baler, then passing two long wires through them. If a young boy was present he could be set to threading the wires back again for the knot to be fastened. The two bale stackers had a slower job but it was heavy work - many bales would be made and several stacks as well. As the stacks reached higher, an elevator was sometimes used, but whichever way, it was hard work and made the chaps grunt!

The chaff job was a dirty, awful job. The chaff man placed a sheet under the machine where the chaff was blown out. As soon as the sheet was full it was taken away. Although chaff was fed to the horses heaps of it were also burned later, well away from the stack yard. Bait time was 10am, when the men would have scones, tea, apple pie, followed by dinner about noon, when there were always plenty of spuds and meat. We would have bait again at 3pm.

If all had gone well, the bay would be finished by 2pm and we would move the machine and set up again and maybe start on another stack. Threshing was done in the winter and we would work until it was dark.

The Race

At weekends there were usually a few people hanging about the farm - some who helped out at hay time and harvest, others to talk. Someone said, 'Let's have a race to Horbury Bridge and back.' I don't know to this day how far Horbury Bridge is, I would say four miles each way. Anyway, race we did. Six of us entered and we each put half a crown in the kitty, so there were fifteen shillings for the winner.

It was a hot, sunny, summer, Sunday morning when we ran the race. We set off from the green and ran away along the track that followed the river all the way to Horbury Bridge. I was the young 'un and the others were off like hares. Bloody hell, I was left well behind but I hadn't gone very far when I passed D Jowett, and not long after another and another. We had to go through Healy village. Just after that I was on my own, a chap on a bike alongside of me to make sure I touched the bridge. When I got back to the farm the other lads were sat with their feet in the water trough. It was a hard earned fifteen shillings - my feet were tender for days after.

On summer days I was out in the fields with a horse, among the mangolds, with the scuffler knocking the weeds about. The skylarks would be singing, everything growing and growing, even me! Sometimes a spark from a railway engine would set a field of corn alight. People would appear, maybe men from another farm that were working that way. All would help to put the flames out.

Scarborough
We were lying about the green at the farm one Sunday afternoon when I was about eighteen. 'Let's have a trip to Scarborough. Yes, we will go to Scarborough.' A week or two later we went, five of us. Harvest had just started, it was lovely sunny Saturday morning, we got aboard a train and arrived at Scarborough about 10.30am. 'Who's for a pint?' Pints all round, I was enjoying this, we didn't often get away from home.

And so we started. I was the youngest of them and didn't know much about drinking. They being some few years older were going to show me. 'How about a whisky?' I was all for it. 'Let's have another,' and so my legs started to wobble and so did my head.

The lads were laughing, 'Some joke,' I thought. 'Look at that Brian!' I had been watching a parrot for a while. It was in a cage that was hanging on some sort of a stand. Now, I being familiar with the parrot at Breeze Lee House, the home of the coal man, thought maybe it was related to Polly. I looked again, there were two of them, I was sure that only one was in the cage before. I went to have a closer look, getting up was a bit of a problem, walking over to the parrot's cage was a bit more difficult and the cage was moving about.

I was certainly moving about. I stuck a finger through the bars,

'Polly, Polly,' I was saying to it. I think it must have been hungry and maybe my finger looked like food. 'Ger off you bugger,' I pulling my finger away, pulled the cage and stand over, feathers and sawdust flew in the air. The parrot was screaming, seed flew about with sawdust. I was grabbed not too gently and very unsteadily found myself in the street, alone, my mates enjoying my performance with the parrot.

I was joined by my mates some time later. What we did that day is still a mystery. We missed the train home that night as all the station gates were locked when we arrived. Being warm, we slept on the front on benches, though the police bothered us a bit. Anyhow, we set about enjoying ourselves again, might as well make the most of it. It was only Sunday and enjoy ourselves we did. No more parrots for me, instead it was fish and chips, the hall of mirrors and up to the castle on the donkeys. It couldn't happen again? It had, the gates were locked at the station, earlier than the day before because it was Sunday night. We went back to the benches on the front, this time the police left us alone.

It was Monday afternoon when we got to the harvest field. It was the field by the old Pissing Mary Pit. 'Where the hell have you lot been?' 'On a day trip.' 'Day trip? It's bloody Monday afternoon.' 'We got locked out.' And so ended our days at Scarborough. We were all in disgrace, our boss was mad. It was a long time before we ventured far again. I did go with the older lads to some of the pubs, but I was a bit wary of parrots and other birds!!

Shooting was still my favourite sport. George took us to South Henshall, rabbit shooting. Fred Blakley gave me some reloading tools for 12 bore cartridges and I got more guns from the policeman. I had crossed the river a few times onto the Savile estates in my search for game and almost been caught. I visited Mill Bank, Great Aunt Florrie's old home, and went over to Breeze Field and further. I was grown up.

The Iron Bridge
We used three different routes to get onto the Savile estate land - from Earlsheaton the iron bridge was used. If we were leaving Mitchel Laithes farm, the weir across the river was the most direct if the river was low, which was only in summer. The other way was via Healy village and over the railway bridge. Whichever way you took, it was a long way and nearly always we had a gun and a dog.

So there were three obstacles to cross if you wanted to get to some good shooting land. It seems that the shooting is much better on someone else's land and the land coveted most belong to Lord Savile.

As I looked out towards Thornhill, across the River Calder, some filter beds lay there, strung out between the river and the railway and an old pumping station with a tall chimney beside it. If I remember correctly, there were eight filter beds. Over the railway were some low lying fields, always flooded, maybe from the canal which ran parallel to the lines. This was the view I had from Mitchel Laithes farm - all the land over the river belonged to the Savile estates. Having little or no respect for other people's land, we trespassed often in our search for game.

The Iron Bridge, as it was called, was not made to be used as a footbridge at all. It was built of iron plates and was a square, box section, with no hand rails, just a flat top. Inside were pipes for gas, water, etc. On the Earlsheaton side of the bridge a tall, stone wall reared up to prevent anyone climbing on the bridge. An iron door set into it was always locked.

The river bank was sheer, the stone wall disappeared into the water. I would say it was twenty feet from the foot plates to the water. At some time, iron spikes had been driven between the stones of the wall. It was possible to hang onto these spikes and work your way around the wall and then across the face of the wall and scramble up onto the bridge. Anyone that cannot stand being up high would run from it. I have crossed the Iron Bridge in all weathers. In summer the iron plates were so hot they burned your hands. In strong winds I have crawled on hands and knees and nearly always with a gun and game bag in fear of being blown into the river.

Ice was the most dangerous, as some of the iron foot plates were worn, water tended to settle in these depressions and soon froze. Again you had to crawl your way over. I have seen the bridge in very cold weather all white by frost. I reckon the Iron Bridge was eighty yards long and only four feet wide. In the dark and wet of night it was no mean feat. If you were alone, your gun had to be slung on your back, a piece of cord was always in a pocket. Some people used the Iron Bridge as a short cut to work at Savile town. The spikes in the wall were always bright with use yet I hardly ever met anyone although a well worn path ran away towards Thornhill.

I remember one year, during the 1940s, the river flooded. All the corn was out in the stooks ready for carting to the farm. The flood was so great that the harvest was spoiled and a lot of it lay out in the fields until early the following year. We had some good pigeon shooting from hides built of corn stooks.

Tatie riddling and turnip pulling

That year we had pied the taties by the Old Mary Pit. Uncle Walter said it had flooded so quickly no machinery could be saved. The shaft was covered over, the winding house was the only bit left. I have sheltered in it many times and shot at the pigeons that roosted there.

An old sunken wagon way which ran towards the Bullcroft. George Tebb said it would be grand for the taties, not much covering up to do. Towards Christmas 1949 five men set off to get two tons sorted; the ground was iron hard. The Major tractor stood beside the pie, I was for keeping her running. Ike said, 'turn her off.' 'No,' I said, 'let her run. I want to warm me hands on her.' 'Get bloody going, that'll warm your hands!'

We lit a fire at the end that was to be opened out to keep the taties from freezing. We hacked at the soil that covered the straw - it came away in big chunks, the straw beneath had a coat of frost too. Ike and Jowett were trying to get the riddle closer to the pie; it took all of us to break it free of the ice. The wire mesh screen was clogged up with frozen soil. It was freed and shoved on the fire which thawed it, then it was cleaned.

'Right, let's get cracking.' The straw was pulled away at the end of the pie. Don Spur chucked some spuds on the riddle, the machine chattered as Ike turned the handle. The spuds shuffled along the riddle, the small ones dropping through the wire or eating taties dropping into the sack at the end where they were weighed, tied up, then put on the trailer and covered up quickly before the frost got at them.

'What they like, Ike?' Don Spur asked. He was having a blow. 'A few frozen,' Ike said. I was opposite Jowett on the riddle, our job was sorting the bad ones out. We had the cold job, half an hour later we all changed places, my feet were like ice blocks, no feeling whatever. It was almost midday, the last sack was weighed and loaded, the sheet was fastened down. We set about covering up the tatie pie. Dry straw was used, wet straw would freeze. It was a difficult job trying to soil up, the chunks we had dug off earlier would not seal the weather out. Later we took more dry straw back and got the trailer under cover.

We were running short of cattle feed, the weather was severe, with no let up - frost at night and freezing all day. The swedes were frozen into the ground. The drag, an iron hook with two prongs would not enter the roots, they were iron hard. I kicked at them - sometimes they broke at ground level my boot toes suffered and so did my foot. A spade was given a try, the roots were stubborn, the spade jarred my wrists but it had to be done, the swedes were needed.

Old Albert Richardson said it was one of the joys of farming. He went on to say that the winters were more severe when he was a young man. 'Yer don't know yer born these days, you lads.' Once the swedes were cut they had to be loaded - the tractor was driven between two rows. A fork was used to stick two at a time, no luck, the prongs bounced off. Try as we may the roots were too hard. We loaded by hand, the frost on them made them slippery. Our numb hands suffered badly. It was only after they thawed and regained some feeling that cuts were found - cuts that would not heal but grew in size and finally developed into keens that broke out each winter. Gloves were good when ploughing or for jobs where we were out of the ground.

Once the roots have been tipped in the building besides the turnip chopper they did not thaw out until the weather broke. A week later the swedes were still frozen, putting them through the chopper made them dance about, the cutting blades could not cut into them and it took much longer to prepare the feed.

I often wondered what effect the frozen food had on the cattle's stomachs. The feed was always readily taken and the beasts put on weight. At three years old they went to market as prime beef. Veterinary visits were rare in those days, our stock was healthy. There were none of the fancy injections and additives that are shoved into the modern feed nowadays. BSE was far into the future.

Molly

'What's this I hear about yer having to get wed?' It hit me like a bombshell! Mother was washing up, the pots rattled in the sink. It was half past six in the morning and I was eating my breakfast. I shoved away my plate having lost interest in the bacon. 'Who told yer?' I asked, feeling uneasy. 'That woman yon girl lives wid, you know who I mean. She was here yesterday, she said that the lass is expecting. How long's it been going on? Yer never said owt to us about her, we haven't even seen her yet. What are you playing at lad? It's about time the truth came out. Is it right what that woman told me? She looked a hard-faced bitch.'

The girl our mother was on about had come to live in the next village. How she came to know the Burrows family I don't know. I knew she had moved from her home in the town. I had seen Molly now and then when on my way from work. A lad I knocked around with was related to the Burrows and now and then we called at their home. Anyway I fancied Molly and eventually asked her out. Soon we were seeing a lot of each other, most evenings she came to the farm when I was doing overtime. Mrs Burrows seemed to have her under her thumb. I was just eighteen. Molly and me got on well together and soon she was spending a lot of time at our farm, being friendly with Ike Tebbs' wife, who was a scruffy woman.

Harvest had finished. We were on our way home. I was lifting my bike over a stile when she said, 'I think I'm having a bairn, Brian.' I stood as though shot. How long I held the bike seemed ages. 'Are you sure, lass?' 'Almost certain. I have missed my period. I'm worried about it.' 'So am I, lass.' Nowt else was said, we walked on in silence. I took her to the Burrows' gate and left her.

Time went by, Molly was having a bairn alright, the swelling about her middle was not caused by wind. We talked of what we should do. In those days if you got a woman in the family way you were expected to wed her. Men were still being taken to court for breach of promise, that is if you were officially engaged and broke it off. By now I had visited the Burrows' home several times. I was there one evening when Mrs Burrows said that folks about had noticed Molly's swelling and were asking when we were to be wed. It would have to be soon or else the bairn would be at the ceremony wid us!

'Have yer told your mother yet?' asked Mrs Burrows. It was a while before I answered. 'No, not yet.' 'Why not, tha's had long enough? Are yer scared lad?' 'No, I'm not scared.' 'Well, what's holding thee up then?' She went on, 'have yer thought of where yer going to live? Can't you get a farm cottage from George Tebbs?'

My head had been in a whirl ever since Molly had told me she was with child. I stared at the fire. Molly was the first woman that I had been with. I knew nowt about women. In those days girls were not as easy to lead down the garden path as they are now.

Being my first romance, I had not realised what trouble it could lead to and, being inexperienced, I had not taken precautions. Now it was up to me.

Mrs Burrows kept at me. Molly sat in a corner crying. I got up to leave them and said that I would let my family know and hope they would help. Knowing my father's quick temper I could imagine what a scene there would be. 'Tha's made thy bed and now yer mun lie on it. You should have thought about it afore yer got the lass in the family way!'

'It's right then is it?' my mother asked. 'Aye, it's right.' 'How far gone is she?' 'I think she's five months gone.' 'Well, you will have to get wed right sharp. Does the girl's family know? Have yer met 'em at all?' 'Not yet I haven't.' 'Where do they live?' 'I don't know.' 'No, ye don't know owt lad.' 'I think it's the other side of town.' 'Well, find out. We are off to meet 'em on Sunday. Go on, get yerself off to work.'

It was out now and mother had the bit between her teeth. That day I felt a bit better though I was dreading the Sunday coming. It came alright. The four of us got off the bus. Molly led the way through a housing estate, eventually turning down a path, pushing open a door and we entered the living room. The chap standing wid his arse to the fire was introduced - he was Molly's father, the hefty woman on the settee was her mother.

The men shook hands but not with me. 'Sit yourselves down. We've heard news, what's going on then?' 'We only found out on Monday,' our mother said. 'It's been kept quiet far too long, Molly's five months gone, summat's got to be arranged and quick.' On our way home we were all quiet, Molly had stopped with her folks.

It was a register office do, no meal or owt afterwards. We had been offered a home with her parents - a small bedroom wid a single bed was our accommodation. We took it. Later my elder sister, whose husband was in the army, was to go to Germany wid him and their two children. We were offered their home until they returned, giving us ample time to find ourselves a home of our own. Having had my medical at eighteen, I had to leave the farm, go in the Forces or down the mines. I decided I would go down the mines. The baby was born, a boy, we named him Stephen after my great grandfather.

III
DOWN THE MINES

Just after the war had finished in 1945, there was a shortage of men, both on the farms and in the mines. National Service was introduced and when a chap was eighteen years old he was given a medical and if he was fit, he was put into the Forces. If you were eighteen and training in a skilled job you could apply for deferment until you had finished your apprenticeship at twenty-one. Then you were called up.

If you were on the farm you didn't have to go in the Forces - you were allowed so many men to so many acres of land. If you had more men than was stated someone had to leave to be called for National Service. Well, our farm had too many men and I was the young one so it was I that went. Mining coal was also an exempt occupation, so I applied to go down the mines. I was accepted and started at Inghams Pit, Thornhill Lees, a very old pit. They also made coke and gas in the coke ovens there.

It was a great change for me. I had been used to being outside all my life but I turned up for work with all the other men. I had done a little training at a training colliery and had been given some idea of what to expect. Mines in those days got a concession of one ton of coal per month. The day shift started at 6.30am when we went to the lamp room and handed in our cheque, a brass disc with a number on it. The disc was hung up on a board, then you were given an electric lamp that fixes to your helmet. At the end of the shift when you hand in your lamp, the disc is given back to you. That way they know when all the men are out of the mine.

We then went to the pit head where the head frame stands. A man, called the banks man, was on duty there. He was in charge of the two cages. As one came up the other cage went down; signals were given by bells ringing from the pit bottom and a bell at the pit head. Before you entered the cage, the banks man searched you for matches or cigarettes. Chewing tobacco was used a lot and sold at the pit shop. Men were not allowed to smoke or have naked flames on account of gas which would explode if there were any unguarded flames.

As each man was searched he entered the cage. As soon as it was full the bell would ring and down we went. The first time is quite a sensation - as though the cage bottom has dropped out. Seconds later you step out in the pit bottom, where walls are white washed and there are lights and lines of sleepers. There were rows of tubs, steel trucks, four flanged wheels, all capable of being fastened together. The tubs full of coal would wait their turn to be drawn up the shaft, empty ones waiting to go in by as it is called, to the coal face.

I was told to go with some men and that the road haulage foreman would see me in by. It was a long walk, about a quarter of an hour to where the foreman met us. He was in charge of a given area. I was put with another lad to show me what to do. Jack, the lad that was showing me my job had worked on the haulage road for the past two years.

The haulage road in a mine is the main road by which all things that enter the mine must travel. It is the main artery and stretches from the pit bottom to the coal face. Every item of machinery, the men, everything, must travel along this road. The road is more or less straight, but may rise or fall with the contours of the ground. In the old mine at Inghams Pit, the width was about ten feet and it was shored up with large wooden props, every few feet. There were two sets of tramlines with space enough for a man to walk without danger, between them. Between the rails on each set of lines, a steel wire rope was constantly moving. The haulage rope is endless and is worked from the pit bottom by an engine. This haulage rope almost reaches the coal face, where it travels over pulleys and so the apparatus is called a main or tail engine.

The steel rope was the means of moving the steel tubs of coal and anything else coming in or going out of the mine. The tubs are fastened to the rope with clamps attached to chains. Usually four or five tubs were fastened together in a run as they were called by the men.

Our job, Jack and I, was to take the empties off the rope as they came in by from the pit bottom. We worked between the two sets of rails - as each set of tubs had a clamp on the front and back we had to work fast, otherwise there would be a 'mullock' as it was called, caused by the tubs ramming the ones in front of them, which derailed many of them.

A crush stood astride the in by rails. It was made of two heavy horizontal steel girders fixed low down which could be moved to meet each other by turning a wheel fixed on the contraption. In short, when you tightened the wheel, the two girders nipped the tubs and stopped them.

We had only our cap lamps to work by so you could only see where you were looking. It was black dark everywhere else. The haulage road is a draughty place and cold as well, because fresh air is driven down into the workings by a big fan, about thirty feet in diameter, which revolves at high speed. The fresh air not only drives any pockets of gas away but gives the men at the coal face enough air to work, the face being quite warm.

So that was my job every day - the haulage road, tubs in and sending full tubs out. At times stone filled the tubs - this was sent out when the rippers had been driving a heading forwards. Sometimes a tub with a steel cover over its top came to us marked 'Danger Cardox Shells'. These were used to blow down the coal for the colliers at the face. Tubs filled with bags of stone dust came in regularly. This was spread about the ground to help keep the coal dust down in case of an explosion.

While I was at Inghams Pit, I was given a different job for a day or two. It was called 'oppers' or charging. Next door to the pit was a battery of coke ovens and above these ovens was a small gauge railway the same as down the pit. These ovens looked like a row of books if you were on the ground facing them. Pipes ran all over the place and where a pipe leaked gas flames burned, especially at night.

Tubs of coal were sent along the overhead railway. Between the rails were small round iron lids which fitted tight when in their place. When the ovens had been emptied, the huge doors at each end were sealed with clay. The lids were taken off the ovens and the doors, coal was tipped inside them until the right amount was delivered. The tubs were pulled back when empty and the lids put on again and sealed with clay. It was called 'pogging up'. It was hot on top of the ovens and when it rained steam rose in clouds.

Inside the ovens the coal burned without air and the gases given off went through pipes. All kinds of liquids came from the coal. How long the coal was burned, I don't know, but sometime later a huge machine on rails, lifted off both doors of the oven, then a long steel arm called a ram pushed out the red hot coke onto screens where it was cooled by water. When cold it was broken up and sold to the coal men. A lot of it went in trucks on the railway.

Lofthouse Gate

I thought I would move to Lofthouse Gate which was a more modern mine. I turned up at the office on the day of the interview and the clerk asked my name. I said, 'Aston.' He looked at me and repeated, 'Aston.' 'Yes,' I replied. 'Ho.' I was shown into the manager's office. The man behind the desk gave me a good straight staring at and said, 'You're from Inghams?' 'Yes.' 'You don't know me?' 'No,' I said.

He mentioned some names that meant nothing to me. I just stood in front of him. 'Well,' the manager said with a bit of a thought, 'I am your relation, Bernard Aston.' Some time in the past I had heard of a Bernard Aston, when my father and aunts were talking.

'So, you want a job do you? What have you been doing at Inghams?' 'On the haulage road, spraying,' I said. Bernard asked, 'How would you like to go ripping?' My mind was working fast. I knew what that meant and that it was well paid. It was contract work. The more you did, the more money you made. The work was very hard and heavy with rock to drill and shots to fire, sides to straighten, rock to pack to form walls, stone to load and rings to erect and board out.

I told Bernard, 'I should like to go ripping.' 'OK,' he said, 'I will put you with Alf Aston.' I looked at Bernard. 'Alf Aston?' 'Yes, another of your relations. He has just come back from Pennsylvania, America. You start Monday night, 10 o'clock you go down.' That was it, what a day! Relations I never knew I had.

Ripping - Lofthouse Gate

My first shift at Lofthouse was on a Monday night and I met Alf Aston at the lamp room. He was a great big chap, really big. I bet he thought he wondered what to do with a small, skinny lad like me. No handshake, just a, 'How do'. There was also a Polish man called Marion, another member of the gang. The other two men I cannot remember.

Down we went and at the shaft bottom we climbed onto the Paddy train and rode down to the heading where we were to work. Without any ceremony we started drilling shot holes. Steel plates were put down to catch the rock when it was shot out and to make shovelling easier. We went out of the pit at 6am the next morning. I caught a bus home while Alf had a motorbike and sidecar. It was still dark as it was winter.

I got on well with the new gang and they showed me a lot. Alf told me about Pennsylvania and how thick the coal was there - to work it they stood upon trestles because it was twelve feet thick. The money was good but I didn't like the travel - it was about ten miles to the pit and I was working when other people were going to bed. In the end I decided to pack it in at Lofthouse. I got in touch with my manager at Inghams Pit and told him about the travel involved. He was very good and said I could start back at Thornhill Lees any time. I said goodbye to Alf and the lads and went back to my old job. It was good to be back on the day shift - we finished at 2pm so I could still spend time with my mates. I had not been back at Inghams when something happened that changed my life once again.

The day shift had started as usual. Jack and I busy with the tubs. I think what I noticed first was the haulage ropes seemed to shudder and come to a stop - they stopped too quickly. When the main haulage road stops, it is like the main road in any town, nothing moves anymore. Minutes later the road foreman came along walking quickly. He said to Jack and me, 'There's a mullock in t'drift.' Away we went and about 200 yards up the road we came to where the mullock was. Props were down and so was the roof - a great piece of rock almost the width of the road and about six yards long and at least two feet thick lay square in the road - a right mullock.

Some tubs must have come off the rails and as they went along they pulled out the roof props which caused the roof fall. 'Right lads,' shouted the foreman. By now there were men everywhere, including the safety officer, shot firer and haulage men. 'Stand back you lads.' The shot firer set some explosive pills on top of the rock and piled more small rock on the top of them. 'We must get the road open sharp,' said the foreman, 'we are holding everything up.'

'Get back lads, everybody get back,' shouted the shot firer. We all walked down the road, two minutes later he fired the shots, two of them. 'Right then, let's get it cleared,' said the road foreman. We all walked back to the fall - we could see through the smoke that nothing had changed.

A second later I heard a sharp crack like a rifle shot and that was all. I was knocked to the ground. I could not move, all was dark and I had dirt in my mouth, my body hurt and a great weight was holding me down. I think I was lying on my side. I thought I could hear voices, but it seemed as though I was half asleep. Eventually

I saw a light and men were everywhere. I was being dug out. I was trapped by my legs and couldn't move. The men were lifting the weight off my legs and at last I was free.

Hospital

I remember being carried out on a stretcher and being laid out at the pit head. Ambulances took us all away to hospital. In the hospital ward we lay on beds just as they had got us out - covered in muck. Some men died in the second roof fall, including the safety officer and the road foreman. The shot firer was also very mashed up but survived a few years. Others had bad injuries and I was the lucky one - I am now the only survivor of that team of men.

When the shots had been fired it was the job of the safety officer to go and make sure all was safe for the men to start work clearing the fall. A lot of the men would still be alive today - but it was the same old story, rush in, go on lads we cannot waste time, we shall have to get the road open. A mistake was made, a mistake that cost men their lives.

My injuries were slight compared to the ones of my workmates. Thinking back to the second roof fall, it seems that hearing the crack before the roof came down, I took a step backwards before being knocked down and buried with stone and muck. Evidently they found that my left leg was twisted causing my clog sole to be turned on its side and the wooden sole was supporting the weight of some very large rocks. The sheer weight split my clog sole lengthwise as well as my foot, causing an eight inch gash under my instep. I had some broken fingers and was badly bruised. I was very sore and shaken for a while afterwards and my ribs and head had been knocked about as well.

I had been wearing a wrist watch at the time of the rock fall. It was bent and eventually I got rid of it as too many memories came back when I looked at it. I had been very lucky and I knew it!

I was released from hospital after a week or two. Before I left I visited some of the less lucky men, my mates. I never saw any of them again. My life was to change once again, a new chapter was about to start. I had had enough of mining. After I got myself mended, I started back at the farm. George Tebb had been good to me to take me on again and so I was back at my old farm and shooting again. But not for long.

IV
NATIONAL SERVICE AND GERMANY

The Army and after

The day after New Year's day, an envelope addressed to me arrived. I couldn't believe it - my calling up papers, after all I had been through. I had been for a medical when I was eighteen years old. Now I was twenty and was called up for the Army.

I was to report to the Kings Own Yorkshire Light Infantry at Strensall Barracks two weeks later. If I had decided to go back down the mines I would not have to go but I had had enough of mines - I was lucky to be alive, so that was it, I was to be a soldier.

There was snow on the ground when I arrived at Strensall Camp along with twenty other new recruits. We were marched to our new home - a red brick built barracks big enough for thirty men. Two iron stoves were all the heating we had, and one bucket of coal for each stove which was only lit in the evening.

By the end of the first week us new recruits had settled in as much as we could. We all came from a fairly stable life at home, into one of shouting and being told what to do and don't be long about it, and of course, we all had an Army number which we had to remember. It was easy for some of us and hard for others. The number was put on all our kit, on everything. My number was 22762786 Pt. Aston.

Basic training

The drill started the minute we stepped through the camp gates and continued wherever we went. We all wore strong, leather boots and each boot had 26 studs in the sole on iron heel plates and were highly polished at all times. The bugle was our clock - 6am Reveille - out of bed sharp, the sergeant shouting at us, 'Get a bloody move on you lot.' We washed, dressed and shaved - in cold water. Beds were made up and we went outside for breakfast parade at 6.30am.

There were drill parades and kit inspections all the time. Later we were introduced to the Enfield rifle .303, the Bren gun and the Sten gun. We learned the art of throwing the Mills bomb or hand grenade. I took to the shooting side of it like a duck to water. I was in my element with the rifle, or any other weapon. Some of the lads found it a hard life. A few had joined the Army from offices, shops and even hotels, and some could hardly wear strong boots. Some lads took to it badly. We were sorry to see them being so unhappy, but you had to make the best of it.

We had completed our basic training at the end of twelve weeks and had all passed out at a parade at the end of this period. We did not know where we would go on leaving Strensall. All sorts of rumours went about and Korea was very much in our minds. We had just finished a drill parade one morning, when our sergeant brought us all to attention.

'Right you lot, anyone of ye drive a car or a wagon, any of you ride a motorbike? When I say, one pace forwards march, you that can drive.' I was one of the would be drivers. The sergeant, 'Attention, you drivers one pace forwards march.' I stepped forwards. 'Stand fast. The rest of you dismiss.' Away the rest went. Our sergeant came up to us would be drivers. We were marched to the CQMS stores where we were each given new uniforms and equipment and marched back to our barracks.

Berlin

'You drivers,' said our sergeant, 'are on your way to Berlin tonight.' Two nights later we were in barracks in Spandau, right up against the Russian border, or the Russian Sector. I was allocated a Ford Willis Jeep - little did I know what I was in for! Some of the lads were given lorries - Austins and Bedfords, 3 tonners, while some had scout cars and Bren carriers. We were in HQ Company. Our new barracks had been Hitler's Cavalry Barracks - they were very well set out.

Soldiering in Berlin meant guard duty - almost all our time was guard work. Spandau Gaol was very close to our camp. Twenty-eight men had to guard the gaol every fourth months. Villa Lem was where the officer commanding our troops lived. He had to be guarded too. It was a lovely villa, set beside the Harvel, a large waterway on the river.

Another guard duty was I.S. Patrol - that was guarding the border. If you were on I.S. Patrol there were four men - a corporal and a driver and two others. We were all armed with Sten guns which were light machine guns. If you were on I.S. duty, all four of us paraded in front of the guard room and were inspected by the orderly officer. On being dismissed we all entered the guard room where we had a small room with four iron beds, with no blankets or mattresses, just bare springs to lie on. My jeep was parked handy for the camp gate. We went on duty at 8pm and stayed there until 8am the next day. We could be called out at any time during that period and often were. If we were called we would rush out and I started the jeep, the others piled in, and away we would go. The wireless operator was in the back with his set and told me where to go. We had 1000 rounds of ammunition with us yet we were not allowed to use it - it was a bit of a farce.

We didn't have much spare time. I did get to see quite a lot of Berlin but only the English sector. The rest of the city was out of bounds to us. It was spring when we were there - things looked very nice though many buildings were just ruins, all marked by bomb blasts and shell fire. Many acres were totally flattened. The Reichstag stood alone, a burned out shell. I saw Hitler's bunker where he died. The Tiergarten about Brandenburg Gate was badly burned, although people were busy building again. Lots of tall buildings were shored up to stop them crashing down and people still lived in them. I went to the Grunwald, a forest on the outskirts of Berlin. Berlin must have been very lovely before the war.

The German broadcasting station was a NAAFI Club - a huge place in the heart of the city where we soldiers of different regiments could spend our leisure time playing games or having a drink. I spent thirteen months in Spandau and Berlin. Our battalion were moving out to Suez Canal zone in Africa, but the soldiers who had not much time to serve were not going with the battalion. We were to be sent to other units in Germany. I was sent to Wuppertal in the Ruhr and was transferred to the Durham Light Infantry. The 2nd Battalion, the Durham Light Infantry was my next home posting, as Germany was called. Things were a lot easier at Wuppertal - there wasn't all the bullshit that we had to put with in Berlin.

I was given a BSA 500cc motorcycle and was a despatch rider going from our camp to wherever mail was to be taken to other units out on manoeuvres. Later on some Matchless 250cc bikes arrived and I got one of those. We had much more time for ourselves at the D.L.I.S. Our camp was on the edge of a forest and I was able to do some scouting about. I borrowed a .22 rifle from a farmer and shot a roe deer and took it in a sack through Wuppertal on a tram. I was told that if I had been caught with the deer I could have landed myself in serious trouble as all game was state owned and it was a serious offence to kill game without a licence.

Private Whitby

Whitby was in the crowded N.A.A.F.I. at Keighley Barracks, Spandau. The old Army song, *Now my Army days are over*, had been sung twice over and the crowd were in a right merry mood, much beer had been downed as it was pay night. Whitby told me that, feeling patriotic, he had done a damnable thing - he had signed on for three years, making him a regular solder and that now he was regretting what he had done and was feeling very depressed. Later on that night he told me that he was going to work his ticket and get chucked out of the Army. I told him many chaps had tried that game and come in for a rough time and ended up in a 'penal battalion'.

We both got off to a good start while on a manouevre and doing a river crossing in collapsible boats, our boat capsized. The River Harvel at this point was wide. It was 6am and just getting light - our crossing was being done under a smokescreen - fifteen men all floundering in the cold water. We all wore Mae West life jackets beneath our webbing equipment. The boat was upside down and, being flat-bottomed and having a rail it offered something to hold on to. There was plenty of shouting and splashing around. The sergeant took charge and made a head count - fifteen heads bobbing about, everyone treading water.

We were towed ashore where a captain took charge. The NCOs were quickly briefed that the enemy (some Americans) were over the hill. 'Who's on the Bren gun?' 'Me, Sir,' Whitby shouted. 'Where's your Bren?' the officer asked. Whitby looked back at the river. 'It's in there, Sir.' 'In where man?' 'In there, Sir' Whitby pointed to the dark river. The magazines and much more equipment had gone to the bottom with the Bren gun.

We were drawn up to charge the enemy position. The whistle was blown, away we went up the bank, over the top then down towards the Yanks who were concealed in a line among some trees. There was a hell of a racket going on - all kinds of weapons opened up, firing 'blank' ammo. Thunder flashes exploded to simulate grenades. We ran towards the Yanks screaming and shouting - our line of men were within a 100 yards of the enemy lines and going to over-run them. 'What the...' my legs went from under me. I was rolling down the hill, so were scores of our lads. Trip wires had been set among the tall grass - we had run right into them, head on!

The shouting had stopped abruptly. Before we could re-group the Yanks ran forwards, firing as they came. We lay winded. I was taken prisoner with many more chaps. We sat massaging our ankles where the trip wire had bruised the skin - we were in the bag. The manouevre was over for us. We were held in a compound of ropes and the referees said we were out of the war.

At the court martial some weeks later we were charged with losing military equipment - most of the lads from our boat had lost their weapons. Whitby and I were charged with losing the Bren gun and magazines. We were told that £33 would be deducted from our pay towards the cost of them.

Whitby was on a right downer. 'I shall work my ticket, I'll show you.' He turned up late for parade, unshaven, the buttons of his uniform undone. He was charged and put on 'jankers', confined to barracks. He had to answer all calls from 8am until 10pm. Instead he went over the wire and was later picked up by the military police. Whitby was then put on Cos Levee and was awarded 28 days detention, clapped up in the town guard room. He took the bed in his cell apart and with it he set about the walls, shouting and raving and would not shave or wash himself. Whitby threw food over the provost corporal. All he had in his cell was a bucket and a blanket.

Two provost corporals went to his cell with the intention of taking him for a shower. Immediately the cell door was opened, Whitby rushed out naked, except for the shit he had daubed his body with. He grabbed a corporal and hugged him close, shouting 'I love ya, I love ya!' He was eventually dragged to the showers, and long-handled yard brushes were used to scrub him.

Having behaved himself for a few days, Whitby was given a job in the guard room where an eye could be kept on him. How he managed to steal a potato and a razor blade, God knows. The blade was stuck into the spud and with the nasty weapon, he went for the provost sergeant, chasing the poor chap around the guard room. A corporal on guard on the landing, hearing the commotion, dashed into the room. Whitby charged at him. The outer door being now open he made his escape down the stairs and passed the sentry at the camp gate.

Whitby ran down the road with the provost sergeant and his squad in pursuit. Whistles were blown and the guard turned out - they too joined the chase which ended on a bomb site close by. Whitby had lost his plimsolls - the laces had been removed in the nick. Standing on top of the heap of rubble, Whitby bombarded anyone trying to approach. The site was surrounded. One or two of the provost's men had come close to being hit with lumps of concrete and kept out of range.

In the end poor Whitby was knackered. He sat among the rubble cursing his tormentors. What rubble lay at hand was too heavy for him to throw. He was finally brought down and helped into camp, his feet in a sorry state, bloody and cut. The medical officer attended to him and Whitby remained quiet for a while though he cursed the prison staff.

When on duty one of my jobs was taking food to the town guard room for the prisoners. I saw Whitby now and then. He had changed - there was a determined look on his face. There was another court martial and Whitby was sentenced to a term in Bielafeld, the military prison or 'glass house'. He ended up among the hard cases. How Whitby ended up I do not know. When I was drafted to the D.L.I. at Wuppertal I lost touch with him. Whether he did finally work his ticket I never knew. He was a good Yorkshire man.

Demobilisation
Well, I managed to do my time in the Army, knowing that when I had done two years I was free to do as I liked, so I just soldiered on until demob day. We were demobbed at Wakefield in Yorkshire, about a dozen of us. Of course we had to celebrate with a drink or more, and more was the word. Several of us went to a pub in the Bull Ring in Wakefield for a farewell drink before we all went our separate ways. We really enjoyed ourselves and finished the night with a fight with some miners who seemed to enjoy it as much as we did.

Well, that was it. I was free to do as I liked. I looked about for a job. There was plenty of work but what kind of work did I want? I'd had enough of the mines and no one wanted me on the farms. Some Irishmen had been talking to me and said it was good money on their job. They worked for a firm that erected electric lines, digging foundations for pylons and holes for poles, then erecting them and stringing the cables.

When I got home I found my wife had moved to a different area.

Eventually I found her new home, thinking it would be mine too but times had changed. I had been away for two years and Molly hadn't told me she had a new partner. It was a shock seeing him in the doorway. I was only a young man and life must go on but I was sad to leave Stephen. My mother kept me informed of his life. Sadly he died from cancer when he was only twenty-six.

Calenders' Cables and the Paddies

Calenders' Cables was the name of the firm. I was taken on and sent to work with the lads I knew. They were a good lot - the problem was the drink. The foreman, Paddy, always carried two bottles in his duffle coat - one of gin and the other bicarbonate of soda. The poor chap's mouth was always white from the bicarbonate - he suffered with a bad stomach - no wonder with all the gin he downed.

Our gang was all Irish except me. I soon learned their ways. I was earning 50/- a day, which was good money in 1954. Some days I earned £5 if the digging was good. We were working on the Yorkshire Moors above Hebden Bridge, snow covered everything. We had to blast some of the pylon holes out of rock. Paddy, our foreman, was shot firer. I watched him bite the detonators onto the safety fuse we were using, thinking, one day Paddy, you will bite too hard and blow your bloody head off!

I did quite well with the Irish and started to use the climbing irons to scale the poles when fixing the cross trees and insulators. I was asked if I would like to be a linesman - that meant being up aloft and fastening the cables to the insulators with copper wire pigtails as they are called. I did have a go several times and found it very easy. The line we worked on came to a close after the work was done and we had to move on. We went to West Yorkshire, near Doncaster. The travelling and working on Sundays was bothering me. The money was very good, but I had been thinking for a while of going back to Germany. I liked the way they worked there. So I packed up and said goodbye to the Irish - next stop Germany!

Working in Germany

I had an awful job to get a passport. It took a long time. I got £15 changed into Deutschmarks, 12 marks to the pound. I had decided to go to Wuppertal, because I knew the farmer there, where I had borrowed the rifle when I was in the Army. I arrived there about 20

June, and found the farmer OK. On his land were some old wooden barracks, just inside a small wood beside a quarry. Three of these barracks had been made habitable and some families lived there. I was able to get a room without any bother.

My next problem was to find work - there was plenty of it but without a work permit no one would set me on. I found the building where permits were allocated. They were not much good at English and I was not much good at German. In the end and with some help, I was issued with a permit for three months. I soon found a job digging - a huge cut was being driven through Wuppertal Barmen. Yes, I was just the lad they wanted. Could I dig? Could I dig! The foreman was willing to let me have a go. 'I will give you 100 marks a week if you are good,' said the foreman. I worked three months with that gang, about 100 of them and I was the only Englishman.

The cut we were driving was about twelve feet deep so all the spoil had to be lifted onto stagings. The man at the bottom or the 'getter' as he was called, threw the spoil onto a stage above him about four feet high. Another man on that stage threw the spoil up onto another stage about four feet above him and another man threw the spoil out onto the bank where another man saw to it.

The sides of the cut were shored up with heavy timbers. The explosives and the firing were all done very professionally and blasting mats were used to stop rocks being blown out of the cut. The organisation was good and I enjoyed it. Work hours in summer were 5am until 2pm, which gave me some time for a pint and the long evening to myself. The weather was good and the job was going along well. I visited the lads at the camp and bought things in their NAAFI.

My accommodation was not much to speak of - just a room in a wooden barracks. After I went to bed I put the light on and a while after, bugs came out of the boards of the walls. I started to squash them but after a while I gave up. The walls were covered with blood spots where I squashed them. In the end I got some empty bean cans and put paraffin in them, then stood the bed legs in them and pulled my bed away from the walls. That helped a bit.

The place where these three old barracks stood was very pleasant. Trees were out in leaf and lots growing in the small gardens about the place. There was quite a big area in front of the buildings where three or four wooden privies were cantilevered out over the quarry that ran along opposite our barracks. It was all quite peaceful. In the evenings people sat out in front of the buildings talking - there were no cars to spoil the scene. Little did I know that the place had not always been so peaceful? Some of the older men, the ones that had been in the war, would try to talk to me in English.

An old man who used to sit about told me that there had been more barracks about the wood and a high fence around the whole place. Russian prisoners of war were kept in these barracks as slave labour. Those that died were thrown into the quarry where our privies were sited and buried there. It wasn't a very nice thought when all was so nice and restful.

My work permit expired and I went back to the office where I had obtained the first one. I managed to get another permit for three months more. I was told I should not try again as I would not be granted one. I changed my job - this time I was taken on by a large firm that did track laying for the railways.

Railway work

The work gang met on the rail platform each morning at 5am. A special work engine took us out to where we were track laying with trucks of stone ballast, sleepers and all the tackle we needed. It was hard work - we laid the ballast stone to form the rail bed and all the work was done with shovel, pick and bar. Then the sleepers were set out and gauged for distance. Steel chairs were then screwed down to the sleepers and all levelled up. Rails were thrown down from flat cars. Twelve men, six each side of the rail, took hold of it with special long tongs, two men to each pair of tongs. At the command everyone lifted together and the rail ws carried and placed in the chairs attached to the sleepers. That done, two fish plates were bolted on and connected to the other one that was laid before it. Next, hard wood chocks were driven between each chair and the rail making the rail firm in the chair. This was repeated scores of times a day. Some days all I did was unload ballast - two men to a forty ton load of stone. In the middle of the side of each truck was a door that dropped down. We heaved the ballast out each side of the truck. A whistle was blown and the engine moved forwards one truck length and we shovelled more stone out.

We used a long handled fork rather than a shovel. Each tine had a blob of metal on the end to prevent the tines sticking in the wooden floor. The weather was very hot and I was now as brown as a conker. Many of the men in our gang had fought in the war. Sometimes as we sat at our food I looked about me and some of the faces were not too friendly. I was taken under the wing of a small Austrian man called Emil Isonclimb. We worked together unloading ballast. He was a very happy chap and a bit of a comfort. I was one Englishman among many Germans. I met men of several nationalities. It was only a few years after the war, and it could have been different as a few Nazis were among our gang.

Leaving Germany

My visa expired and once again it was time to say goodbye. The powers that be made it quite clear that I should return to England and so I was a bit sad and a little glad to see my parents again. I arrived home very unsettled and immediately started to look for a job. I started to go about with some of the lads, who were newly married. I was still keen on shooting. One day one of my uncles said why not be a gamekeeper. That was it - I would be a keeper. I went to see the estate agent at Farnley Hall, Otley and an interview was arranged. I turned up on the day to see Major York at Marston Manor, near York. The major was a very tall man, and was taken with my Army service and the jobs I had done since my demobilisation.

IV
Game keeping in Yorkshire

Marston Manor, Long Marston, York

And so another chapter opened in my life - I was taken on as under-keeper at Marston Manor. The head keeper, Dick Rudd, was in charge of the game department. I arrived and was met by Arthur Bloss and taken to my new home, Chapel Hill Farm. It was about a mile and a half out of the village and the farm itself was called Hutton Grange. The house had previously been called Shepherd's Cottage as the farmhouse had been enlarged over the years from a small shepherd's cottage.

Mrs Lewy Goat, a widow, rented the farm from the estate. Tom, a son of hers who was not married, farmed the land. My accommodation was the old part of the house, separated from the main house by the dairy. There was one room downstairs with a small, black iron range, a horsehair couch, a table by the window and a chair or two. Upstairs were two single beds, both of them iron and very old, a couple of chairs, a piss pot, and a few coat hooks behind the door.

Sometimes my place was referred to as Grandma's Room. Everything was just as she had left it many years ago. The window looked out across the gravel pit where there were a lot of rabbits. It was said that a long, long time ago, the village church stood there. I know that a few years ago some men were rabbiting on the gravel pit and several skulls were found. It was thought that they might have been killed at the battle of 1644 at Marston Moor. We have no way of knowing how true that is.

I started my work as gamekeeper and was given around a thousand acres - a beat as it is called in the shooting world. There were three beats on the estate. The head keeper had one where most of the woods were on the low side of the estate. Tony Dick's son had the Marston Lodge beat on the high side of the estate and my beat was called the Angram beat. It was ideal partridge country. Crops of sugar beet, potatoes, barley, wheat, turnips, sometimes beans were grown.

A gamekeeper has many jobs to do depending on the time of the year. After Christmas the keeper will start to mend the tunnel traps sites. Four inch gin traps were set inside tunnels made of three two feet long six inch boards. The boards were nailed together, two of them on their edges and one flat on the top. If there were stones or bricks handy, they would be used instead of wood.

The wooden tunnel would be placed alongside a small mesh wire fence, outside a wood where young trees were planted. Then the keeper cut sods or clods of earth and covered the tunnel, leaving both ends open. The trap with a chain and a strong peg were installed. They were set inside the tunnel so that only small animals going through the gap would be caught. Two small sticks were stuck into the ground about three inches apart to stop partridges entering the tunnel.

Many traps were used in this way. I would say at that period, there were 200 tunnels at work and these were all visited at least once a day. Some traps were set in holes under tree roots, a favourite place for stoats. Others were in tunnels made through banks in hedges - in fact we set them wherever there was any sign of vermin. The gamekeeper kills all ground vermin before the partridges and pheasants start to sit on their eggs. The fox is the worst killer of partridges. If there is a litter of cubs anywhere within a mile they were killed. Stoats, weasels, rats and hedgehogs all take their share of game and their eggs. Badgers will take birds from their nests, but the badger has a very wide variety of food. I did not persecute him too hard.

Cats that go wild can be a menace, but the cat will by choice take young rabbits. Even so he can be a nuisance and is easily caught. Dogs that are allowed to run loose at nesting time can spoil many a nest and the farmers are asked to keep their dogs tied up at this time of the year. There were also winged vermin such as carrion crows, they being one of the worst, to deal with. We used to shoot at the nest when they are sitting on the eggs, or trap them to a piece of rabbit or a rat bait. When we used to poison we would nail a rat on a tree branch, cut it open, put a small dose of poison in and the crows were soon dead. The bait was always out of the reach of humans, dogs and children and all dead birds were picked up.

Jays are real ghouls. They take eggs, chicks and also song birds. The magpie another of the crow family was another killer of small birds and taker of eggs. Owls will take young pheasant poults just when they start to roost. They knock the bird off the tree and take the head off and leave the rest - that is the tawny owl. All hawks will take young birds whether they be on the rearing ground or in the wild. We did out best to keep their numbers down. As the keeper went on his rounds, he made a mental note of the nests of vermin.

Major C. York, Swinton Castle - grouse shooting
While I was employed as game keeper to Major C York at Marston I had the pleasure to attend the shooting parties at Swinton Castle, the home of Lord Swinton who had been of some importance in government during the war. He was an Air Vice Marshall. The nearest town to the castle was Masham where there was a brewery owned by Theakstons.

Many famous men shot with Lord Swinton. He was an old man and a gentleman. Harold Macmillan, the then Prime Minister was present on some occasions when I was there. Mr Douglas, the American Ambassador, was another guest. He only had one arm but he was a very fine shot. Major York, my employer, was MP for Harrogate. These were great days on the North Yorkshire grouse moors. The head keeper on the moor was a grand old chap called Adam Rough. His son, Jack was second keeper and Peter Brough was under-keeper. The head keeper on the low ground was called Billy Edgar. He was a short fellow and could be a bit dour at times.

We would leave Marston in the Major's old Jaguar car, nearly always late, and travel the old A1 or the London Road, at speeds up to 110 miles per hour. It's a wonder we arrived at Swinton Castle some times. In the mid 1950s that was a fast speed, especially as two way traffic was using the road at that time. These were great days for me, and it was a new experience meeting people like the Prime Minister and more besides and at night sitting in the castle kitchen awaiting my employer. Other keepers were at the kitchen table, from estates all over the country. There were lots of different dialects to be heard and all the talk of shooting and dogs.

Rudding Park estate, Harrogate
While I was a keeper at Marston Manor I met my wife, Joan. Several of us had been to the fair at York one Saturday night. Before I came to Marston, Dick Rudd, the head keeper was helped by his son Tony. Shortly after, Tony was called up for the Army and so Dick and myself were left on our own. I learned a lot from Dick

who loved horse racing and cricket, too. I made quite a lot of friends in the village. Joan and I would visit an old keeper at Askham Richard, the next village. He was a bit of a character. The old men are now all gone and I am the old man now!

My stay at Marston was a very pleasant one. When Tony came out of the Army, Major York, my employer, said he could not afford three keepers. One day the Major said a friend of his who I knew, wanted an under-keeper at Rudding Park, near Harrogate. I went to see Captain Ratcliffe at Rudding and met the head keeper, Fred Dowker. It was arranged that I should move to Rudding Park soon. Fred came for me with an old Ford van. I piled my few possessions in the back, said goodbye to Tom and Mrs Goat, my landlady, and away we went.

My new home was a room of about ten feet square in the kennels. The kennels were the home of the Bramham Moor Foxhounds. The hounds had been taken away a few days before my arrival but they had forgotten to take their smell with them. The kennels were built in red brick and outside were five runs, topped with iron railings. The hounds had access from the inside through holes cut in the doors to the runs.

My room was on the left hand side. A passage divided up the inside of the kennels where the hounds lived on the right hand side. There were also store rooms for food and butchering any fallen stock that were sent for the hounds to eat. My room had bare brick walls painted yellow, a bit of a fireplace across one corner of the room, an old sink and cold water tap, a double bed, a calor gas cylinder and gas ring. I put my suitcase under the bed and Rusty, my border terrier soon made it his bed. Mrs Dowker had a family of two boys and three girls and lived in the keeper's house which was also called The Kennels.

The railway ran through Rudding Estate and became my source of coal which I used to cook my food. I used the railway as a footpath as it ran quite close to the kennels and so I could go from my home to the far end of the estate fairly quickly. Thorn bushes grew very plentifully on the railway embankments as the rails ran through a shallow cutting before entering a tunnel. I have picked lots of coal up on my way back to my accommodation.

Rudding was a pheasant shoot, though a few partridges were to be found on the Haggs as they were called. There was very little arable land - it was mainly grass for sheep and other stock.

Rudding House, a stone Regency house, stands at the top of the park. It looks out towards Knaresborough. At the bottom of the park are two small lakes and between them is a cemetery where the Ratcliffe family lie buried. As a small pheasant shoot it was good. The bulk of the shooting was done about the park where some good high birds were shot from the fox cover. The deer park, as it had been, was surrounded with a stone wall. At the Folly Foot village side, a lodge with an archway provided the entrance. It must have been very imposing in years gone by.

I was soon busy at my new job. Fred Dowker was a totally different man to my old boss, Dick Rudd. He was a real keeper whose life apart from Army service was spent among the game. He had served some time on a game farm and he was very knowledgeable about the different breeds of pheasants. A few thousand pheasants were reared at Rudding - the hatching yard was where the front garden should be at the Kennels, the Dowker's home.

The estate had a number of outlying woods and a couple of streams running through it which were a good source of water for the birds. The land undulated and was more rugged than what I had been used to at Marston. I soon got cracking with the traps and other devices for catching vermin. There were plenty of foxholes and some badgers on the railway sides. There was also plenty of winged vermin but we soon made them a lot less.

Two hundred hen pheasants were in pens close to the Kennels in a small, young plantation on the side facing Harrogate. The hens laid well and by the time we had gathered enough broody hens we had a lot of eggs ready to set. The rearing field was at Dibben Dale, about one and a half miles by road from the Kennels. It was on a fairly steep hillside, with the railway at the top side of the field and a beck at the bottom.

Dibben Dale

You had to pass through Billy Mitchell's farmyard to get to Dibben Dale where there was a cabin on big iron wheels in the middle of the field and a boiler with a load of wood to fire it with. There was also a crate of eggs, sacks of meal and greaves, a mincer on a table, buckets, traps, snares, lamps, oil, cartridges, bottles of medicine supposed to cure ailments in birds, and a camp bed. This was my home for the next nine weeks. I moved onto the field with the first batch of chicks and came away when the last lot were about five weeks old. All my water was carried from the bottom beck - this was for drinking and all other needs. It was a hard climb from the beck with a bucket in each hand.

Rusty, my border terrier, kept me company. I chained him under the cabin during the day and at night he slept with me. Just imagine the cabin - eight feet long and about six feet wide and filled with the feed bags, my bed and shelves full of all sorts. It was a bit cramped, especially on wet days as Fred would sit there with me. There was nowhere to dry my clothes and smells of meal, meat, Rusty and me.

The rearing field was an old meadow ideal for the birds. They did well and there were no diseases for it had never been reared on before. My first lot of chicks numbered 500. The coops and guard boards were all ready and the weather good. I had time to look at the traps which were set up all about the field and my lamps were already for lighting. I went to my bed - old Rusty doing a bit of scratching! About 4.30am I could hear some rooks - the cabin had sliding shutters, no glass. I eased the shutter back and saw that all was well on my field.

My day started with a wash, followed by taking Rusty for a short run, then chaining him up. I then made a bit of feed for my chicks - hard boiled eggs minced up, dried off with meal. I let the chicks out and fed them, gave the mothers some wheat and maize and watered them. The coops were spread out over the field, twenty yards either way. The grass was fairly short, so the chicks could get about alright. I made some breakfast - bread, butter, marmalade and some tea, and set the copper to boil and put twenty eggs in a sack and put them in the boiler. All the time young pheasants are out a close watch on them must be kept. Hawks, jays, crows, weasels and stoats are always on the hunt. The gun was always close to me and if it were possible, I carried it with me. The lamps were extinguished at dawn. I don't know if they ever deterred foxes or other vermin in the night - anyway I did not have any trouble.

On Thursday mornings, Fred took over the field and I went to the village for my groceries. That took about an hour, then I was back on duty in the field. Dibben Dale was a good place and at the end of the rearing we had done well. Just before I left the field, having a bit of time to spare, I walked up the beck. Underneath some low bushes I saw a dead fox lying in the water. He had been dead for some while and I had been drinking that water all the while. The last lot of birds were to be mine. I had taken over the Park beat and about 1000 poults were put there, some in the fox cover, some in the Low Wood and some in the School beat.

My courting had almost stopped while I was rearing, but now my birds were settled in their new home, I could resume my courting. I would get on my bike and ride fourteen miles to Longmarston, do my courting and bike home to Rudding in the early hours of the morning, having spent four hours with Joan.

Captain Ratcliffe offered me the Lodge House near to the Kennels if I wanted it. Yes, I wanted it. Joan and I were engaged before I went to Rudding so I started to get a home together. Friday evenings Fred and I would travel to Acombe near York to Hook's sale rooms and there I would purchase anything that I could afford to get my home started. I wasn't fussy. I didn't have much money, but got some furniture for only £1 or 30/-.

Married

I had been at Rudding Park about eighteen months when we married at Marston Methodist Chapel. Joan and I went to Scarborough for our honeymoon for three days. It was misty all the time and I remember the fog horns blowing all day long.

We arrived back at Knaresborough in the evening having travelled by train as we didn't have a car in those days. Taxis were not plentiful as they now are, but we managed to find a man who hired out as a taxi now and then. He took us to our new home at Rudding Park. When the driver found we were newly wed he would not take the fare - it was a present from him to us. The next day I was back in the woods with my pheasants.

Joan got a job at Boots the chemist in Harrogate and we were quite comfortable. About a year later Heather Ruth, our first daughter, was born at Harrogate Maternity Home. I had been on the look out for another job with more prospects, on a bit more money, as my wages were only £6 per week. We did not pay rent and our electricity was free plus I got a suit of clothes and an allowance for the dogs. We looked through *The Gamekeeper & Countryside* every month - plenty of keepers were wanted in those days.

I applied to several advertisements and went to a few interviews. One estate I was interviewed at was Mulgrave Castle, near Whitby, North Yorkshire. It was a fine estate, all pheasant shooting. I was shown about the estate and the keepers' cottages. There was the choice of two - one was a cottage on the cliff top at Kettleness, it had been the railway station at one time - or a whitewashed bungalow at a village called Sands End at the mouth of the River Esk. The bungalow was alright - inside a passageway ran the full length of the building and all the rooms opened off from it.

The interviews took place just before Christmas. I remember I was lucky to get away one night as it was snowing heavy on the moors which I had to travel over. My luck was in, at the castle the same day was a person who was travelling back to York. He was very good to me and gave me a lift with him. I arrived home very tired and cold on a snowy night and decided not to take the keeper's job at Mulgrave Castle.

I then went on an interview at Betisfield Park on the Shropshire borders. Again I travelled by train and bus. It was in a lovely part of the countryside. I met the estate agent in the estate yard - he had just come in on a bicycle. I thought all estate agents drove Land Rovers! I and the agent walked to the keeper's cottage - it was so small, with tiny little rooms, almost like a doll's house. I didn't say anything at the time but I was thinking plenty. We walked back to the estate office and talked about the duties I would have to perform and how much pay I would get - it was less then I already received. The agent said, 'I suppose you would like some food?' 'Yes, please.' Away he went. I looked about the office - there was not much to see - a wooden form, a chair and a high desk, like something out of Charles Dickens, plus one or two books and a map of the estate.

The agent arrived back with a tin plate on a tray. On the plate were two potatoes, a few bits of carrot and a small piece of meat. I sat astride the wooden form, the tray before me - my meal was soon finished. I looked at the agent and he at me. 'What do you think?' he asked, 'are you interested?' ' I shall have to talk to my missus about it,' I replied. 'Alright, you think it over and let me know soon. What about travelling expenses?' Ho, yes, how much did it cost? 'About £5,' I said. What a scrat he had to find enough money for me. I left the place a lot wiser and did not take the situation.

Life at Rudding Park, 1957

I had been under keeper at Rudding Park for one season and now lived in the Lodge just across the road and a field away from Fred Dowker, the head keeper. The one thing that our home lacked was a bathroom window. It was like a small box, very claustrophobic if you were that way inclined. I liked the kitchen - it had a low roof and had been built on at a later time. It had a glass light set into it. The rest of the Lodge consisted of a good sized living room, another room of similar size which was our best room and seldom used, plus two bedrooms. It was all quite cosy.

Outside there was a walled-in yard and a low wooden shed that was the wash house. I also used it to boil pheasant and dog food in, as it had a large gas boiler. A long wooden baker's trough under the window was where I mixed the boiled corn with other ingredients prior to feeding the birds. Behind the wash house and backed onto the park wall were a row of four kennels enclosed in a fair sized exercise run which was made of strong wire-netting, six feet high. At times I took people's dogs to board at £1 a week and also trained them for shooting men.

Behind some trees and shrubs were the large walled-in kitchen garden, potting sheds, glasshouses and boiler houses and two gardeners' cottages made up the remainder of the buildings. Rudding House was built of sandstone, with large bow windows and had a grand view from the elevated position at the top of the park. Below and in front of the Park Wood, were two small lakes, divided by the family graveyard hidden away among yew trees. To the left and standing lower than the main driveway, were some old buildings - workshops for joiners and painters - which also belonged to the estate. There was also a small sawmill and places where tools, wire-netting and fence posts were stored.

At the top end of the cobbled yard was a low bothy where old Mr Larkin lived. Behind the stone buildings and facing onto the park were three cottages in a row - these were very old as were the residents. Mr Shepherd lived in the end one nearest my house. He told me that as a young man he was employed as coachman to Sir Everard Radcliffe. Old Shepherd had lived at Rudding all his life and worked at many different jobs before being pensioned off. When Rudding Park House opened to the public, old Shepherd was brought out of retirement and sat in a small wooden sentry box by the tiny car park and took the money and gave tickets to people visiting the place. You had the choice of walking in the grounds or doing the whole tour which included the house and church. A coach house had been made into a cafe. Earlier the coach house walls had been covered by glass cases containing a superb collection of birds from all parts of the world. Many were destroyed but I kept a few.

Mr Davis lived next to the Mr Shepherd. He was very ancient too. I only saw him now and then. He too had been employed on the estate most of his life. He had been a butler to Sir Everard and later to his son, Captain Radcliffe. Who lived in the other cottage, I cannot remember now. Charlie Butters worked in the wood and sawmill.

Old Mr Larkin lived in a bothy which was only a good sized room with a large open fire, a deal table and a few odd chairs and his bed. He was cosy and appeared to be content. The room smelled of pipe smoke and was homely. I had lived that way when first I arrived at Rudding. Each evening Mr Larkin's son, Pat, called. He was a car salesman. We sat talking many a night and sometimes I went with Pat for a pint. Fred Dowker did not care for Pat and said he was a poacher. I had been thinking of getting a car. Pat turned up one day in a 1926 Morris 8. We liked it and paid £25 for it. Joan and I thought it great to have our own car.

Captain Radcliffe was a Catholic and had his own priest who lived in the Manse near my Lodge. Opposite the Manse there was a gate in the park wall and a path led to the private chapel which was beside the big house. On Sundays, the local village people went there to worship.

Follifoot village had a shop, a general store, two pubs - the Radcliffe Arms and the Lascelles Arms. Follifoot Lodge guarded the drive to Rudding House from that direction. The living quarters were at one side of the road and the sleeping accommodation on the other. It must have been awful leaving a warm room to walk the few yards to the bedroom on a wet, windy night. The lodge keeper could be called from his bed at any hour to open the gates and let any coach pass.

The village stocks used to stand on a tiny strip of grass called the Green. Later they were moved onto the footpath by the barn. A Wesleyan Chapel stood beside the Knaresborough Road, perched above the valley where the Cripple Beck flowed. Looking back at the chapel from Warren Wood, the few Scots fir trees and the chapel made a picturesque sight. I often stopped a while to look at the view. Just inside the park walls, by Follifoot village is the cricket field with a wooden pavilion. On summer evenings while among my pheasants in Low Wood, I could hear the crack of the ball being hit and the cheering from the spectators.

The whole of the park was surrounded by a sandstone wall. At times gypsy people camped on the wide grass verge by the Black Plantation. Sometimes I remonstrated with them for tethering horses and ponies to the copings on the wall. I used to tell them, 'Camp if you want but please don't leave your rubbish.' Usually they shifted elsewhere during the early morning leaving their rubbish behind.

Poachers came from Knaresborough, Harrogate, Leeds, from everywhere, and at weekends keepers were ever vigilant. I patrolled the land and roads at all hours. Rudding was fourteen miles from Long Marston, so we paid regular visits to my wife's family and were able to keep in touch with Dick Rudd, the keeper there, who I had worked under before coming to Rudding.

Sunday Poacher
One Sunday lunchtime I was looking out of the window at a car being driven slowly past. I said to Joan, 'I think those buggers in yon car are after our birds. I'm off out for a while.' Our lodge stood within the park walls which were about seven feet high. I ran to where I could see the road through a hole and I could also see some pheasants in a field opposite.

As the car came into view it was moving at a walking pace and the two occupants seemed very interested in the birds. I scratched the car's registration number on a stone beside me and prepared to leap over the wall. I hadn't long to wait - the car stopped opposite my hiding place and a shot was fired. The passenger jumped over the fence to fetch the pheasant as I jumped over the wall. The driver set off when he saw me, though not too fast.

By now the poacher had the dead pheasant and was running towards the moving car. I ran to where he was climbing the fence and shouted, 'I'll take that bird!' The poacher swung the pheasant hard and hit me in the face with it. It took me by surprise and he got away. I immediately rang the police and gave them the registration number. Later that day the bobby called to say the car was local and was found outside a pub in Knaresborough. The owner was traced - evidently he worked at the goods yard at Wetherby Railway Station.

The next day the policeman and I hid a short distance from the workers' canteen at the station. The policeman said, 'See if you can spot any of the poachers and point them out, but don't let them see you.' Sure enough I saw the chap who had hit me with the pheasant.

An arrest was made and I was given notice to appear at Knaresborough Court to give evidence against the poacher. Lord Mowbray was chairman of the court. He owned Alerton Park Estate and was a keen shooting man. He dressed like a Victorian, complete with side whiskers and a heavy moustache. He was severe to say the least.

However the poacher was found not guilty and the case was dismissed as he had been in a pub at Knaresborough at the time of the offence. The court awarded the chap £5 in damages. I later found out that the man had an identical twin. The local paper article was titled, 'Gamekeeper identifies wrong man.'

Keepers and keepers

I was taken by Fred Dowker on visits to see other keepers. Alec Wolstencroft was head keeper at Harewood Estate. I later applied for a job there but the keeper's house was too far from any road. I had to think of the time when Heather started school.

Vic Thompson was keeper at Bramham Park and we paid him regular visits. I bought a .32 calibre pin fire pistol from him. It was an 1876 American model in almost mint condition. I also bought a British Bulldog .450 pistol from Alec Wolstencroft complete with a box of 50 cartridges in a tin box lined with felt. I paid £5 each for them.

Dick Dale was keeper at Ribbston Park, near Knaresborough. Wilf Parkinson was keeper at Ingmanthorpe Hall. Wilf was a great friend of Fred Dowker and often paid visits to Rudding. Just before we moved to Kent, Wilf gave me a .303 carbine which I used on deer in Kent. Old Carey was keeper at Tockwith. I paid him visits now and then and got news of his area.

Vincent Banks was part-time keeper at Askham Richard. I also kept in touch with him. I bought a revolver from him, a .32 RSW revolver which broke open to load. Vincent kept tumbler pigeons. On summer evenings we would lay stretched out on reclining chairs and Vincent would clap his hands making the birds fly high, then they started the tumbling routine they are famous for. Vincent had two wives. The first one baked super cakes and I often had a meal at his home. He kept terriers kennelled about the paddock and an ancient horse called Violet - he thought a lot of her. Harold Shipley was keeper for Sir William Brooks Banks at Wighill Park. We never came in contact with him much.

Ernest Percy was part-time keeper at Thorpe Arch and was employed on the War Agricultural Vermin Destruction. His mate, Fred Young, worked for the government as well. We had regular visits from them - they organised fox drives at various places in Yorkshire. A lot of tree-planting was being done near the moors. These were driven at times on Sundays and many foxes killed.

I was introduced to Jim Wilson. He was keeper for Silcocks, the cattle feed people at Bleasdale Tower in Lancashire. He was a Scotsman and very hard to work for. He had a reputation for large bags of game - 1000 pheasants a day sometimes. They reared many thousands of them. Sometimes Jim Wilson and Fred exchanged pheasants to get fresh blood into their own stock. I remember once in Clitheroe we met Jim on a pub car park and were changing the crates. Somehow a few escaped and disappeared over the roof tops.

Charlie Triffet had lived at Bilton in Ainsty and did some part-time keepering on Marston Moor. One night Charlie had set out for home across the land from Marston. His son later phoned to ask if his father had left the head keeper's cottage. Later a search was made and eventually Charlie was found - evidently he had been crossing a dry ditch when he collapsed and died, his dog was with him when he was found.

Charlie Heslop was keeper at Stockheld Park. He was a Geordie and was a great talker. I had a black Labrador dog from him on trial one spring. I had taken the dog out and on the way home he picked up a dead jackdaw. I took it from him and put him in the kennels. We had my father and mother staying that weekend and after breakfast I took my father to look at the new dog. At the gate I shouted the dog's name - all the other dogs appeared but not Charlie Heslop's dog. I called again, no dog appeared. Turning to my dad I said, 'The dog must be dead.' Entering the kennel I saw he was indeed dead. I had been using poison baits for vermin and the dog had eaten part of the jackdaw he had picked up. How Fred squared it with Charlie I don't know, but I never paid the £10 he wanted for it. While I was at Edenhall, I met Charlie again. He was keeper at Flakebridge, near Appleby. He always called at my home in the evening, would talk for ages and never knew when to go home. It was so bad that I would avoid him.

John Gregg was a keeper at Clarendon Park, Wiltshire. He was an easy going chap. We became good friends and when I left Clarendon Park we kept in touch. I told John of a keeper's job at a place called Barnwell-Wold. Duncan Marsden was in charge of the syndicate. The Greggs were offered the position and moved to Barnwell and appeared to be happy there. About three years later I had word that they were leaving. John had been given notice just before Christmas, it was a great shock for us and them. He went to work for the prison service. They had had enough of tied cottages, keepering and especially syndicate bosses. A few years later we heard the sorrowful news that their only son, Simon, who was in the Air Force, was killed in a motorcycle accident. I have not heard from them for many a year.

Norman Dunn was keeper at Winderwath, across the river from Edenhall. He took over the same year as I took over at Edenhall. We helped each other on shoot days and met at keepers' shoots and clay pigeon shoots - they were always there when anything was happening. I was taught that a keeper should be about his work and should not to be seen in pubs or other places of enjoyment - the job came first.

Jim Overs, was keeper at Melkinthorpe, part of the Lowther Estate. I helped Jim to move when he went to Lazonby Hall to be keeper there. Their belongings were very sparse and the cottage in bad repair. A while later at their new home at Fogg Close, the Overs seemed to blossom. It would appear that they had prospered by the move to Lazonby. The home took on a new appearance, furniture and the rest of the chattels were new or near new. We visited the Overs now and then. Jim had a near breakdown in health when keepers had to turn to incubators and brooders to rear the pheasants, because broody hens were not available. He came to tell me of his problems. I went to Lazonby and did my best to show Jim what temperatures the incubators had to be set at and other things to do with the hatching. He managed somehow and eventually got well again. Some good days shooting were had at Lazonby. Jim eventually retired and died several years ago.

Jim Wilson of whom I wrote earlier, was living in an old caravan in a wood somewhere in Lancashire. His wife was living in a council house. Jim would not give up the old ways. He was an old man then. Jim Wilson never recovered after his only son was killed at Bleasdale in a road accident. The lad was riding in the back of a van and had been to the pub with his mates. The van left the road - Jim's son was thrown forwards onto the gear lever which pierced his head because it had no knob on it and was killed.

Monty Fairish, was keeper to Major Hassall of Dalemain House, Ullswater. Monty told me about his cottage - it stood in a small wood, a field away from the road. There was no electric and water from a spring and the wages were hardly enough to live on. I was in Penrith one day and came across Monty. I asked how were things with him? 'I am working for the council now, on the bins and have a council house.' Evidently he had differed with old Major Hasell and had been sacked. His furniture was put out of the cottage onto the field. Poor Monty, his son was a keeper at Barrock Park, towards Carlisle, a nice young chap. Monty helped his son on shoot days.

Hughie McGinn, a Scotsman inclined to temper, was keeper to Mr Stafford Howard at Greystoke Castle, near Penrith. Hughie was a frequent visitor to Edenhall. He was a picker-up, usually having a useful dog or two. I met Hughie at various shoots. Racehorses were one of Hughie's vices - the racing stables of Gordon Richards were on the Greystoke estate and Gordon was a neighbour of the McGinn's. Hughie attended most of the northern race meetings - he couldn't drive yet he got there somehow. I have not seen him for many years now and he will be very old if still alive.

Donald Wilson was head keeper to Lord Lonsdale at Lowther. I often called at his home, a large house which stands alone, close to the old barracks where the Lowther troops had their quarters many

Brian and daughter Heather.

years ago. The barracks are now homes for the estate workers and all have been modernised. Donald, another Scotsman of even temperament, was a typical head keeper - stern looking and smartly dressed, like the older generation of keepers. He haled from Dunkeld.

Bill Wright was keeper at Warwick Hall which had a fine stretch of the Eden, famous for its sea trout fishing. I fished the water late on summer evenings and Colin Armstrong from the fishing tackle shop in Penrith fished there with me. Bill Wright was a first rate keeper and always had a good dog. He came picking-up at most of our shoots at Edenhall.

Walter Drysdale keepered Reagill, part of the Lowther estate. He was employed by Mr Derek Pattinson, agent to Lord Lonsdale. Walter was another Scotsman, quite a small man and a good keeper who trained some good dogs. Walter came to our shoots and it was a pleasure to have him. He also used to buy and break horses and later worked in the saw mills on Clifton Moor.

Charlie Sweetman was employed by Colonel Ogden on the Cowan Bridge Estate. I went there with my employer, Airley Holden-Hindley, who was brother-in-law to the colonel. We had some good days shooting there. Charlie Sweetman's brother keepered the adjoining Leck estate, which belonged to Lord Shuttleworth. Both the Sweetmans helped us at our shoots. I enjoyed going to Cowan Bridge or Park Hall. We had great days there. The colonel was a good man and very generous but died quite young.

Charlie Raynor was head keeper at Eastwell Park, Ashford, Kent. The estate belonged to Captain George Broderick. Charlie was a tall, thin man, who rolled his own cigarettes and enjoyed a joke. He had been a sergeant in the Army and his legs had been wounded by a mine. Charlie Raynor was a very competent head keeper. Stan Martin was a beat keeper at Clarendon Park, Salisbury, Wiltshire. He was a Berkshire man, soft spoken and would always agree with you.

Adam Rough was head keeper on Lord Swinton's grouse moors. He was quite old in 1955 when I was loading for my employer, Major Christopher York, MP for Harrogate. Adam had a Lakeland terrier that would retrieve grouse. He was often used when the other dogs failed to find a bird. Jack Rough was Adam's son and was second moorland keeper. He eventually took over from his father.

Peter Young was the third moorland keeper and had worked with Vincent Banks years before. Peter's home was isolated, stuck way on the fellside. It was a hard life those keepers lived. I know they enjoyed a drop of beer and met now and then to let their hair down.

Dick Rudd was the first keeper I worked with. He was a small, thinly built chap, liked horse racing and attended Wetherby and York fixtures. Dick came from Eskrik. When he came back from the war he took over at Marston Manor, near York. His son Tony was also a keeper. Years later Tony left keepering and turned to farming on the same estate which was owned by Major Christopher York.

Dick Evans was at Plumpton Hall. The stable block or yard was huge by today's standards, the buildings forming a large square with a cobbled yard in the centre. An archway led into it and the gate was always kept shut. In the far corner, on the right, the Evans family lived. Old Dick Evans was the head keeper on the Plumpton Hall estate which belonged to Lord Harewood. The rest of the Evans family consisted of George, Dick's only son and a daughter, Mary, who were both in their forties or fifties.

Dick Evans was a big man and would have been retired but keepers don't retire they just fade away. I remember having cause to visit their home, during the late spring, the rearing season. The gate to the stable yard had wire netting fixed to prevent any animals entering. I was surprised to see about twenty coops each with a clocker installed with a brood of young ducks. The door of Evans's house was open and Dick was seated on a chair watching over his rearing ground. 'Sit yerself down, lad.' Dick talked of the great days he had seen at Harewood and Plumpton. He remembered well the fox hunts with Lord and Lady Lascelles, or Lord Harewood. Mary Evans helped Dick with the duck rearing. I was told how handy it was having a fine yard like this, as an eye could always be kept on the broods of ducklings and if heavy rain came on suddenly, the ducks were driven into the kitchen of the Evans's home.

With Dick Evans getting on in years, I was given permission to kill foxes in Warren Wood and Birkham where I worked my terriers and killed many foxes. We often drove the woods at Plumpton for foxes. Old Dick would take a stand in the corner of Birkham Great Wood. I can picture him now, leaning with his back to a tree. Dick was a fine shot - though was an old man he could hold his own.

The Gardener's lad, Rudding Park

Grant, the head gardener, had left Rudding Park and was replaced. The new head gardener turned out to be uncooperative and was hard to talk to so I left him alone. I had been used to calling in at the walled kitchen garden where the glass houses were. I knew that someone would be about and would have a sit down and talk about the estate, etc. In fact I enjoyed our talks. If the gardeners were having problems with rabbits or grey squirrels, I would do something to help them.

The head gardener and his family lived close to my lodge - his wife was a school mistress. They had two children, a girl of about twelve and a lad who was fifteen or sixteen. The new people kept themselves to themselves and seemed a bit aloof. Maybe they thought they were superior to Joan and I.

As time went by I had to warn the gardener's son to stay out of the woods in the park that was stocked with pheasants. Traps I had set for vermin were sometimes sprung, gates left open letting sheep enter the woods and causing the farmer to search the wood looking for the strayed sheep. I had found the raft on the lake cast adrift several times and had great difficulty in retrieving it. Alarm guns had been tampered with and feed cabin doors left open to the weather. I knew it was the gardener's son doing the mischief. In the end I had a word with his father but there wasn't much joy from him.

One Saturday afternoon I was eating my dinner and heard an alarm gun go off - bloody hell, I could not get a meal in peace. I had to go and investigate. Picking up my rifle I made for the park wood where I thought they would be. It could be that bloody gardener's lad or it could be poachers. I went straight to where the alarm gun was set - it had gone off and the wire was pulled out. I stood a while and listened, then walked to the edge of the wood from where I could get a view across the deer park.

I set off towards the Deer House that overlooked the Low Wood and Fox Cover and stood there for a long time. Towards the sawmill I saw someone by the wall that surrounded the park - there were two of them and the way they were trying to hide themselves between the trees, it was a good guess they were the ones I was after. Right, my lads, you are in for a surprise, I thought. When you get to Low Wood I shall be waiting you.

I walked quickly down the park behind Fox Cover Wood, well out of sight of the intruders. Entering Low Wood I made for the lakeside where the raft was moored. I hid myself among the rhododendrons that grew thickly by the lake bank. I heard them coming along the ride behind me. The trap was set and I was there! The pair of them were on the raft and poling out towards the island. I let them get there before showing myself. 'Good afternoon,' I shouted at them. They froze. 'Caught you at last. Now you are for it.' I stood, rifle under my arm - they seemed shocked and knew they were trapped.

It was the gardener's son and a mate of his. They poled the raft to the far side of the lake hoping to make a landing there. A dozen yards from the shore the raft stuck in deep mud. The lads pushed the raft off again and tried further along the lake, again the raft grounded yards from the green grass of the park, deep mud preventing any escape. I had made myself comfortable, knowing the only way the raft could be brought to land was where I stood on guard.

How long the voyagers tried I don't remember. The long pole was heavy and at times had to be pulled from the mud. In the end they were exhausted and made for where they had started their journey. The raft was still some feet from the shore and the mate of the gardener's lad had leapt ashore. I let him go and he disappeared along the ride through the wood. I jumped aboard and charged the lad with my shoulder - he went into water around ten feet deep. I quickly tied up the raft as he was just surfacing.

'Now you bloody sod!' He was hanging on to the raft side. The raft was made of four 45 gallon oil drums with a stout staging. It floated high out of the water. I sat down and placed my foot upon the head of the lad and pushed his head under the muddy waters - each time he surfaced I repeated the ducking.

I looked across the water and saw his mate a long way off, watching me. I took up my rifle and fired over the watcher's head. The last I saw of him he was running towards the sawmill yard. I returned to the gardener's lad in the lake - he was about done. Eventually I allowed him to crawl ashore. I had no fear of him running away. When he could stand I told him I was taking him to Captain Ratcliffe, my employer.

To start the lad on his way I gave him a kick up the arse which put him on his knees again. Out of the wood and up the park we went. The prisoner was bawling and turned to me and asked me not to go to the captain. I spun him about and started him on his way with another hefty boot behind him. My short temper was fired up. This bugger in front of me had caused me much trouble and time.

At the gate that led from the park into the gardens, the gardener's lad pleaded with me again, 'Don't take me to the captain.' I had no forgiveness in me. In the stable yard at the back door of the big house I rang the bell. The butler who opened the door said that Captain Ratcliffe had gone to London the night before. I walked my prisoner behind the stable block and told him he was lucky. 'Bugger off and don't try it again.' I knew he would be many days before he annoyed me again.

The following day, Sunday, I had a visit from the police. They wanted a statement. I was careful what I said and denied that I had fired a rifle over one of the culprit's heads. I said that the lad was mistaken, it was a gun I used and the range was a few hundred yards so there being little fear of injury to him.

The police said I was to be charged with assault with intent and that the parents of the lad wished them to proceed forthwith. I was called to the estate office, where Major Ives, the agent said I was in serious trouble and could maybe go to prison for the offence. The major asked me to go to the gardener and his wife and apologise to them and their son. Major Ives said he would do all he could to get the lad's parents to drop charges against me. Only they could get the police to stop the prosecution charges.

The gardener did not want to lose his job and appeared to have been swayed from pressing charges. His wife was the opposite and would not relent. Fred Dowker, the head keeper, asked me to go and apologise to them all, if only to get the charges dropped, pointing out that Joan and I had only been married a short while. I relented and went with the agent to the home of the gardener. The whole family were there and I stood in their doorway.

I did my best to apologise to each of them in turn although there was no remorse in me. The agent said his piece and hoped I would be forgiven. We left them - they hadn't said whether or not my apologies had been accepted or not. I was called to the estate office the next day and was told that my apologies had been accepted and that the police were dropping the charges against me.

I heard later that the police were reluctant to drop charges against me and asked the parents to press the case as it was a serious offence I had committed. But in the end the charges were dropped and things quietened down but were never the same. The gardener left the estate the following year and so did I.

Trouble at Lodge Wood

This incident happened on the Rudding Park estate. A few hundred young pheasants had been put in a one acre wood - it was the first time this had been tried, the wood being on the edge of the estate. The wood consisted of larch and spruce with the odd hardwood tree scattered among them. A stream ran along the bottom side and the whole wood was surrounded with a post and rail fence. To get there you had to travel the Haggs Road which was a quiet, little used way and only served a few farms. One track led to Lodge Farm at the far side of the shallow valley where Lodge Wood lay. To reach the wood, two fields had to be crossed on foot or by tractor as there was no track.

It was a lovely, peaceful place and only keepers and farmers went there. It lay in a valley and could not be seen from the road. I was working among my pheasants one mid-September afternoon. I had taken some light fence posts and stacked them against the fence with a roll of wire netting which I had been using earlier. It was a great day - ideal for a bit of trout tickling - there were some good fish in the stream. Alec Dowker and I had caught a good bag full a year ago.

Leaning against the fence I watched the young pheasants dusting along the wood edge. Many were wandering in the meadow where there were plenty of insects and they were busy chasing moths and pulling at buttercup flowers. It was an ideal place. I had placed a few coops with the mother hens facing out onto the field - if there was any danger the hens would give the alarm.

The sun was very strong and made it difficult at a distance to see who it was coming towards me along the beck side. As the chap got nearer I could see he was in his late teens and a stranger. He hadn't seen me until I spoke. 'And where are you going?' I asked. He had pulled up by the fence on the beck side. Seeing me he came up, 'I'm going down the stream, mate.'

'There's no footpath or public right of way along here. This is private land belonging to Rudding estate. I think you had better go back and get onto the road again. This is private property.' He stood before me evidently wondering who the bloody hell I was. The pheasants caught his eye. 'What's them?' he asked, pointing to them. 'Nowt to do with you, lad, it's about time you were back on the road.' 'Else what?' 'Alright,' I said, 'I'll tell you who I am. I am employed by the estate owner. I am a gamekeeper, employed to look after the estate, that's who I am.'

He, the trespasser, was softening now. 'I was only going down the stream for a walk. I'm doing nowt wrong, just having a walk.' 'Where do you come from?' I asked. 'What's it do wi you where I come from?' 'Look, lad, I am not going to argue with ya. Now bugger off the way you came in. I told you, get moving or else.' He stood beginning to get cocky with me again. 'Are you going or not?' 'NO!'

I walked towards the beck, then over the fence on to the field. This was it, he was daring me. He stared at me. I was close now, close enough. 'Are you going to go the way you came?' I asked. 'NO!' My blow caught him right - it was a good one. Standing over the lad I was waiting to do the necessary should he try anything. He lay shocked. I was trembling as I do when about to explode. My temper starting to subside, although I was ready to strike again at any aggravation from him. It was quite a while before the trespasser gained his feet and slowly set off back the way he had come, his legs a little wobbly.

Sitting on an upturned bucket I contemplated my spoiled afternoon. I had lost interest in fishing for the moment and fetching two buckets of water I set about cleaning and filling the drinking fountains. I heard a sound and looked up. I thought it must be among the stock at the farm, as it was getting on for milking time.

Another shout - I shaded my eyes, looking along the beck side the way the lad had gone. What was he shouting for? Was he going to have another go at me? It was cool in the wood, the shade easy on my eyes. I watched the figure approach - he shouted again. This wasn't the lad I had dealt with earlier, but another stranger, another trespasser.

He appeared to be in his forties, about my height but heavier. He could certainly shout. It would be hard for him to see me as I was in the shade. What the hell was there to shout about? 'What yer shouting about, have yer lost summat?' I was thinking maybe he'd lost his dog. I was now standing by the fence and in the light he came and stopped a dozen yards before me. 'That you that hit my lad ?' he shouted. He was agitated whoever he was, fairly mad.

'If that was your lad, it was me.' The chap could not keep still. I told him who I was and what had happened and that the lad was being clever and that was it. The chap started shouting about what he was going to do to me. He was good at shouting.

Oh, hell, I thought, here we go again. He was by the fence and his foot was on the rail when the stake hit him at the side of the neck. He fell back onto the field and lay there. There was no movement - first the son, now the father. I was in trouble now alright, the way he fell he could be badly injured, even dead! But he wasn't dead, I leaned on the fence watching closely. He was breathing. I was strangely fascinated by what I had done. I had had enough of Lodge Wood for one day. The stake was still in my hand. What if I had hit the chap on his head and knocked his brains out, made a right mess of him? Well, he had shouted what he intended to do to me. I threw the post down and set off home at a good gallop.

The two miles to the kennels where the head keeper, Fred Dowker, lived, seemed to take hours. On the way I had thoughts of being gaoled, losing my job and my home. Fred was in the kennels. 'What's up with you?' I sat on some sacks of corn getting my wind back. 'What's up?' I told him that I was for it any time and the police would come for me. 'What have yer done this time?'

Fred listened to the tale, dragging on his cigarette, interested. 'What have you done?' He started laughing after a while. 'Don't worry, lad, don't worry. You were doing your job, that's what keepers are paid for.' 'I thought I had killed him, Fred. He's bound to go to the police when he can. He might still be lying at Lodge Wood.'

We sat in Fred's home and Mrs Dowker made some tea. When Fred told of my doings she said, 'What shall I say if the police call?' 'They won't come, forget about it.' Fred seemed sure all would be well. He was right. I never heard anything. We kept it quiet for a long time. Eventually it was told to one or two of the older keepers who said, 'Yer did right, lad, you stick at it and don't stand any nonsense, thou should make a good keeper.'

Rats at the Water Slakes
One day I visited what is known as the Water Slakes, an area of about half an acre with a small clump of tall old willow trees surrounded by rough grass with a hazel and thorn hedge. In wet weather the place would flood and in summer it was dry. Over the years farmers had tipped all kinds of things there - buckets, churns,

sacks, iron sheets, bits of worn out machinery, bailer twine, spoiled hay and sweepings from granaries and outbuildings.

The day I visited was in winter and the Water Slakes was flooded. The water was about six to eight inches deep but deeper around the trees. I had come to check some tunnel traps but had my gun ready as the place was a favourite for ducks. Some ducks flew up but they were too far away for a shot. I came upon some heaps of threshing muck - chaff, barley horns, weed seeds and small corn and rats were darting about and then disappearing among the rubbish.

I stood quietly for a minute until a rat came out. I shot it then out came another and I shot it. I could see rat tracks all about the rubbish - bloody hell there was a drove of them here. They must have moved in recently as a couple of days before there was no sign of rats. I went to tell Dick and he said, 'Get your bike and gun and take Rusty.'

So, Dick and I with Rusty my Border terrier, plus Lynn and Mandy, Dick's two Cairn terriers set off. We left our bikes and the terriers were soon in the threshing muck and rats were shooting out and setting off across the shallow water. Dick was shooting and there were rats everywhere. I shot one, a terrier grabbed it and shook it and parts of it flew everywhere. The terriers were nosing deep into the threshing rubbish and would then back away with a struggling rat in their mouths, howling because the rat had sunk its teeth in.

Dick came over to ask if I had any cartridges. We were almost out so decided to tie the terriers up and go to get some more. I got on my bike and went to Tockwith, a village about two miles away where I could get cartridges at the blacksmith's shop behind the Spotted Ox pub. Mr Gosney, the blacksmith, gave me fifty 12 bore cartridges to charge to Major York. I stuffed them in my game bag and set off back to Marston.

I pedalled as fast as I could as it was getting dark and I was out of breath by the time I got back. 'Have a minute,' said Dick, 'we'll soon have these rats out now.' We let the terriers loose again and they were straight into the muck. I shot and shot but it wasn't easy as the rats kept hiding behind tufts of grass. The smoke from our guns hung over Water Slakes. After a while things went quiet. I took my rabbiting spade from my bike and started digging into the threshing heaps - now and then a rat would bolt but the terriers soon finished them off.

I fetched an old wheelbarrow from the tip and had piled the dead rats in it. The barrow was brim full. I didn't count them. The next day I returned to the scene of the rat massacre and all was still. The rats must have arrived in one lot - rats on the move together. I had heard of hundreds of them being seen before but I hadn't believed it. The magpies had a feast on the rats in the barrow. It would have been an ideal place to kill down some of the winged vermin - some poison would have rid the countryside of the black and white hoard.

One time I had some traps set from Peggy Rash Wood across to the Askham Whin Wood and took a visit to each trap twice a day. I shall never forget the day when a chestnut and white magpie was caught by the leg in one of the traps. I would have killed it immediately if it had been on ordinary one. But this one was special, unique and had to be preserved. I cut its broken leg off - it still had a good stump - and put it in my game bag and set off for home.

Ernest Percy, a rabbit catcher on War Agricultural Service, wanted to buy the bird to stuff it. I told him to get stuffed as I would not part with my magpie. I kept him in a poultry ark but one day when it needed moving Tony Rudd, Dick's son, lifted it too high and the magpie was gone - but not for long. A few days later he was caught in the same bait trap as before - all that was left of him were two brown and white wings as a fox had had him. He must have been stupid to get caught in the same trap twice.

Late night revellers, 1957

I know we hadn't been married but a few months and had settled ourselves at the lodge at Rudding Park, Harrogate. Just before Christmas, it had been a busy time as we were feeding the birds hard as we called it, carrying corn to all the woods twice a day. Some woods were several fields away from a road or track and it was heavy going if the land was sodden or had been ploughed and sown.

We had gone to bed about 9pm - we didn't have a TV set in those days. I was soon asleep but something woke me. I lay for a while listening. I looked at the clock - it was 11.45 pm. I heard the noise again - it sounded like shouting and more shouting. Whoever it was, was coming up the road towards my lodge. Joan was awake, 'What's going on?' she asked. 'I don't know but I shall soon find out.' I was out of the bed, dressed and was soon downstairs. The sitting room had a bow window and it was possible to look up and down the road. I didn't put the light on but I could see quite plainly as it was bright moonshine. The shouting was much louder now but I still couldn't make out where they were at that time.

My dogs had been barking for a while. Now and then they would be quiet as though listening, only to start again the instant the shouting started. I stood at the window and finally could see two of them; they didn't appear to be in any hurry. Eventually as they approached the lodge they quietened down a bit. As they passed my window I recognised the pair. They were some of the travellers that were camped at the Long Plantation at the top of the park.

The dogs were making a hell of a racket by now. The kennels were backed up to the wall that surrounded the park and there was only a wide grass verge between them and the road. Opposite the kennels the late night revellers stopped and the shouting started again. The noise was awful and it had gone on long enough. I went out to the entrance gates and shouted at the pair to shut up and get away. Eventually they saw me approaching them and quietened down. They were a rough pair and were the worse for drink - some bad language was spoken between us. I made it plain that I would be at their camp in the morning and if any horses were tethered to the coping stones of the park wall, I would cut the tether ropes, so they had better be away now.

I left them and went back indoors. I had only just got into bed and the dogs started again, so did the shouting - the bloody travellers were back! The more my dogs barked, the more the pair shouted and bawled. More trouble! I dressed again but didn't put the light on. Downstairs I loaded my gun and went into the yard. I shouted to them to bugger off, then got some step ladders and leaned them against the wall and climbed up and sat astride it.

When the shouters saw me I suppose they thought I was about to jump down to the road and began to retreat again. They stopped some sixty yards away and renewed their abuse. The night was bright and I could see them without any trouble. The lights at the kennels were on - evidently Fred Dowker, the head keeper, must have heard the racket and his dogs were barking.

My temper got the better of me - I had had enough. I raised the gun and fired both barrels at the road some few yards in front of the travellers. Sparks came from their boots, but they were away this time, the shouting ceased and eventually I got the dogs quietened down and went back to bed but not to sleep. I was up very early.

  The day started - breakfast, mix the feed for the birds and away on my rounds. Joan was making the Sunday dinner - it smelled good and the table was set. I walked to the window that looked onto the road. 'Ho, bloody hell,' I said aloud. 'What's wrong?' 'There's two coppers coming with that pair I shot at last night!' Joan said, 'You're too bloody handy with the gun.' I said, 'I bet I let some shot into them bastards.'

  When the police arrived I went outside. They were friendly, not at all what I had expected. There was no mention of any shooting or anyone being injured - that was a relief. I was asked, 'Had I heard anything last night?' 'Yes, I had,' and I told the police about the disturbance and that I had seen the two men that were with them on the road at midnight and that the disturbance had gone on for about a half hour. 'Would I be willing to give evidence?' 'Yes, I would.' The pair were marched away. At the gate one of the policemen turned to me and said that the local pub had been broken into last night and that the two travellers were prime suspects. It turned out that they were the culprits and were convicted. They pleaded guilty so I was not called as a witness. It had been quite a night. This was the beginning of married life, what would the rest of it be like?!

V
Game keeping in Kent

Eastwell Park, Ashford

I had an interview at Eastwell Park, an estate near Ashford. I travelled there by bus and train, and was met by Ollie Pyke in a Land Rover. I was taken to the estate office where I met Captain George Broderick. He was a very nice gentleman and greeted me warmly

He and Charlie Raynor, the head keeper showed me around the estate - about 9,000 acres all told. It was superb countryside, with rolling hills, plenty of really old trees and miles of coppice woodland. The estate had been a training area for tanks during the war. A deer fence had enclosed the park but the Army had destroyed it. Now the deer were everywhere and beginning to be a nuisance.

I was shown the keeper's cottage, which was called Church Cottage and had once been where the parson lived. The old church stood about a hundred yards away on a low hillside and a medieval timbered barn sat up on staddle stones close by it. Church Cottage had been divided into two. It had a heavy oak Norman door, all studded at the front side with arched windows. We looked inside the cottage - the kitchen had a brick floor and a Rayburn cooker, then there was a lavatory, bathroom, large front room with an inglenook fireplace and three bedrooms. The whole was surrounded by about quarter an acre of land and some snow fencing enclosed the lot.

Captain Broderick and I discussed the terms of employment, and I received my travelling allowance, then took my leave and was driven to Ashford where arrangements had been made to put me up for the night at a small pub. I was very impressed with Eastwell Park and the way I had been made welcome. On the train I thought a lot about it. By the time I got home I had been away two days. Joan and I talked about my interview and decided that we would move to Kent soon.

Arrangements were made at Eastwell Park and I worked my time out at Rudding. We started packing things into tea chests. We had three written estimates for our removal from Harrogate - the one that was accepted cost £72.00. We loaded our furniture one day and that night Joan and I slept on a mattress. Early next morning the van with our stuff called for us. We loaded the mattress, and the car into the back of the van.

We had said our goodbyes some while before and now we were on the road. There were no motorways then and we went through London. We stopped a while at a cafe, the two van men, the two of us and Heather, just a baby in arms - what a journey. We arrived at Challock, the nearest village and had to ask the way to Church Cottage - it was black dark and raining. Down through the woods we went, the van scraping on the low branches. The cottage was about a mile out of the village. Our van pulled up, 'This looks like the place.' There were no lights on and it was about thirty yards from the track to our front door and about six steps down to our path.

I got Joan and Heather out of the cab and into the house. The room was thick with smoke from the inglenook fire because the wood was soaking wet. I went out to the van men - the tailgate was already down and we started to roll our Morris 8 out. As it started to come down the ramp, the exhaust pipe caught on something. After a bit of shoving about it came free and I soon had it parked away but the exhaust pipe was damaged.

The weather was awful. I managed to get some lights on in the house - the generator made a hellish noise. The rain continued to fall as we struggled to get the furniture into the house. I had also packed tea chests of hens, ferrets, mice and dogs, which all went into the stable. We had three dogs with us. Eventually the van was empty. The men were good and went away with a small tip each,

There we were among our possessions in a room full of smoke. We didn't know where anything was and we were tired out. Joan fed Heather, we put a mattress down and went to sleep. What a day! We had made our first move - all those miles and for just ten shillings a week more!!

Next day we started to get our house sorted out. The kitchen would only take the round tip up table, one easy chair and two ordinary chairs. That was soon done. The rest of the cottage was all put to order by noon. Both fires were lit and hot water was soon available. I started to make dog kennels and a large enclosed run so that the dogs could go in and out of the kennels at their own will. A small cabin at the bottom of the garden was used as a store for dog food and other things, along with my white mice.

All our power at Church Cottage was made by a generator driven by a Lister one cylinder diesel engine. The engine used about fifteen gallons of fuel a month. The money for our diesel was deducted from my pay every two weeks - most estates paid out monthly or by the fortnight. The generator was very efficient - as soon as a switch was put down in the cottage, the engine would start up, even for a kettle or one light and so it paid to run a few electric appliances at one time when it was running. The noise was quite loud as the Lister was in what had been the old privy about a dozen yards from our back door and the exhaust pipe stuck out through the wall. The cottage was in a valley with woods all about us so the echo was very noticeable. I could hear the noise of it a long way off when on my rounds.

I soon found my way about the Challock beat which was my beat and met the other keepers every Friday at the estate yard where we would have a natter and the head keeper would inform us if we were to have rabbit shoots or fox drives or whatever. We were paid our vermin money - so much for a fox tail, deer skins 1/6d - some estates paid vermin money, others didn't.

Joan and I went to Ashford market once a week. It was a good country produce market, and you could buy anything from a ferret to a gun. A gunsmith from Canterbury, who was also a collector, had a stand there. I became friends with this man and he supplied me with ammunition for the guns in my collections. At Christmas the market was a wonderful sight - all sorts of game and poultry hung up in the big barn-like covered market and there was holly and mistletoe, which was grown in Kent. Many farmers and people of the land were to be seen there, though we found it difficult to understand the dialect at first.

As it got round to the rearing time, a field was put out for our use. I was in charge of the field. Charlie Raynor and his son, John, ran the hatching yard. The usual things were brought to the field - the cabin on wheels, boiler, a load of wood - all the tackle that was needed. Old Bert Haskell, a keeper for many years, lived at Westwell at the far side of the estate. The old Pilgrims' Way ran through the land on that side - it had been used many years ago by pilgrims on their way to Canterbury Cathedral to pay their respects to Thomas à Beckett who was murdered there long ago.

Bert Haskell
Bert Haskell lived in a house by the side of a 44 acre lake with an island in the middle. Some short piers ran out into the bay, as it was

called, at the side of the house. The place was ancient and stood beside the remains of Westwell Church - only the tower was left standing - it had been bombed in the war. Bert lived alone in the old place which was covered in ivy rich with bird life. How long Bert Haskell had lived there I never knew. His wife had died there. I would go and visit Bert in the evening sometimes and listen to him talk of the days before the war, before Captain Broderick took over.

Bert reared his birds by the lakeside - he preferred doing his own rearing. During the rearing season, he would row out to the island and set lines baited for pike. The following day any fish that were caught were kept alive and placed in a wired part of the pier. These fish were kept there until such time as they were needed. A fish was killed, put in the boiler and cooked, then taken out to cool. Then it was put through the large mincer and mixed with the meal and other ingredients and fed to the young birds. Care had to be taken not to overfeed with fish as this would cause scouring in the birds and kill them.

Bert Haskell was quite a character. He used to umpire at cricket matches and took with him two tame badgers which were left fastened up while he was out on the field. He chewed tobacco and after a while it was taken out of his mouth, then put inside his hat under the sweat band. Charlie Raynor couldn't stand to see him do that, and called him 'a dirty old sod!'

I met Bert one day where our beats joined. We were talking by a corn stack when a stoat caught my eye as it came around the stack. I immediately raised my gun to shoot it. 'No, no, don't kill he. Leave him, he will keep the rats down, he has been about a while now.' So we went our ways, Bert to the home beat and I to Challock. We had another old keeper, Bert Tollman, who was a grand old chap. He looked after the Kennington Ground where some hop yards were and a few small woods. Bert Tollman had keepered there many a year.

We had two men, Len and Jack, who were employed as rabbit catchers. Jack would turn up on shoot days or rabbiting days, on a motorbike and sidecar. He always wore an old gabardine raincoat and cap and usually had a bottle of rough Romney Marsh cider in his pocket. I have seen Jack laid out on the ground laughing away to himself, having drunk cider early in the morning. Len was a bit younger than Jack, perhaps thirty years old and more reserved. Come to think of it, Jack had the look of a rabbit, with prominent teeth and a narrow face.

A while later, a young fellow called Ken Pickles, was taken on as keeper. He said that he was just out of the Army. He talked with a Scottish accent but he was as Yorkshire as I was. He came from Bradford or Keighley. Ken took over from Bert Haskell when he retired. If I remember right there was a bit of a to do with Ken. Evidently he had been parading up and down in front of the big house in the early morn, playing the bagpipes. He was a bit of a daft bugger. Ken said he was a friend of David Imry, a keeper in the Lake District.

Most of my beat consisted of old, established woodland, broken up by rides and cart tracks. It was very wild but lovely, with a lot of sweet chestnut trees. It was very hard to show pheasants there as there was so much cover but we had some good days on the Challock Ground. Before the young birds went to the woods, each bird was marked by having an aluminium tag fastened to one wing. On the tag were the year and the name of the beat where it was released. With the tags on the birds we could tell where they came from when they were shot. It was all very interesting and showed how the birds tended to move about from one beat to another.

There were many fallow deer on the estate. They were completely wild and had very dark coats unlike park deer, with russet coats and spots. I had to kill them whenever I could. I had a .303 Enfield rifle and I shot them frequently. The meat was supposed to go to the yard but we and my dogs ate it. Foxes were plentiful and we caught a lot of them.

We had some very good days shooting. The estate was shot over by a syndicate of the captain's friends. Different beats were shot each week and so the birds had time to gather up before being shot at again. Some beats were better than others owing to the way the fields were sown. If a crop that attracted the birds was driven towards a wood, some good shooting could be had. Our employer seemed happy the way things went and so were the keepers. The forestry department were busy putting the woods right following on from the Army's use of them during the war.

The best beat at Eastwell Park was Charlie Raynor's. The woods were smaller and low lying on some of the beats and if the weather was windy and cold the young birds would seek shelter there. In the smaller woods almost any bird could be shown and put over the guns. Sunflowers were grown - these provided cover and feed for the birds. The flower heads could be cut off when they were ripe and hung up at feed places for the pheasants.

We had a lot of travellers in that part of Kent. At a place called Great Chart there was a council tip and many of these people were squatting on that tip. It was more like a reservation. They lived in all kinds of abodes - in hooped vans or under corrugated iron sheets, under sheets of plastic - anything at all would do for them. A lot of stealing and poaching was done by these people, nothing was too heavy for them. Many farmhouses were broken into on market days when the farmers were in Ashford. Often guns and rifles were taken. Some of the shooting estates suffered at the hands of these poachers. They were hard to deal with as there were so many of them.

Joan was working the strawberry fields during the spring time. In the second year at Eastwell we were expecting another baby. While at work on the field she had a miscarriage and was taken to hospital. I was left to look after Heather who was only about 18 months old. I was busy at that time and so I got a sack and cut two holes in the bottom. I put Heather in the sack with her legs through the holes - that way I carried my daughter while I went on my rounds. It was at this time that I fell ill and collapsed on the kitchen floor where I was found by the postman. Some people in Challock village whom my wife worked with took Heather to look after her while I recovered. Joan was soon home again and I recovered fairly quickly and we soon got back to normal.

The rearing season had been a good one - the birds had done well and were enjoying freedom in the woods. We started preparing for the first shoots - these usually consist of small outside days as they care called. The first day was at Kennington, Bert Tollman's land, on the outskirts of Ashford. There was a fair amount of game and we had some pleasant days among the root crops and hop yards. The oast houses and hop yards were all new to me. They were picturesque and the orchards with fruit - cherries, apples and mistletoe. In spring when the trees were in blossom, Kent is the Garden of England. I was very impressed by the loveliness of it all.

We had some outside days at Westwell Large, a large field of kale and a few small woods. For these days we used only a few beaters, all wearing white oilskin aprons that covered them from neck to ankles. These aprons were a godsend when walking kale, for kale tends to hold a lot of water in the leaves.

About the second week in November the big shoots took place

where most of the pheasants had been released. For these big days about thirty beaters were employed and were paid £1 a day. On my beat, it was hard to show birds as the woodland was so vast - about 1000 acres of trees, woods running into woods. The birds would run instead of fly. We did have some good days there and everyone enjoyed them. As one of my guns said to me, 'You never know what will come out of the woods at Challock.'

The Elephant and Castle, London, 1959
The Morris car stood there for days on end while I trudged the miles on my beat carrying the rabbits I caught to the estate yard or home, whichever was nearest. What I needed was a horse or pony. The more I thought about it, the more the idea appealed to me. I was in Ashford Market where cattle dealers were easy to find but no one in the horse business. I asked various farmers and they said the best place to buy a horse was the Elephant and Castle. Where was the place I asked? London, I was told. One day I set out to the Elephant and Castle. Boarding a train at Ashford I was soon in London - where did I go now? A taxi driver said he would take me there and told me what the fare was. It was a fair ways to the Elephant and Castle which the driver said was well known. I enquired at the pub where I could find the horse sales? 'Don't know,' the barman answered. I tried more people, could they give me any idea where horses were to be found or point me to any horse dealers in the area. All said they had no idea and gave me queer looks - I was hardly dressed for the city.

My heavy tweed keeper's suit, plus fours and heavy brown boots were I suppose not seen every day in the city. I walked miles and made lots of enquiries and always the same answer - don't know mate. Three hours and miles later I had enough of the Elephant and Castle district. London was not the place it used to be. One old chap mentioned that when he was a lad horses had been sold, many of them, but not for sixty years. I have no good memories of that day and would advise any person wanting to buy a horse to keep away from London. Tattersalls maybe but not the Elephant and Castle!

Johnny Turner and the shells
In front of our cottage was a small, shallow valley surrounded by woods on three sides, rising gently up away from our place and a cart track ran up the middle of it. Over the years the piece of land

had grown wild. Mr Buckland, the farm manager, decided to clear the rubbish and plough out the land. After the scrub had been cleared a sheep netting fence was erected around the sixteen acre field.

Johnny Turner, the ploughman, turned up one day and was soon busy turning the light, chalky soil over. Later I went to see the ploughing - there were sticks stuck up hear and there where the soil was turned over. Being nosey, I waited until the machine came to the head rig and asked, 'Johnny, what's the sticks for?' 'Them be shells, unexploded shells.' Evidently that part of the estate had been part of the wartime target area and seventeen pound shells were turning up all over the field. I would not have ploughed that field for a gold clock! Later the Army came and took the shells away or blew them up. I found four mortar bombs stuck in the soil, in one of my woods - a man was felling and burning not far from where these bombs were. I took him and showed him where the bombs were and told him to be careful where he made his fires. Many unexploded shells and mines were found even though the land was supposed to have been cleared.

The Burst Gun

I bought the gun from Alec Worsencroft, head keeper at the Harewood Estate. It wasn't a keeper's gun but it was made by a leading gunsmith - the double barrelled twelve bore was made by Ian Hollis, number 44777. It was a hammer gun with fine rose damascus barrels, thirty inches long and it was made before 1880.

I bought the gun during the early spring of 1959. One morning I went to shoot jackdaws in Young's Plantation. I had a new box of cartridges open in my pocket. I shoved two into the gun as I approached a hollow tree - a likely place for a nest. I tapped the tree with a stick a few times and out flew a bird. I fired and the explosion dazed me for a considerable time. I didn't know what had happened but my ears were ringing and I was in a dream world. I looked at my gun and saw that the right hand chamber or the breech end had gone - blown clean out and there was just ragged metal where the chamber had been. The gun was a wreck. I was lucky - if it had been the left barrel I would most certainly have been killed.

Alec Greenfield, a gunsmith in Canterbury, sent the gun to the London Proof House. They sent back a report to say the barrels had crystallized with age. The gun was meant for use with black powder and the person who had fired it, if not seriously injured, was a very lucky person indeed.

I now didn't have a gun so my employer said he would pay for a new one and the cost would be deducted from my wages. The replacement gun was made in Spain and cost £46. It was a double barrelled twelve bore *non ejecta* made by AYA Aguirre & Aranzabal. I still have the same gun. It has seen much service but is still in excellent condition.

The Hollis gun was on display at game fairs many years ago. I saw it and told a friend to go and look and check the number. He did and it was the old gun which nearly killed me. What caused the gun to burst I am sure was a small button from my waistcoat. If a button was loose I'd pull it off and put it in my pocket. I later tried one in the crimp end of a cartridge and it fitted nice and tight - it would have been enough to cause the gun to burst. Mud or snow in a gun barrel is enough to split or bulge the barrel.

I had another lucky do with a .22 automatic pistol in 1948. I hadn't any ammunition so I used it as a muzzle loader putting a .22 blank cartridge down the breech with a small amount of gun powder from a shot gun cartridge, then some paper for wadding and some small shot and more paper on top. The pistol blew to bits in my hand - I was burned but lucky again not to be seriously injured.

The dealer at Ashford Market
I was viewing livestock - ferrets, hens, a few ducks, many rabbits of different colours - the market was busy that day. I wandered down to the bottom end - some old bicycles and various pieces of machinery lay on the ground and some leather leggings that had seen better days lay on top of some cart harness. Ashford market was a joy - owt could be bought there and I mean owt!

I was talking to Alec Greenfield, the gunsmith. He had a closed-in stall with wooden shutters. There were quite a few customers and I had ordered some pistol cartridges and turned to leave when someone tapped me on my shoulder. 'I hear you are looking for a pony?' I recognised the speaker, I had seen him at times at the market. 'Yes, I am wanting a pony.' 'What kind of pony?' 'Something about fourteen to fifteen hands, a cob type,' I said. The chap was quite tall and dressed like a dealer - buff trousers, narrow legged and hitched up to show the high tops of his brown boots which were clean, not covered in shit as some men wore them. His checked shirt matched his tweed jacket and the tie he wore was done up tidy, in fact he looked a gentleman. His hair was wavy and quite grey and his face was long and well weathered. 'How much do you want to pay?' the man asked. 'Not more than £50,' I said. The man leaned on the railing of the cattle pens. 'You should get something decent for that money.'

We chatted about horses for a while. I asked him where he came from and was told the name of some distant town. He told me he had a pony that would suit me and described the animal. He said he would bring the horse to the market next week if I was interested. 'No harm in having a look at it,' I said, 'bring it along. I shall be here next week and maybe we can do a deal.' The dealer asked, 'How do I know that you will keep your word? I might arrive and you don't turn up. Tell you what,' he added, 'this pony is worth all of £50, give me half of it now, then I know you will turn up.' I didn't know the dealer but had seen him several times before. 'I'll give you a written receipt,' the dealer said. 'If it turns out the pony isn't what you want, I'll give you your money back, cannot be fairer than that.'

We had talked a long time and it was time to pick up Joan and Heather. 'OK, write out a receipt and sign it.' I said. The dealer asked, 'Is it cash?' 'Yes, it is,' I said. He used a blank postcard for the receipt and I handed over the £25, then we shook hands.

I was talking to Bill Baldock who worked as a road foreman for the council. His wife worked with my wife in the strawberry fields. 'Bill,' I said, 'I may have a pony by this time next week.' And I told him about having met the dealer. All week I was thinking what would the pony be like - I was like a child at Christmas and the next market day saw me away to Ashford very early. I was alone and did the shopping and loaded it into the Morris 8, then set off for the market to see my pony. People were bringing things to be auctioned and it was busy by the livestock pens and cages. Already some scruffy travellers or redskins as the locals called them, were mooching about, always on the look out for summat to steal.

I walked to Alec Greenfield's gunsmiths stall. I think Alec was Canadian and he lived in Canterbury where he had a proper shop. He had a nice collection of antique firearms and we talked a lot about guns. Later, I started to look for the dealer. I hung around where we had arranged to meet and time went by. I was getting impatient and by now it was 10am. Taking a walk through the pro-

Doing a deal.

duce market hall I met Bert Tollman, one of our old keepers. I then went looking for my pony dealer again. By 2pm I knew he would not turn up and disappointed, I drove home. 'How did you get on?' my wife asked. 'He didn't show up.' 'What about your money?' 'He will be there next week,' I said. But I was beginning to have my doubts.

Three weeks later and I still had not met the horse dealer. I started asking about - some people knew him but they didn't know much and didn't know where he came from. I finally met a chap who put me on to the dealer. I was told that he lived at Herne Bay and had an antiques shop there. When I next met Bill Baldock we had a beer together. 'How are you doing with that chap who you were supposed to be getting the horse from?' he asked. I told him that I had found where he had his shop and that I would be paying him a visit. 'You're damned right. I'll go with you Brian. I don't like the way that chap operates.'

The following Saturday afternoon Bill and I arrived in Herne Bay on the south east coast. 'Shouldn't be hard to find, can't be many antiques shops here.' It was winter, the days were short, but by 4.30pm we stood in front of an antiques shop. It was all lit up and very quiet. There was only one person in the shop. 'It's him, Bill.

It's that bloody dealer.' 'Leave it to me,' said Bill.

The door was opened and not too gently. I followed Bill, his broad back blocking my view of the dealer. 'Can I help you?' the dealer asked. I stood beside Bill and wondered if the dealer would recognise me. He did not seem to. 'You owe my friend here £25.' 'Yes, you do, remember me, Ashford Market,' I said. Now he remembered me. I pulled out the receipt that he had given me. 'I want my £25, mister.' Bill flung up both arms, 'Wouldn't take long to knock a few hundred quid to the floor,' he said. Bill swung his arms again, just missing some glass decanters on a shelf.

The dealer said he was sorry that he had not been able to meet me and started to say that he wasn't well and had many problems. His hand held a bundle of bank notes. 'Give him his £25,' said Bill, 'we want to be away.' The money was shoved into my hand and the dealer was keen for us to leave his shop in case Bill took a swipe at his precious antiques! On the way home I was on top of the world. I had £25 in my pocket - it had been quite an experience. I would be more careful next time. I have never trusted anyone since that happened to me. I did eventually buy a pony but not from a dealer.

I bought Gipsy from a farmer. She was a light cob, stood 14.2 hands and cost £55, including the saddle and bridge. She was eight years old and anyone could ride her. She made my work a lot easier, especially when it came to rabbit catching time. I would lead

her along my line of snares, taking out any that were caught and setting up the snares again. Sometimes in the evenings I would ride along a wood side, my .22 Martiny Henry rifle across my knees. The rabbits hardly took any heed of the pony and I shot a lot of them. Gipsy was steady and the rifle shot never troubled her.

I loved to gallop her on the cart track which went towards Westwell. It was known as the mile straight and I used to let her have her head and have a good work out. Gipsy wasn't made for hard riding - she was too heavy and soon started to blow, so I only galloped her now and then. I took a few falls. I remember my parents were staying with us one time and Dad was sitting out behind the cottage. I had been in King's Wood and coming onto the field, Gipsy could see home - she always went a bit quicker knowing she would be fed. I let her go faster than I should have; it was quite steep all the way home. It happened too fast - I could not save myself - the Gipsy's leg went through a shallow rabbit hole and down on her knees she went. I slid over her neck catching my groin on the pommel of the saddle. Gipsy was alright, no damage done, but I was sore for many days after. Dad said, 'Call yourself a horseman!' and laughed. I was too sore to laugh. I sold Gipsy for the same amount as I had bought her, before we moved to Wiltshire. She went to a farm at Detling.

Starr Walk Cottage and Harry Jones

No-one lived in the cottage while I was at Eastwell Park. Why it was called Starr Walk Cottage I know not, but it was a lovely, quiet place. The building was timber framed and clad in red tiles. It stood facing down a wide avenue of very old sweet chestnut trees. During summer cattle grazed among the lovely mature trees. The avenue led to Challock village, a good ten minutes walk away. Behind the cottage were a row of low built loose boxes, very much like you see at riding stables, but these boxes were for deer that were caught and brought there.

Years before a proper deer fence had surrounded Eastwell Park. It was made of strong strand wire mounted on iron posts set in concrete. Beside the loose boxes there was a large square pen made of the same materials. Deer, with antlers removed, were turned into the pen a few days after being caught. They were fattened and later killed for meat. There were also some kennels on the other side of the cottage.

Giddy Horne or Angels Roost Wood started behind Starr Walk Cottage. I often passed there and looked about the old place - all very serene on warm spring days. I had heard how the Jones family came to leave. Harry, the keeper before me had been driven from Starr Walk by poachers' threats. Harry must have been a very frightened man indeed to leave such a peaceful home - evidently it wasn't all that peaceful!

Harry Jones had been the gamekeeper on the Challock beat before I arrived in December 1958. He was an elderly man and one afternoon, early in the pheasant shooting season, Harry was doing his rounds when he heard rifle shots in one of his woods, Young's Plantation to be exact. He went to investigate and, arriving at the feed ride, he saw some men in the act of killing the young pheasants that were hanging about awaiting to be fed. Some had .22 rifles, others had catapults. The birds had been fed corn and were tame as they had never been shot at.

Harry had approached the poachers and began to tell them they had better be off. He tried to bluff them but as there were several of them, they took hold of Harry and roughed him up a bit. They didn't hurt him too much but they made threats as to what they would do to him and his family. Harry went home to Starr Walk and had locked the doors and stayed there for two days. He was obviously a frightened man. On pay day Harry had gone as usual to the estate yard for his wages and he told the people in the estate office he was handing in his notice. He never said anything about the poachers. It was obvious something was wrong, but no-one knew what.

A day or two after this poaching gang had done their work, a young policeman on duty in Sittingbourne saw two men enter a butcher's shop carrying sacks. The policeman saw the tail feathers of a pheasant sticking from one of the sacks. The officer followed the men into the shop where the contents had been tipped upon the floor in a back room. There he asked the two men where they had obtained the birds. These men were in rather a scruffy state and looked as though they didn't have two shillings between them. They said they had some shooting and the pheasants in question had been shot on their own land.

The policeman phoned for assistance and the two men and eighty-six pheasants were taken in charge. Not satisfied with the story from the two men, the policeman phoned all the local shooting estates to ask if any of the keepers had lost any pheasants through poaching? Several keepers turned up to see if they could identify them but one pheasant looks very much like another.

Later, Charlie Raynor, head keeper at Eastwell Park cut some of the birds' crops to see what they had eaten. Boiled corn was found in them - wheat, maize, barley, catechu, pepper and spice. This was the feed used at Eastwell Park. The other keepers were feeding pellets and wheat. Charlie Raynor claimed that the birds belonged to Eastwell Estate. More men were caught selling pheasants on a street corner. They were charged with killing game without a licence and selling game without a licence. Their homes were searched and stolen guns and rifles were found along with more stolen property. It was only then that Harry Jones said what had happened and why he had decided to quit keepering for good. The poachers were sentenced to three months each at Sittingbourne Court.

The dream

Many years ago I had the same dream several times. The first one was while I was keepering at Marston Moor, then again whilst at Rudding Park. In all, I would say that over five years I had the same dream once a year. I mentioned it to my wife and would say, 'I had that dream again last night, about the fox cubs under the tree root.' But there was no response from her, she wasn't interested.

It used to bother me at times, where were the cubs? Everything was so vivid in my mind. The place in my dream was an old wood on a steep hillside with plenty of old oak trees, beech and much hazel coppice wood, heaps of bramble and a fair amount of bracken. Midway down the hillside, a huge tree root lay where the gales had blown it years before. The ground was bare about the great root and most of the trunk had rotted away long ago. Underneath it were two holes and by the look of them, cubs were in residence. Some feathers and bits of rabbit fur were around the holes and judging by the way the soil was paddled down, the cubs were quite big. I killed many foxes but I never found the place in my dream. Now and then my mind would return to the place - where were these cubs?

In the spring of 1959, just after we moved to Eastwell Park, the keepers were busy killing vermin. I set off from my cottage and went away up the valley to spend the day a long way off at the far side of my ground. I had started in the early morning and had a busy day. During the afternoon on my way home, through Star Walk Wood, I left the track and was looking on the steep hillside for rabbits or vermin. Seeing a large tree root stuck up in the air I made my way towards it.

What I saw by that root came to me in a flash - this was the place I had been in my dreams, years before. It was exactly the same! I know that I stood a long while taking it all in - there was only one small difference - two mortar bomb tail fins lay by the holes. The bombs, being bright and shiny, were some of the cubs' toys.

I climbed over the fence at the bottom of the wood and looked back at the foxes' home. Yes, there was no doubt about it. I couldn't wait to tell Joan that at last I had found the place in my dreams. 'Maybe we shall have some peace now that you have settled the affair,' she said.

Mount Ephraim and jays

Another interesting experience occurred in about the middle of October 1959. It was a Sunday morning, and hearing gunshots not far from the cottage, I took my gun and set out to investigate. The shooting was in a wood called Mount Ephraim, on Charlie Raynor's beat.

As I approached the wood, I could see Charlie in the corner of the wood. When I came up to him I wished him the time of day and asked him what he was shooting at. 'Jays,' he replied, nodding towards four jays lying beneath a Spanish oak. 'Look out!' Charlie's gun went up. After the shot he picked up another jay. 'They just keep coming for these acorns,' said Charlie. 'Get yourself to the other side of the tree.' They are usually a wary bird but that day they were intent on the acorns and didn't bother about the shooting. We could see acorns in their mouths as they flew away.

The jays had definite flight lines - coming in on one and leaving on another. Between Charlie and I we killed forty-four jays that morning. Where the acorns were being taken we never found out. I had never seen so many jays before, nor had I ever heard of anyone witnessing such a determined lot, so intent on the task that they weren't afraid of two men with guns. I do know that jays will hide food in the deep forks of trees and among dead leaves, maybe the Spanish acorns were being hidden - there were too many to eat.

Poison seed dressings

In the spring of 1959, when spring sowing was almost over, I was going on my rounds and had picked up wild pigeons - some dead and others lying on the ground, not quite dead. I had seen a pigeon fall from a tree as though shot. All the birds looked to be in good condition - their plumage bright and their bodies plump.

Each day I found more dead birds - they were all over the estate. I saw one flying over a field, suddenly it nose-dived to the ground, its wings still driving it on. Something was very wrong. My attention was drawn to an article in the local paper about foxes found wandering about in a dazed state. There were reports of foxes on village streets and some had been found dead. I don't think anyone apart from the hunt were concerned what happened to them - but what was causing them to behave so?

The answer was simple. After post mortems on the pigeons it was found that the cause was the seed dressings, 'aldrin' and 'deildrin', on the corn. These were pesticide dressings, based on mercury. The brains of the birds and animals were affected by the mercury - first the pigeons died, then along came the foxes - pigeons lay everywhere and a good feed off these dead birds was all it needed.

People were warned not to eat pigeons. Today these seed dressings are banned but how much damage was done? I was in contact with these poisons - my eyes were affected and I had to get glasses. How many more people were affected too?

VI
Game keeping in Wiltshire

Clarendon Park

I had been thinking of moving to a home where my family would be a little nearer a school and village, so I applied for a situation in Wiltshire. I went for an interview at an estate called Clarendon Park, about four miles out of Salisbury. The estate belonged to a gentleman called Major Christy Miller. He was very tall, quiet man, who interviewed me along with the head keeper, Jack Dorling. I was shown around the estate and the beat I was to look after should I decide to accept the job.

Arriving back at home at Eastwell Park, we discussed the change of jobs if I was offered it. A few days went by, then a letter arrived from Clarendon Park saying that I could have the situation. We had made our up our minds we would accept and wrote back to confirm it. Captain Broderick was surprised that I was leaving the estate, but he wrote me a good reference which I have to this day. We started packing things up and a removal date was set.

This time we wouldn't be moving too far and it could be done in one day. Once again we said goodbye to our friends and I sold Gipsy. I had one last walk about my beat at Challock. I was sad to leave as I had grown fond of the wild old place. However Joan wasn't sorry to leave Eastwell - it was a bit isolated and we had to think of Heather when she started school.

We arrived at Pitton, which was the nearest village, about a mile away from our cottage. Salisbury was about four miles distant. There were two cottages, side by side, in a nice old wood, called Pitton Copse. The cottages were quite modern, built before the war. All the woodwork inside was natural varnished wood. The walls were brick finish, no plaster, apart from the ceilings. We had some neighbours called Acker - he was a tractor driver on the farm and his wife, Joyce, was later to be our babysitter.

We soon had the home tidy. The kennel for the dogs was a bit small and right beside the track that fronted our cottages. There was a small cabin to store things in. Joan seemed to like it - having neighbours and their two children just a bit older than Heather.

Gamekeepers at Clarendon Park were paid every two weeks. My beat was what was called the Council Ground - a mixture of arable and grassland - none of the farms were more than sixty acres. Some small belts of trees provided some shelter and in all there was about 1,200 acres. Partridges and hares were the game on this land. The place had not been properly keepered for some while - I could not find anywhere where traps had been set.

Very soon I had made trapping tunnels and had snares for foxes set in all the likely places. I was introduced to the farmers on the Council Ground. It was nice rolling land and a lot of it had never been ploughed until the war. Now that the war was over the land was used for growing barley.

The rearing season came round again. The rearing field was quite a way from my house and I had to walk each day through the woods. I loved the place - ideal for game. We used the pen system for rearing the pheasants, but we only had fifty pens. The young birds were fed on crumbs - no boiling up to do and no shutting up at night. Stan Martin and I ran the field between us. Stan was a Berkshire man and very civil too. He was a few years older than me but we got on well. Jack Dorling brought the chicks to the rearing field in the Land Rover. Sometimes Chris Chapel, the head keeper's lad, was with him. Chris would open the gates and also looked after the hens and dogs at Dorling's place.

Jack Dorling lived in a thatched cottage which stood in a large clearing in a wood, alongside the main carriage drive - a very picturesque setting. All sorts of fowl were to be seen there. Mr Dorling, as well as being head keeper had a small holding and a lad to look after it into the bargain!

Fair Oak Cottage, Pitton Copse

There were some more cottages a few hundred yards further along the track from our home. There were four of them in a row and more estate workers lived in them - woodmen and more tractor men. These houses were set back a bit and had gardens in front, all very well kept. Pitton Copse ended there and fields started. There was a fair sized green where washing was hung on wash day.

We could take a short cut through the wood and there our path met the one from the cottages further along. A 'phone box stood there and a shop where we bought our groceries and I my tobacco. Some very old thatched cottages stood on the left of the street - they were in a very dilapidated state and uninhabitable - their roofs sagging in the middle, ready to fall in at any time.

Coming back to our cottage by way of the proper track that passed our house, there stood a white thatched lodge where Ernie Taylor lived. He was a small, oldish man and spent his days in the coppice woods making sheep hurdles in two sizes - four and six feet. When he had about a hundred ready, a lorry would come to pick up the load.

After leaving our house the track continued for another mile passing two more cottages where another keeper lived and another farm man. Fussells Farm stood at the end of the track, on top of the hill that overlooked Edward Wood. John Gregg and his wife, and their son Simon who was about Heather's age were our friends. Woods surrounded our home and I had a garden front and back.

I was very happy with my work. The keepers were paid three pence per tail for rabbits killed. I kept the tails in a tin and every so often the head keeper took them and paid the money. I sold some of these rabbits to the butcher who called at our cottage - someone must have told the head keeper as I got a good telling off about it!

The shooting season came round and we had some good days. There were no large bags - three hundred pheasants being the best bag. The average day was about a hundred and fifty. On the King Edward beat, most of the shooting was done out or over belts of trees. It was the best beat on the estate and there was some good sport there. My friend and neighbour, John Gregg, was the keeper on the King Edward beat.

We had hare drives after the game season ended, usually at the beginning of the year. Many men with guns were present on these drives and large areas of land were driven in. The land was alive with hares running in all directions. As the men moved in, the circle of guns got smaller - only the hares that were breaking back were shot. In the end all the hares would break out to escape and the shooting would be hectic and the gun barrels would get hot. I remember on two occasions when five hundred hares were killed in two days. The men were offered a hare each but most declined. The remainder of the hares were buried - it shamed me to see that happen. Today those hares would fetch many pounds and pay for the cartridges and more besides.

Judith

On Saturday evenings, Joan and I would go to Salisbury Market Hall and watch the wrestling. We were both keen on the sport and it was nice to get out together. Les Potter, another of our neighbours. went as well. We had a lively time on the bus with the three of us talking and another chap who would sit with us - we had some good nights out. On the way home we walked along the path from the village and I would think how different it was to Eastwell. We would say goodnight to Les Potter where our path left his and we would go through the wood to our door. We were fortunate our neighbours looked after Heather, while we were away.

Joan was in child again and she wanted the baby to be born at home. Someone brought the maternity things that would be needed when the time came. We got on with every day work and when Joan started in labour, just after midnight on 9 June, it was, quite dark. We put a rubber sheet on the bed and everything was handy - all that was needed to deliver a baby. I had been told to 'phone the midwife when labour started. I had the 'phone number in my hand and away I went, my legs going as fast as I could. The midwife who answered the 'phone said she couldn't come until her husband got home! I ran home, Joan was breathing through a mask connected to a small cylinder. It was 1.30am when the midwife arrived and about an hour later Judith was born. It was just getting light. We soon had Joan made as comfortable as possible. The midwife was on her way and she sent me up the wood to bury the cleansings all wrapped in newspaper. We christened our daughter Judith Dawn, as she was born as the dawn was breaking.

Our family was growing - three women in the house now. My mother and father arrived and stayed about a week. We had a small black bantam chick, Dicky, we called her. She was the sole survivor of a brood of bantam chicks. The mother had hatched them out in the woods, then a fox killed the mother when the chicks were only about a week old. Dicky, the only one left, was found and brought into the house where she wandered about where she wanted. At night a cardboard box was set by the Rayburn cooker. It had two holes in it, one on each side of the box and a stick pushed through. That was Dicky's perch. A tea towel was put over the box after Dicky went to bed. The towel just touched her back and must have felt as though she was being brooded.

We also had a tame pigeon and a tame jay - all three of our pets wandered about the garden. Dicky would scratch about among the spud rows and the pigeon and jay followed, picking up bits and bobs. We were quite happy at our home in Pitton Copse. It was a quiet place and the work was easy. Salisbury was handy and it was only a short walk to the village to catch a bus.

The winter of 1962-3
We started with frost at Christmas and on Boxing Day snow fell, about a foot of it, winter had really started. The wind got into the east and the temperature fell day after day. The wind blew - some of the fields were blown clear of snow. In hedges and hollows the snow drifted and where root crops, like turnip or kale were, the snow was trapped. Flocks of pigeons arrived and soon stripped the leaves from these roots. In fields that were bare of snow the wind burned the grass off and laid them bare. Wild life was soon suffering and the pigeons quickly started to lose condition and get weak.

By day the sun shone and the east wind blew. It was always well below freezing and at night it got even colder. Where there was snow there was a thick crust of ice and walking through it was hard work as it was not strong enough to bear my weight - it hurt my lower legs and cut my leggings. I was carrying feed out each day onto the Council Ground for partridges and pheasants. As the days went on and ran into weeks, the crows started to wait about the feed rides and as soon as I fed my birds they would come down as well and take the corn. I couldn't do anything about it. I shot a few crows and left them lying on the feed rides but every creature was so hungry, and the crows were taken away by foxes and badgers.

This winter was a problem. The temperature was always below zero and there was nothing for the wild life to drink. The hares and rabbits were very weak and some died. The foxes were doing all right as there was plenty for them to eat. Still the winter went on, the east wind blew and the sun shone each day. Our cottage was sheltered by the wood but we still had burst water pipes and ice on the walls inside our home.

Each day I set off with feed for my game birds, I saw dead birds and animals everywhere. The small song birds suffered very badly, what with the ground being so hard and the hedges full of snow and frozen hard. Herons died and some swans were frozen into the ice on the ponds. I found five blackbirds frozen hard. They had all gone into a hole in a tree where a large branch had broken off. The blackbirds had slept only to freeze to death.

Weeks went by and still there was no let up in the terrible cold, sub-zero weather. My partridges were by now weak. They were so weak I could pick them up. I brought many of them home and put them in a wooden cabin with some feed. Sadly they were too far gone and died. I thought the world was coming to an end. It was hard to keep warm. The pipes for the water kept bursting and there was ice on the wall in the passage by the bathroom - it was hopeless to try to bathe.

One afternoon at about 3pm I stood on a hill of tall beeches on the Council Ground. I put my gun against a tree and looked out across the valley in front of me. The sun was going down - it was blood red and everything quite so still. I felt as though I was the only person in the world. There was no movement anywhere. It seemed to get warmer for a few minutes, then a steady drizzle of rain started and this lasted for three to four minutes. The red sun came out again, just before it disappeared behind the hill. Wherever I looked a strange red light shone upon everything - the drizzle had frozen on everything it touched. The twigs on the trees, the village roof tops, the barbed wire of the fences, everything shone, glazed with ice. I was sure the world was coming to an end. Even today, what I saw is bright in my mind. It was all very wonderful and frightening too. I have often thought what religious people would have made of such a spectre. It was a marvellous sight.

The great freeze lasted for eleven weeks. When it finally broke on the first day of March, it took a long time to get back to normal. Before I finish about the 1962-63 winter there is one more story about starlings. I had a two acre wood called Griffins Firs. It was mainly fir trees with a few other trees such as elder, thorn and brambles. Thousands of starlings roosted there and the ground was covered some four inches deep with their droppings. These droppings were killing the trees so I made up my mind to thin these starlings out a bit. At one end of the wood stood a large dead spruce tree, all life gone out of it. Just at dusk I arrived with my gun and 25 cartridges loaded with No. 8 shot - that means small shot, the higher the number, the smaller the shot.

The starlings arrived in their thousands, landing all over the wood. The noise was terrible. The trees were open in the bottom, the snow quite deep and stained with droppings. I walked towards the dead spruce tree and clapped my hands. The birds flew in front of me and soon the great spruce was black with starlings. I stopped about fifty yards away and raised my gun, fired both barrels into the black crowd. There was a hell of a racket as they took off and many birds fell dead. I didn't bother to pick them up - I had more shooting to do. I walked back up the wood then repeated the process again, walking towards the dead spruce tree, chasing the starlings before me and again discharging my gun at about fifty yards range into the crowded tree.

The moon was coming up and the temperature falling. Again and again I shot and shot until my cartridges were gone. The ground around the spruce tree was littered with dead starlings. I went home for my supper and a rest. The next morning I was at Griffin Firs early - some wounded starlings were running about but my terriers soon got them. I started to gather up the dead bodies. There were hundreds of them - my game bag was full in no time. I tipped out the birds in a small clearing beside a fallen tree. It was a right mess trying to pick them up. There was starling shit everywhere on every branch and twig. It was a good thing I wasn't bothered about a bit of shit.

Eventually I had all the frozen stiff bodies gathered up. Sitting myself down on my game bag I set about cutting off their wings - a firm of fur and feather dealers would pay two pence per pair for them. I shot starlings for three nights and each night I made good bags. I later recorded that, on average, I killed eighteen birds with each shot. The pile of dead starlings was huge but as the weather was so cold it kept them from smelling.

I took home the wings and laid them on newspaper in the spare bedroom to get any moisture out of them. Then we packed them in cardboard boxes in layers of twenty pairs. In total six hundred pairs of wings were sent to the dealers, Horace Frend and Son. We received £5 from them - we needed the money. Mr Dorling said I was wrong to shoot at night. I tried to point out what damage was being done by all those starlings. The birds moved to King Edward wood on John Gregg's beat. I put the pile of dead birds into sacks and put them in an old dried up well in the ruins of a long abandoned cottage just below the wood.

I came across a young badger one day, wandering about a wood. I took it home and kept it in an old war-time air raid shelter with a heavy duty wire netting door to let it look out. I fed it on strawberries, worms, slugs, snails, milk and rabbits. It would climb up the netting door and Heather called it the monkey.

Dogs among the sheep
One afternoon I heard dogs barking. I stood a moment - what were dogs doing by Fussells Wood? Harold Ling, the shepherd had some ewes about ready to start lambing beside that wood. I set off and as the field came in sight I could see two dogs attacking the sheep which were crowding into a corner. Both dogs seemed determined to get a hold of them. Running toward the flock I shouted. The dogs didn't hear me they were so intent on getting the sheep. When I reached them I kicked one of the dogs - it let go of the sheep but immediately dived into the flock again. I was out of breath. Some of the sheep had blood on their flanks - the situation was out of hand. Waiting until I could get a clear shot, I killed both dogs and dragged them into the wood.

Later that day, Harold Ling, the shepherd passed my cottage. I told him of the sheep attack and that the dead dogs were in the wood. Two nights later, just after supper, Jack Dorling called on me. Could I come outside to the Land Rover, Major Christy Miller would like a word with me. I was told to get into the rear of the Land Rover and was driven away up the track. Stopping the engine, the Major, my employer referred to the day I shot the dogs among the sheep. I should not have done so and was given a very severe reprimand. I tried pointing out that the dogs were intent on killing the sheep. It was no good, I was in the wrong.

I was dropped off again at my home, feeling very disillusioned with things. I had done my best to protect my employer's sheep and been reprimanded for doing so. I had been told off for shooting the starlings and for selling rabbits. I was beginning to think it was time that I shifted myself again. I could do nowt right!

The badger was soon full grown. I had a breast harness for it and took it for walks now and then. Then I saw an advertisement - a chap wanted all kinds of animals for his zoo at Appleby Park, on the Isle of Wight. The badger was sold to them. I lined a tea chest with sheets of aluminium and sent the badger by rail. I often wonder how it fared?

The Murder

Another season started and went. About Christmas I had a letter from Fred Dowker, my old head keeper at Rudding Park. He asked it I was interested in a head keeper position - the pay was far better than I was receiving where I was now. Joan and I talked things over. We would be going north again, to Garstang in Lancashire, if we took the situation. It was arranged that I should go for an interview to Barn Acre Lodge Estate. Mr Robert Benson who lived in the mansion there, was in charge of a syndicate that rented the shooting. So, after a few 'phone calls, arrangements were made and I set off for Lancashire. Mr Benson met me at Lancaster Station and we drove to Garstang. The estate was about three miles further on by road.

I noticed many fields were grassed down and hen cabins lay scattered everywhere. I had never seen so many poultry before. As we approached the lodge gates, the scenery improved, woods and a stream ran at the side of the drive up to the big house and stable yard. I was told that the owner of the estate, Shepherd Cross, was a tax exile and lived in Jersey.

It was dark when we arrived at Barn Acre. I was taken into the big house where Mrs Benson had some food prepared for us. The Bensons lived in just a few rooms in the house. We talked about the job but I was tired and soon went to bed.

We set out in a Land Rover the following morning and I was shown about the place. It was very different to the south, with no arable land but hills and reservoirs and the River Wyre running through the estate. The M6 motorway was being built right across the estate land, parallel to the railway. The keeper's house was quite big and stood by the stable yard, where all the buildings were used by the keepers. Another young keeper, George Wilson, was employed as well. He had been there a year or two with Nat Mortimer, the old keeper who had just retired. Nat and his wife lived in the next cottage.

Mr Benson and I had discussed most matters concerning the situation and I had seen all I wished to see, so I was taken back to the train station at Lancaster and set off for home and family.

Joan and I decided we would take the situation at Barn Acre Lodge, Garstang. I told Mr Dorling that I had found myself a better job and gave one month's notice. I had been at Clarendon for three seasons and just before we left a woman was murdered in one of my woods.

I was feeding my pheasant one Sunday afternoon and heard voices in the distance. There was a footpath not far off so I thought none of it. It was a very cold afternoon and the sun was starting to set. I finished my feeding and went home. We had our tea as usual and spent a night by the fire. Next morning I had done some jobs about home when the police were all over the place.

Monty, one of the young keepers was feeding his birds up in a wood by the palace, as it was called and he had come across a woman's body - her throat was cut and she was covered in frost. I was told later that Monty had panicked and ran all the way to the head keeper's house and was in a very upset state on arriving there.

The police were informed and the estate sealed off. All the roads onto the estate were guarded and a search was started. A day or two later a man was caught - it would seem that it was a lover's tiff. Maybe the voices I heard on the Sunday afternoon were them?

VII
Game keeping in Lancashire

Barn Acre Lodge

We were packing our belongings again and were getting expert at that job. The removal van turned up and all was loaded aboard - dogs, ferrets, hens, no car this time. The motorway had been partly built and this took quite a lot of time off the journey we had made to the south. We soon settled in our new home and I started to find my way around. George Wilson, the other keeper, showed me the estate. George lived in the bothy above the stable block and had his meals with us. Our house had a large kitchen, a good sized living room and a big front sitting room where we stored things we were not using. It also had three bedrooms and a bathroom. A van went with the job and my wages were more than at Clarendon by a good bit. In the stable yard was the proving room where all the feed for the ducks and pheasants was kept and a boiler for boiling the dog food. The kennels were out at the back of our cottage on higher ground. There were garages in the stable yard too.

There were three hundred hen pheasants in four large pens. Laying time was on the way. A fairly large room next to the proving room was where the large electric incubators were sited - they were 'Hammers' 3000 egg incubators, made for hatching hens eggs. A room next door was the egg store. It had a table with two sheets of corrugated plastic fixed to it, tilted up at the back. The corrugations ran horizontally.

The pheasants started laying about the first of May and the eggs were picked up from the pens about four times a day and stored on this table. We had to keep a close watch for crows, magpies or other vermin. Eggs were taken to the egg store and placed on the corrugated sheets. When turning the eggs, one egg was taken out at the end of the row and that let all the eggs turn over half a turn. The one that had been taken out was put in the space at the other end. When a thousand eggs were gathered, these were set in the egg trays of the incubator.

These incubators ran for a week before any eggs were set in the machine so that the correct setting could be made. The temperature was all important and if anything went wrong, all the eggs could be spoiled. The temperature was 99.9F. There was a thermometer in a small recess on the incubator door and a constant watch was kept on it once the eggs were set in the machine. There were three compartments in the incubator - the two outside compartments contained racks into which were slid the egg trays and the central compartment housed the electric fan which gave a constant flow of warm air around the egg trays.

Every day the eggs had to be turned half a turn, just as they would be if under the mother bird as she settled herself down to sit. The day before the eggs were due to hatch, warm water was introduced into the incubator - rolls of cotton wool were laid on the trays to get the necessary humidity to help the chicks hatch. The humidity stopped the membrane drying out too fast. There were also containers for water attached to the inside of the machine, these were kept filled with warm water. Most keepers in those days had one or two small paraffin oil incubators made of wood, which could hatch 150-250 eggs. They were used mainly when chicks were chilled or late hatching, not for setting eggs.

At the entrance to Barn Acre Lodge stood a red brick lodge. The drive was about a mile long and parallel to it was a small stream. Behind the lodge a pen had been made to keep ducks. Duck eggs were gathered and hatched in incubators before the pheasant eggs.

On the estate there were three reservoirs, high on the fellside at Harris End, belonging to the Manchester Water Authority. Nicky Nook was the name of the lower reservoir. It was situated in a lovely steep valley, a stone dam held back the water and the beck which fed it was very good for trout, as was the reservoir itself. The water from this place was condemned as it was polluted by a pig farm higher up the fells. The shooting rights over the land surrounding these waters was held by Barn Acre Estates and a few grouse were found on the land bordering the heather beds or moors. I was to look after in all about 3,200 acres. My season there was quite successful. We shot many duck from the ponds where they had been released and the pheasants did well and we had some fairly good bags.

I had one problem - the syndicate I worked for could not agree - some wanted to shoot pheasants, others wanted to shoot duck. Some wanted to shoot the middle of the estate where the bulk of the birds were and the others would want to do something else. There were ten people in the syndicate so I had ten bosses! I had members ringing me up asking about what we were going to do. When I told them we would be going to shoot such and such a part of the estate, they would argue and say we should be doing something else. The syndicate came from all walks of life - a dentist, a haulage contractor, a butcher, three farmers, one owned a coach company - they were a right mixture.

Lancashire, I am sure, has more poachers than any other county in England. Being not many miles from Blackpool and Preston, it was fairly lively at weekends. The estate was intersected with narrow roads and lanes, ideal for the car poacher. As soon as the young pheasants started to move out of the woods, the poachers appeared. Some of the woods were beside the lanes - the pheasants would sit on the walls, showing themselves off.

Farmers would 'phone to say that they had heard shots fired in some wood or roadside field. It could be difficult to catch these people as there were many roads and lanes. The police were very helpful but evidence of poaching and the bodies of the shot game must be produced in court. I caught about nine poachers while I was at Barn Acre and others were warned off.

The first shoot at Barn Acre Lodge

On my first shoot day at Barn Acre the guns were standing around a 'Duck Pit', as they are called in that part of Lancashire. It was just a fair sized pond with some scrub trees around it, made for cattle to drink from originally. A few hundred ducks had been reared and put out on several of these pits that were sited about the estate.

I looked at the line of guns, what had I let myself in for? Seated on an old fashioned piano stool was old Tom Cowell. How old he was I've no idea - he was a typical farmer, nowt smart about him. Old Tom Cowell could hardly walk at all and had to be driven up to the place he shot from. He sat, his gun across his knees and behind him, young Tom, his son stood, a cartridge bag over his shoulder.

The day before young Tom came to me and said his dad was to shoot today and he would keep an eye on father. I blew my whistle to set the one or two beaters off and put the ducks in the air. There was much quacking and some shouting and eventually a few ducks took off from the pond. No sooner were they in view when a barrage was opened up on them. Usually the ducks are given time to climb into the air so as to make good sporting shots. More ducks were getting up and began to circle the pond. The noise of shooting was deafening - everyone was blazing away. I looked at old Tom on his piano stool - as he put his gun up he almost fell off - his son had to hold on to him while he fired, then let the old man lean against him while he loaded the gun again.

The smoke from the shooting hung over the circle of guns and the ducks kept a steady circling above the pond and the shooters. I looked again at old Tom Cowell. He had been set on his feet by his son who was trying to hold the old man and shift the piano stool. That done old Tom Cowell could now lean his back against the front of his Land Rover. Each time his gun was raised old Tom almost fell from his seat and the gun was pointing anywhere but at the flying ducks!

Dogs were running about all over the place - one spaniel, a white duck in its mouth, was looking about for its master. Two more dogs were fighting over a duck. The shooting was dying down, then someone shouted, 'They're coming back.' The shooting started again. Old Tom joined in - by this time his piano stool had sunk into the wet grass and appeared to have short legs.

'Stand up,' dad, shouted his son. Old Tom, with the gun in his hands struggled to his feet and leaned against the Land Rover. The piano stool was pulled from the mud and set down afresh and old Tom settled on his perch. I wished that the duck would fly away and then I could see who had been shot or wounded. I was thinking of the beaters by the pond - it must have been hell among the trees with all the shot flying around.

I blew two long blasts on my whistle for the shooting to stop and set off towards the pond. Just as I got into the trees the shooting started again. A few ducks had hidden under some brambles - they set off for the pond then changed their minds and took off. 'Look out!' someone shouted as another volley of shots blasted out. I was among my beaters, hiding behind a tree, making sure it was between Tom Cowell and myself! I would just have to be patient and await the outcome. As the shooting died away again I blew two long blasts on my whistle and poked my head around the tree. Finally, the beaters and I decided it was safe and left the duck pit on the far side from Tom Cowell.

The bare grass field could hide nothing. There were a few dead ducks lying about. These were collected and counted - 45 killed - with ten guns shooting and hundreds of cartridges fired, it looked like bloody poor shooting! The shooters were delighted with their first drive and said if all the drives were like this one I would have to send for a van load of cartridges and sharp!

We visited three more duck pits that day and nothing changed. I had no control over the shooters once the duck were in the air. We finished the day without anyone being shot, but my nerves were bad for days after, in fact I was dreading the next shoot.

The morning of the first cover shoot dawned. Beaters and dog men arrived and assembled in the stable yard. This was my 'big day'. I had worked hard for this. I had a young lad with me as George Wilson had been dismissed. John Pickersgill was a useful lad - he was a quick learner. We started with a drive from the big wood in the centre of the estate. There were plenty of birds and they flew well, maybe too well for the shooting was not at all good. We made a mixed bag that day - 343 pheasants, 7 ducks, 5 rabbits and 6 hares. We shot every week and the syndicate continued to disagree. If I shot Heald Wood, I was told that I should have shot Toppins Wood first. There were half guns and quarter guns, it was a right mix up at times. As the guns gathered on a shoot morning I looked at them with suspicion. Old rusty hammer guns were the mark of a farmer. The gun would be left in a barn like as not and never cleaned. The man with it would be a pot hunter and not used to driven game. God help the beaters and me!

On one occasion a member turned up with two dogs and said they were good at catching game. I asked him to leave his dogs behind while we were shooting. Beaters turned up with terriers. In some of the woods rhododendrons were rank and the terriers could be heard yapping and dashing about, putting the birds back. They were never under control. It was a nightmare time for me. Towards the end of the season a duck supper was put on at a local pub for everyone who had helped with the shoots. We all had a whole duck but it was too much for me. I haven't eaten a duck since that night! I had had enough of the syndicate and of Lancashire. Poachers were everywhere and there was nothing but grass fields and duck pits. I had been in court many times and it was hard work. I started looking for a fresh job and eventually found a lovely place at Edenhall.

Tractor v. van at Whinmarley

I had only just settled in at Barnacre Lodge when George Corpes called upon us one dark Thursday night in winter. Evidently Thursday night had always been George's night to visit Barnacre even when Nat Mortimer had been keeper. I asked him in and introduced him to Joan and the children. I was told of what to expect of the syndicate I was working for and that they were a hungry lot.

It was late when George decided to leave us - I walked with him into the stable yard where his van was. 'Come and see me some night, Brian. Come and meet the missus.' he said as he left giving me instructions how find his home. One evening a while later I set out to visit Whinmarley where George Corpes keepered. I crossed the A6 and drove along the lanes, it was a real dark night. From what I could make out the road was raised up well above the surrounding fields. George had said that his home was just about a mile across the A6 but I had travelled much further than a mile.

The farms were a long way apart and I was lost. I decided to turn round at the next field gateway and go back. I stopped at an open gate, there was a ramp down to the field which appeared to be grass. I drove onto the field and swung the van round to come back to the road. The engine was labouring, I changed to low gear but the van wouldn't move. I revved up and tried again - the wheels were spinning. Looking behind the van there were deep marks where the tyres had gone through the sod. I was stuck, bloody well stuck. It would take a tractor to pull me out and where was I to find a farm with a tractor?

I locked the van up, once the lights were out it was even darker but my eyes were soon used to it. I made my way back on to the road - I hadn't passed any other vehicles on my way, no sign of life anywhere. I could see the lights of Blackpool in the far distance. Turning my back on them I set off at a fair pace. I had not noticed the farm on my way, it stood well back from the road but I could make out a couple of dim lights. I found the farm track and was looking for a door at the side of the house when a dog started to bark somewhere in the buildings. A light went on. I made for the light and suddenly a door was opened. I could see the silhouette of a man. 'I wonder if you could help me,' I said, 'I'm sorry to bother you, I'm stuck in a field down the road.'

'Hang on a minute, mate,' he said as he disappeared - I could hear shouting away back in the house. 'You want a pull mate?' said a young man as he stepped out into the light. 'Yes, could you bring a tractor and a rope or a chain?' 'Come on, mate.' I followed the young chap to a building. He climbed aboard a big tractor. 'Get on mate.' 'What about a rope or chain?' 'They're on mate, always carry them on this land. It's all moss land you know.'

At the gate he asked, 'Which way mate?' 'Right,' I told him. 'The first gate on the left.' The tractor turned into the field and stopped in front of my van. I got down and fastened the chain round the front bumper bar. 'Take it steady will you?' I got into my van and started the engine, putting it in gear. I shouted, 'OK, go on.' Off went the tractor, the chain tightened, there was a ripping of metal - away went the tractor and my bumper bar!

'I said take it easy!' He had the bumper in his hand. 'Sorry, mate,' he said, 'what now?' 'Do you reckon that we could pull her out backwards?' I asked. 'Yep, I could do that.' I fastened the tow chain on and got into the van and started it up. 'Right, go on,' I shouted. The tractor set off, the van lurched backwards, there was the ripping of metal again and the tractor disappeared towards the road with my rear bumper bar bouncing behind it!

I got out, I could not believe what was happening, my van was literally being pulled to pieces! 'What now mate?' he said. 'Look, I will drive the tractor, you sit and steer my van.' 'Can you drive a tractor, mate?' asked the youth. 'I've been driving 'em since 1949,' I said, 'you get yourself in the van.' The chain was put about the chassis, letting in the clutch of the tractor I slowly took up the slack in the chain and eventually had the van on the road. I had about £2 on me and I gave it to the tractor man. I looked in the van at my scrap bumper bars and was glad to be on the hard road. I gave George Corpes a miss that night.

Early the next morning I went to the garage and had the two bars welded back on my van. I did eventually find George Corpes' home, in the daylight, early one afternoon. I didn't say a word about my nightmare night with the mad tractor drive at Whinmarley! Later on I drove through that part of Lancashire - the whole of the area was what is called locally 'the mosses' - nothing but peat and piles of bog oak, trees that had been ploughed out of the land. Beware if you happen to be in the area mentioned - don't leave the road in your vehicle or you may have your car pulled to pieces by the mad tractor man!

The pheasant rearing season was on us and the eggs were set in the Hammer incubator and more trays were filled ready to be set. The hen pheasants were laying well - close on 300 eggs a day were being picked up from the laying pens.

I was having my tea when I saw George, 'What's George Corpes doing this time of day? Come on in, sit yerself down. What's ta doing? It's the wrong day isn't it, George?' 'I'm in trouble, Brian, there's been a disaster.' He went on to tell me that the fertility of the pheasant eggs he had set was less than 50%. They only wanted a few hundred birds at Whinmarley and George was working to a tight margin. If what he said was true he was in trouble. 'Drink thy tea,' I said, 'it's not all that bad. Yer can still set more eggs, George.' 'I haven't any more eggs to set, Brian.'

We went out to the egg store and I said, 'There yer are, help yerself to 300 of them. Pick 'em where yer like George. I have plenty left for myself. Use them hen egg trays, go on, get cracking.' I left him to it. 'Thanks, Brian. What can I do to repay you?' 'Forget it, George. I might need a hand one day.'

Joan and I had been to Garstang shopping one hot afternoon. I stopped outside the Kenlis Arms. 'Fancy a pint, missus?' The tap room was nice and cool, only a middle aged chap there, the beer was refreshing. 'Grand day.' 'Aye, it is a right good one,' the chap answered. We were soon having a good crack about dogs and things in general. 'This weather will suit the game,' I said. 'Aye, it will. I do a bit of rearing,' the chap said, 'Usually rear a few pheasants. I bought some eggs a month ago.' 'Did yer get 'em from a game farm?' 'No, I bought 'em locally from a keeper,

The author with a line of fourteen grey squirrels - a morning's work.

George Corpes. Do you know him?' 'Aye, I have met him a few times.' My blood was boiling - I had been done, done well and truly by George. We left the pub directly. 'What's up wide ye?' my wife asked. 'Them eggs that chap bought were my bloody eggs. That's what's up, lass!'

Sure enough when Thursday evening arrived, so did George Corpes. I met him at the door and then took him into the stable yard. I told him what a liar he was and that he was not to come to my home again. I had learned a lesson.

Poacher at Spar Wood

'That was a grand meal, lass.' We had filled ourselves with spuds, liver and onions with mashed turnip and rice pudding. After lunch young John Pickersgill and I set off for Spar Wood to check the rabbit situation. I put my gun in the van and drove down the drive. There were plenty of young pheasants, picking over the fallen leaves where earlier I had thrown some corn. I said to John that we'd have to keep an eye on the penned ducks as I'd spotted some mink in the area.

Parking the van we headed for Spar Wood which was crescent shaped and stood on a low hill following the contour. Entering the wood we looked for signs of rabbits - there was little in the way of ground cover. At a rabbit hole there was a footprint and some disturbance in the soil around it. 'See that,' I said quietly to John, 'that's a peg mark, someone's been here and not long since.' We advanced quietly. Rounding the bend we could see along the rest of the wood. We stood watching the poacher who was on his knees looking into a hole, a lurcher dog beside him, looking intently into the hole, too.

There were fifty yards between us and he could not escape. We were on him in seconds, though we were quiet about it. 'Now then, me lad, who's telled ya to catch rabbits here?' The chap was still on his knees. I looked him over - he wasn't much of a poacher; his ill-fitting clothes had seen better days. He wasn't much younger than me. The broad bandage around his head was dirty and showed signs of blood. 'What's up wid yer head?' I asked. He turned back to the hole, 'I'm waiting for my ferret.' 'Look lad, bugger yer ferret, what are yer doing here?' The poacher decided to stand up. We faced each other on the hillside. A thought flashed through my mind, this chap could have been myself not so long ago, before I became a gamekeeper. He was the same height and weight as me, a double.

I looked at the dead rabbit and again at his dog which was wagging its tail as I put my hand towards it. 'What's up wid yer head?' The poacher's face looked at me in defiance. 'Nowt to do with you anyway,' he said. 'No, but poaching is, I am in charge of the estate and the shooting. This wood you're in belongs to it. Has the farmer given you permission to ferret rabbits?' No reply. 'OK, come on, I am taking you into Garstang Police Station. John you stay here and catch the ferret, I'll see you at home.'

I turned to the poacher who moved away from me. 'I'm not going, I'll set the dog on yer.' He was challenging me now. I pointed the gun at his dog. 'Go on, then, are yer coming easy way mate? Yer know what you will get if you offer violence don't you? Probably get sent down for it.'

We walked across the field to my van, the dog in front of me. I felt sorry for the lad. The dog and rabbit were in the back of the van and the two of us sat tight in the front. Sergeant Ashworth was at the desk. 'Hello Vasey, what have you been up to? Bring him in here.' The interview room was small. 'Right, turn out yer pockets, Vasey.' He had half a dozen purse nets, a knife and some small change, a bit of old rag and a dog chain and collar.

'So, yer've been at it again, have yer Vasey? What's the charge keeper?' 'Killing ground game, rabbits, and refusing to quit land when told.' The sergeant wrote and I signed it. 'Yer head, Vasey, yer been at it again?' 'Fighting,' came the poacher's reply. 'Right, you can go, Vasey. Here take this lot,' and shoved the nets across the table. 'You will be hearing from us soon.' At the door Vasey turned and looked at me, I nodded to him and he went.

'You seemed to know that chap Sergeant.' He smiled, 'I know 'em all, the whole family of 'em. We have 'em regular like for summat or other, mainly poaching. They are very fond of salmon; you'll probably come across them again, keeper.'

I was early at Garstang Court and hung about the entrance. A policeman asked what time my case was to be heard. '10.15,' I said, 'I'll stay out here.' I had a cigarette in my mouth, just lit. A voice beside me said, 'I could do with a fag.' 'Here yer are, lad, have one.' 'Thanks, mate.' It was Vasey. 'How's yer head?' 'Mending, not right, but mending.' We talked of one thing or another, steering clear of why we were at court. He kept pigeons and told me that he raced them. Anyone passing would have thought us mates, the talk flowed easy. I turned to him and asked, 'Why the bloody hell when we had you in the wood, didn't you just say it's a fair cop? If you hadn't told me you would set the dog on me and said you had no intention of going quietly, we wouldn't be here now. I would have waited until your ferret came out and then you and I would have walked to the road. I would have given you the rabbit and told you not to come again.'

Vasey changed his plea to guilty. I did not have to give evidence. He got a £10 fine to be paid some time. He had nowt so he said. Outside the court we shook hands. I stood by my van watching him walk towards his bus stop. I felt sorry for him - we were alike in more ways than one.

The man with the suitcase
One Thursday night in November at about 6 o'clock, it was black dark and raining. We had been shooting all day and all my jobs at home were done and the game hung safely ready to be taken away to the dealer the next day.

Having finished my evening meal I was relaxing by the fire. Joan asked, 'Haven't you to go to Garstang tonight?' 'Oh, hell, I had forgotten about that business,' I replied, 'I'd best be off, what a night to turn out in.' I drove the van out of the lodge gates. The rain was fair bouncing on the road. The lights of my vehicle picked out a dark figure as I approached Barnacre Church. It was a man carrying a large suitcase. I stopped and asked the chap if he wanted a lift. 'Yes please, mate, that will help me.' 'Where are you bound for?' 'Garstang.' 'Put your case in the back, the door's open.' He got in beside me. 'Bad night to be on the road,' I said. 'Aye, it is. I have been to see a mate of mine at Barnacre Lodge.' 'Oh, aye,' I answered. 'George Wilson, do you know him?' 'Aye, I know him.'

The chap beside me was talkative. 'I usually call to see George during the shooting season.' 'Do you mate?' I said. 'I usually get a few pheasant from him. I have known George a few years now.' We were entering Garstang. 'Where do you want to be off, mate?' 'Anywhere will do me.' Eventually I stopped by the police station. 'How's that mate?' 'Grand,' the chap said. I got out and went to the back of the van, taking hold of the suitcase. I said, 'Come on then.' 'Where?' 'In here,' and urged him into the police station. 'What are we going in here for mate?' I told him who I was - the game keeper in charge at Barnacre Lodge estate and that the pheasants and rabbits were the property of the syndicate who held the shooting rights.

Inside the station a policeman went to fetch a sergeant. I told him who I was and that I was in charge of the shooting at Barnacre and that the chap I had just escorted into the station with his suitcase had some game which belonged to the syndicate. The case was opened and there were three brace of pheasants and two rabbits. I said I wanted the man charged with receiving game stolen from my employers. I felt a little sorry for the chap I had handed over to the law. He appeared to be dazed by the happenings of the past few minutes. He had not tried to flee when I took him into the station - it had all happened too fast. One moment he had been given a lift, the next he was being charged for having stolen game. He cooperated by giving a statement saying that the game had come from Barnacre and that George Wilson, my other keeper, had supplied it and been paid for it.

A few days later I found that George had also been selling pheasants at a pub where he drank. I thought a lot about what had happened and decided not to charge the chap with the suitcase. I told the police that I wanted to drop charges. I thought it better to get shot of George, which I did, but that wasn't the end of him at Barn Acre!

Barn Acre Estate was so different from what I had been used to. The syndicate were of no help to me, in fact they were the opposite, always groaning. I had been used to private service, one boss, quiet, peaceful places and enjoying life a little. I was now run off my feet after every Tom, Dick and Harry with a gun. It had been a long, hard year, one I will never forget!

Heather, our eldest daughter, had started school, just after we arrived at Barn Acre. The school was at Calder Vale, about two miles away. The village was tucked away in a small valley - a mill stood by the river and employed most of the village people. There was also a Co-op where we sometimes got our groceries. Heather travelled on the school bus with more children from a farm a bit further on from us. Just after Christmas I heard a head keeper was wanted on an estate in Cumberland. I had been out with a friend of Mr Benson's who was a very keen gun dog man. We had been shooting over some land and I was told it was a nice situation at Eden Hall.

VIII
Game keeping in Cumbria

Edenhall Estate, Penrith

Allan Mason, the person who knew the estate owners and head keeper at Edenhall. I was a bit disillusioned with the syndicate at Barn Acre and knew there were better jobs about. I told Allan that I was unsettled and was thinking of a change. One night, not long after, Allan Mason rang me and said he had talked to Bob Simpson, the old head keeper at Edenhall and he had been in touch with the owners who wanted to meet me. A week later, on a Sunday morning, Joan, Heather, Judith and I set out for Edenhall which is three miles east of Penrith. It was a nasty, wet day and we travelled the old A6 road over Shap Fell. It wasn't a long journey as we were on the same road all the way from Garstang.

We arrived at Edenhall in good time and met Mr Airly Holden Hindley, the eldest son of Mr Arthur Hindley. We were made welcome at Bob Simpson's home, which was called The Pheasantries. We were shown the Edenhall Estate, taken to the River Eden and went to see the West Lodge which was to be the keeper's home. The lodge was an impressive place, built in the Grecian style, mounted on huge stone blocks. The front entrance door was reached by climbing eight wide stone steps. On each side of the front double doors, stone fluted pillars supported a big carved stone porch. The windows too were high with arched tops. The lodge was a strange shape, looking at it from above, it was laid out as a square cross and everything about it was ornate. The roof was covered entirely with sheet lead - I would imagine several tons of it and the round stone chimneys were decorated with twisted fluting and sat in the middle of the building.

Two huge stone piers stood at the wide drive entrance - they too were very ornate and about eighteen feet high. On top of each pier, a pair of arms in armour was set, each holding up a ring and a trophy. The Musgrave coat of arms were carved into a panel on the piers at each side. At the rear of the lodge were the dog kennels and a wooden building with slate roof where tools, animal feed and wood were stored.

We looked inside the lodge, what a place! There were four rooms downstairs, just two of them on the same level. Stone stairs led to a back bedroom with one more step into the bathroom. I had never seen any house with so many steps in it. There was an unusual Yorkist range in the kitchen.

The gun room was in what had once been the schoolroom. It was very small so wouldn't hold more than ten children at their desks. It was a typical gun room with a large table, racks of guns and cupboards where fishing rods and tackle were kept. It was all well laid out and clean. It was still raining when we left Edenhall and drove home. Joan and I discussed what we had seen and been told. We were not at all impressed with the keeper's lodge with all those steps and only two rooms on the same level. It had been a miserable day weather wise. During the following week Bob Simpson 'phoned and wanted to know were we going to take the Edenhall job? 'No,' we said 'we were sorry but the house was not suitable.'

A few nights later, Mr Airly Hindley rang. He and his brother, David, would call on us on their way to Edenhall at the weekend. They arrived on Sunday afternoon and we made them welcome. Joan made some tea and gave them some of her special cake - she was good at making cakes. Airly asked would I reconsider and have another look at Edenhall as he would like us to look after the estate. We talked for a long time - the conditions were excellent it was just the lodge we did not care for. Anyway it was arranged that we would visit Edenhall on the following Sunday.

We had a good journey to Penrith in lovely weather. We had a walk around the town and liked it. We then went to Bob Simpson's and he took us around the estate again. From Dolphenby Farm the view of the eastern fells was superb, with snow capping the fell tops and everything in sunshine. The fells to the west - Saddleback and Skiddaw - were also covered in snow and could be seen from West Lodge. We looked over the keeper's lodge again and out of the sitting room window on the east side, we could see pheasants picking about among the trees. Looking down the drive that led past the front door I wondered about the people who had lived there years ago.

I was impressed at the peacefulness - everything looked so different in the good weather. I made up my mind and I was sure we would be happy at Edenhall. On the way home we were full of what we had seen. I 'phoned Mr Hindley the following evening and said we would like to move to Edenhall. Airly was very pleased and said he was sure we would be happy. Bob Benson was

The Lodge at Edenhall.

a bit upset that we were going and wished us well. I worked out four weeks notice and started packing our things again. This time I hoped it would be for good. Our family was growing and Heather would be starting at a new school very soon.

It was an easy move this time, only about sixty miles. We knew what to do and so all went fairly well and we were at home in no time. Joan soon sorted out Heather with her school - the bus stopped at the lodge and children from Udford and Dolphenby Farms and Big Wood Cottage also caught the bus. The school was in Penrith at Brunswick Road, an old red sandstone building situated just behind the main street of the town.

Penrith was our nearest shopping place. It was old fashioned and I thought a nice, quiet place, with some good shops such as Sykes, the gunsmith, a saddler, Arnisons' Gents Outfitters and some good butcher's shops. In the town centre stood a tall, monumental clock tower with the main road to Carlisle running past it. I think there were about twenty-eight public houses in the town - I had never seen so many pubs in one small place before. Some of the pubs were meeting places for farmers on market days, such as the George Hotel in Devonshire Street and the Agricultural in Castlegate. Good meals could be had at these hostelries.

The cattle market at the top of Castlegate was very busy on market day, Tuesday mornings. As well as stock sales there were all the dealings in cattle food and farm equipment, insurance, etc. By late lunchtime most of the dealing was over and farmers would walk down the hill to the town to meet their wives in some hotel or pub where they would have a meal together. I got to know many of these people, as I visited farms for clocker hens which we purchased from them.

Edenhall village lay at the bottom of a hill about half a mile from West Lodge. It was an easy walk there but a bit of a drag back again. There were thirty-five houses and a hotel, plus the stable yard with a clock tower over the entrance. The church was just outside the village towards the River Eden. There were no shops, just the Edenhall Hotel. Langwathby over the river to the east was a good sized village with a post office cum general store, a garage and a cattle feed mill. In those days the mill was called Monkhouses. There was also a tiny little penny shop owned and run by Arthur Whaugh, or 'Taffy' Whaugh. He sold sweets and it was the local gossip place.

The Eden valley was well named. To my eyes it was like the Eden I had read about in books - the river running north to south, the River Eamont joining it at Watersmeet on the boundary between the Edenhall land and the Winderwath Estate. Over the years I enjoyed the fishing, both salmon and trout, and got to know the bailiffs who patrolled those waters.

Some pheasants were already in the laying pens which were sited on a hill a few hundred yards from my lodge. The soil was sandy and well drained. The pens had been erected in 1932 and were built of larch wood. Even after thirty-six years of use they were in good repair. Five hen pheasants and one cock pheasant occupied each section and in all there were thirty pens. I had a look at the rearing equipment - coops with sliding roofs and some fairly new rearing pens. Bob Simpson, the head keeper, told me the coops had arrived at Langwathby Railway Station in 1932 and he had carted them to Edenhall. We, Josie Burn and I, did some repair work on some of the coops and water dishes and galvanised drinking fountains were all scrubbed and cleaned.

A rearing field had been arranged and some traps put out at certain places to catch any ground vermin in the area. We used a twelve seater Land Rover to collect the broody hens - we would need about three hundred in all. The hatching yard was prepared beside a huge cedar tree which provided some shade for the nest boxes and coops. The hen pheasants were laying well so we started to collect the clockers.

Josie Burn and I would set out about 6pm in the evenings and call at farms in the surrounding villages. We drove a lot of miles along the east fell side, and up tracks to outlying farms and cottages. Sometimes we would be lucky and get half a dozen clockers, at other places none at all. The old breeds of poultry were disappearing and being replaced by new breeds which were smaller, bred for laying and did not go broody and, if they did, it was only for an odd day or so. Clocking was bred out of them. Josie and I went out three nights a week. People sometimes 'phoned to say they had some clockers and eventually we would have fifty good, steady hens. These would be given twenty eggs each, so a thousand eggs were set at one time.

During the day we keepers were busy carting the pens and coops to the rearing field, where we placed the coops twenty yards apart. The rearing pens were put by themselves at one end of the field, close together. Our cabin on wheels was parked against the fence about midway down the field - all the tackle and feed we needed was there. The cabin was our headquarters at that time and our only shelter from the weather. When the first lot of chicks came on the rearing fields one man was there all the time with them. Eventually all the hatching was finished and the second man was then there too. During the day the men took turns to look about the woods and fields and return again in the evening for the last feeds and to shut up the chicks at night, usually at about 10pm.

The day started on the field at 6am. I would open up the coops and stand back behind the coop, count the chicks as they came out and write the number on the side of the coop - that way we would know if any were missing. I would feed and water the chicks and hens and mid-morning I would move the coops on to fresh ground. At midday we would feed the chicks again and during the afternoon cart water ready for next day and look at traps.

On fine nights the keepers would sit about the cabin talking or making snares. If it were a cold night the birds would be in the coops early and if a warm night they would hang about outside the coops, not wanting to go in. It could be very frustrating at times. Curlews nested in the long grass in adjoining fields and when we were trying to shut up the coops the curlews would give the alarm call and that would cause the hens to get alarmed and make the pheasant chicks run from the coops. After a few nights of curlew calls I was forced to shoot the bird as I was weary of going without sleep. After a day on the rearing field, I would walk home or ride in the Land Rover if we had one.

Once the young birds were put into the woods, things started to be a little easier. They were watered and fed twice a day but the keeper would patrol his ground and watch the harvest field when the corn was cut. Rabbits were shot and sometimes a fox. I always tried to be there, as it gave an idea what game was on the ground.

In August the berries of elder and blackberry were ripe. Pheasants love the fruit and tended to stray a long way from their home in the wood. Acorns and beech mast also attract the pheasants and other birds. In warm weather birds would 'jug' out in rushes or long grass. Jug means sleep on the ground when they were easily caught by foxes, cats or any ground vermin. The keeper would go in the evenings to these places and using dogs would chase the birds back to the woods. If not, he stood a chance to lose them. Sometimes they would wander over the boundary onto someone else's land. The keeper would hear a shot on the land adjoining and know another pheasant would not be coming back again.

Pheasant shooting starts on 1st October on most estates but little or no shooting is done until the second week in November. By this time most of the leaves are fallen from the trees and the birds are well grown. The shooting season at Edenhall usually started on Saturday afternoons - potato and turnip fields were shot over and sometimes a field of kale or rape would be shot. It would be a light-hearted affair, no serious shooting - the root fields were walked over in line with the odd beater or two. The idea was to shoot the boundaries so the pheasants made towards the woods and were going home. These short autumn afternoons were very pleasant.

On the east side of the estate at what was called the Desert, some shelter belts of trees had been planted and these would be driven on these outside days. For these drives a couple of guns would stand forwards, most of the pheasants there were wild bred and flew well. Coat Gill on the north side of the estate was part of Edenhall Grange Farm and was an interesting place to shoot. Woodcock liked to feed there and made some good shooting. Roe deer would bed down there high up under the beech trees where they had a good view all about them. If disturbed they would make for Slate Quarry Wood, a short distance across the valley. Once in the wood they were safe as we hardly ever shot that wood - it was too big and the trees very thick as it hadn't been 'brashed' up. Brashed means taking the lower branches off. The dogs were tired at the end of the day as they were out of condition at the start of the season.

Eight guns would make up the shooting party on the big shoots - my two employers, plus six of their friends. The guests, if from a long way off, would arrive on the Thursday afternoon. They usually stayed at the Edenhall Hotel which was right next to the estate yard where everyone gathered at the start of a day's sport and where we all finished at the end of the day. After the guests had settled themselves into the hotel, Bob Simpson and I, would join them. There would be much handshaking and the guests would want to know where we would be shooting on the morrow. After a few drinks and beginning to feel very happy, we would go home as the next day we would have an early start.

The estate yard would be busy with people coming and going, from 8am onwards on shoot days. The beaters, and dog men were the first to arrive and were told where we would shoot and what we wanted them to do. Some of the men would be out on stop at the end of a wood or field and not be among the shooting until later. These men were older men and could be trusted to do this important job. The guest guns would all gather about my employer and he or his brother would get the guests to draw lots for places. Number 1 was always on the right but if you drew number 8 you would move to number 1 on the second stand - each time moving up one number.

We had two tractors with trailers. Straw bales were put on one of them for beaters to sit on and the other tractor was used as the game cart and was fitted with rails which the shot birds were hung over after each drive. The head keeper stayed with the employer and the under-keepers went with their beaters. Once the tractor and beaters were gone the host and his friends would follow in the Land Rover, the head keeper leading the way. The under-keepers by now would have their beaters ready lined out, to start at a signal from the head keeper.

The host and the rest of the guns having parked the transport behind the shooting line, would walk to their respective pegs with the numbers painted on a card. The guns were loaded, cartridge bags opened and set handy. The dog men would be about a hundred yards behind the line of guns where they could watch for wounded birds. When everything was ready the head keeper would walk around the wood or field that was to be driven and join the line of beaters, taking up his place in the centre of the line like a army general.

The whistle was blown and the drive started, beaters tapping their sticks. 'Keep a good line, you lads,' you would hear again and again, from the keepers. As the line of beaters advanced their sticks tapping the trees and undergrowth, pheasants and any other ground game ran forwards, until eventually a bird would fly, followed by others. Sometimes the beaters got a little excited and shouted. The keeper would tell them to keep quiet as too many birds in the air at one time is not good. Shooting started and everyone would be excited, with guns banging away all down the line and birds falling from the sky. The dogs wanted to be away to retrieve the game. 'Sit down, Ben, sit down will you!' one of the guns shouts.

The line of beaters stopped. Pheasants were getting up all over the place. 'Hold the line, lads, hold the line.' The keepers were busy trying to keep the beaters steady. 'Just tap your sticks, lads.' The head keeper shouted, 'Josie, Brian, come forwards on your own.' We two keepers left the beating line and quietly walked forwards - more birds rose but not in the same numbers as before. The guns dealt with the birds in fewer numbers. The three keepers stood still. 'Right you beaters, come forward, but keep a line.' More birds got up with the line of beaters upon them and the keepers are in line again and the drive taken right through. Having reached the edge of the field or wood, the whistle was blown twice, 'No more shooting after the whistle.'

The drive over the head keeper makes his way to his employer, 'Good show of birds, Simpson.' 'Aye, not bad,' says Bob, 'I've seen more.' The dog men are busy with the fallen game. The guest guns are retrieving the birds closer to their pegs. The other keepers gathered their beaters together and made their way to the next drive. Having reached the wood or field that was to be driven, they stand a way from it and talk among themselves until told to line out again.

Once the ground around the shooting pegs was cleared of game, the rest would be left for the dog men to find. The dead game was loaded into the game cart and counted. A card was handed to the host who told the guest guns how many head were killed at the stand. The head keeper would then lead the guns to the next stand and see that all was correct and that cartridges were in good supply. Then he went to where the beaters were waiting, and so another drive began.

Lunch was usually taken after the third drive of the day. At

Edenhall guest guns dined in the Clock House, the home of my employer. The lunch was brought from Langwathby, a village just across the river. Mrs Henderson, the wife of a haulage contractor, cooked the meal and it was fetched some while before the guests arrived at Clock House. On Fridays fish pie was sometimes on the menu for religious reasons. The food was always excellent.

The head keeper would give his employer a game card with the morning's bag entered on it - how many pheasants, partridges, rabbits, hares or other sundries. The beaters meanwhile sat at trestle tables in the stables - beer was given to the men and pop for the young uns. There was plenty of talk of the morning's shooting. 'Did you see old so and so, couldn't hit a haystack!' The keeper would tell the offender to be careful of what he said, if the boss heard him there would be no more days beating for him. The place would be full of smoke and the men would be talking of the afternoon's drives. After lunch the keepers, their dogs at their heels would say, 'OK, lads, let's away.' The trailer was loaded up and off we went, soon to be lined out for the first drive of the afternoon.

The guns were all at their pegs for the afternoon drive, some of them a bit jolly after a drink and a good meal. A whistle blast and the drive started. There were two drives in the afternoon and that ended the day's sport. After all the game was gathered up, the beaters and dog men were paid, and told, 'Don't be late tomorrow!' They climbed on the trailer and were taken to the estate yard. The keepers were busy with the dead game until finally everyone was away to the yard and the fields and wood were left quiet until the next day. The keepers sorted out the game and made sure it had space to cool down. We would walk over to The Pheasantries and the gun room where a large table would be filled with cleaning rods, tins of oil, tow and clean rags. The guns were cleaned and put in the racks ready for the next day's shooting. Once the gun room was all tidy and secure, everyone made their way home.

The walk home gave me time to think and sometimes I felt sad for all the killing. Amongst today's bag were a few birds that would run up to me when I whistled to them at feed times. They were so trusting and I was a Judas to them.

Joan always fed my dogs on days when I was busy. After a good meal I could relax a while with my family. Later in the evening I would go to the Edenhall Hotel and have a drink with the guest guns, my employer's friends. What a night we would have.

Beaters and guns pictured at the Farmers' Shoot, Eden Hall Hotel.

Eventually I wandered home, maybe calling in at the estate yard to have a look at the game larder on the way - it was quite a sight - all very quiet in there, the birds that had made the woods at evening echo with their calls.

I would go to bed hoping for good weather, dry with a light wind. I would be up again at 5.30am. Out in the dark owls would be calling and I would go out to open the kennel gate to let the dogs out. I usually walked them for twenty minutes, down Boat Lane, the lane that leads to Udford and Dolphenby Farms. Once the dogs were back in the kennels I would go in for breakfast and light the fire for Joan in the kitchen. Afterwards I would have a walk down Boat Lane, my ears tuned, and heard what sounded like shots a long way off. I knew that only poachers would shoot at 6.30am on a November morning and I hoped that we had not been visited by them during the night.

By 7.30am dawn would be breaking and I would take my waterproofs and dog away to the estate yard and into the stables. The place has been cleaned up since Friday's lunch. Fresh crates of beer and soft drinks would be stacked ready, the floor swept, the smell of tobacco lingering about the place. I would go to the gun room, take down the guns and use a clean jag in the gun barrels to take any oil away. The gun sleeves of my employer were made of sheepskin with stout canvas on the outside. I put the guns in the sleeves and filled the cartridge bags. These along with four boxes of 250 cartridges, were placed in the Land Rover, with waterproofs, dog leads and holding pegs.

Bob Simpson, the head keeper, would arrive and ask, 'How are ya? Everything OK?' 'Aye, Bob, all ready for off.' By this time the beaters had started to arrive and as Saturday was a 'big day' we would have more of them. John Thompson, the tractor driver says, 'Can you get somebody else to drive Brian, I want to do a bit of beating?' I manage to find someone willing to drive the beaters' tractor. 'Everyone happy now?' On the 'big day' we shot the 'middle' - that is, the place where the bulk of the hand-reared pheasants had been released. The under-keepers and beaters went to Boat Lane and then to the back of High Barn Wood.

Today High Barn Wood will be the first drive, followed by the Greens and Round End, shot as one drive. Later, Udford Rise was walked blank into Struma and Struma shot into Big Wood. Big Wood was stopped off by men placed out to stop the birds leaving the woods that were to be shot after lunch. At the first drive number 1 and number 8 guns are placed on the flanks of the line of guns, more or less forming a crescent shaped line. The idea was any birds making back to High Barn would give some good sport to these flank guns.

The head keeper with his beaters started the drive and almost immediately the first birds started to rise. A minute later shots were heard - the big day had started. The shooting was heavy, all along the line of guns while in the wood the beaters stand still, the keepers holding them there. Birds are getting up well in front of them. At times twenty to thirty pheasants took wing together, too many for the gun below to deal with. The shooting went on, the gun barrels would get quite hot, but the birds still poured over the guns. In the wood the line beaters were at standstill - more birds took to the air, more heavy shooting - would it ever end?

Eventually the shooting starts to die away. There are still some pheasants moving about in front of the line of beaters. 'Stand fast you lads,' the head keeper shouts, 'keep your sticks tapping.' The keeper walked quietly forwards - some birds got up, immediately the keeper stood still. A few seconds later the shooting started again, and so it went on with the keeper moving about in front of the beating line.

Eventually the beaters reached a small rock outcrop at the edge of the wood, bracken between it and the wall that surrounds the wood. A few odd birds got up, a few more shots and then two blasts of the whistle and the drive is over. The first drive of the day went very well - a half hour of continuous shooting.

One hundred and fifty or more birds were killed at this stand - and that was just the first drive. The guns were busy filling cartridge bags from the store of magazines in the Land Rover. Beaters went to get ready for the next drive. The second stand of the day was just behind where the guns stood earlier. This time number 1 and number 8 guns walked in line with the beaters until they reached their numbered pegs. The second drive is in a wood called Greens and Round End, roughly half a mile long, with some birch, bracken and a few larch trees. Where the Greens meets Round End, the beaters were stopped, while the head keeper made sure that all was well, before blowing the whistle for the beaters to set off once more. Round End held many birds, some having come from High Barn. Soon the air was loud with shooting. The pheasants that get past the guns make for Big Wood or Sixteen Acre Wood, which would be shot over later in the day.

After the second drive the dogs would be busy finding dead and wounded birds and the game cart would be loaded, with the birds tied in braces of a cock and a hen. The guns would collect more cartridges and then they were ready for the third drive which was at Struma, a wood of about four acres with larch trees and a few rhododendrons, but very open in the bottom, not much ground cover at all. Udford Rise, a wood that meets Struma corner to corner, was walked through quietly by the beaters and the pheasants allowed to run in to Struma to be shot. Birds started to rise almost immediately - a flush of birds got up - a 'flush' being a lot of pheasants. Once the drive was over, the beaters quickly got away for their lunch. The dog men would follow later when all the game had been picked up.

Saturday lunch for the beaters and other helpers was tatie pot and again the talk is of the shooting and the stable fairly buzzed with noise. The beaters seemed to enjoy the day as much as the guns. As the days are short at this time of year, time is of the essence and the beaters would be ready to start the drive again soon after lunch while the head keeper would be hinting to his employer that it was time to get going for the next drive at Sixteen Acre Wood where the guns stood with their backs to Park Clump.

Two men were sent to keep the pheasants in the wood when the shooting started. On a dull day it would be dark under the trees by

2pm. The line of beaters would bring the pheasants through the wood towards the guns, taking care not to make them fly too soon. Once the birds were near the line and took to the air the shooting was fast and furious.

The beaters would try to give the guns time to reload it possible and to keep just enough pheasants in the air to keep them busy. By now the light is getting poor for shooting and the last birds escape being shot. For the final drive of the day the guns stood in a crescent with their backs to the estate yard. The beaters would bring pheasants from Park Clump, a small stand of Scots Fir of not more than two acres with little or no ground cover. Some pheasants tried to head back for Sixteen Acre Wood and some fine shooting was had at these and the dog men were kept busy.

Finally the beaters walked back through the wood looking for dead or wounded birds. It was beginning to get dark and we could see the flashes from the gun muzzles as they fired at the stragglers. The shooting stopped immediately the whistle was blown. The beaters were paid, thanked and told when the next shoot would be.

By this time dogs are everywhere and birds were being brought to the game cart by the armful. Dunlop and Arthur Graham were busy pairing the dead pheasants and tying them. In the game larder, the hot game, that is that day's game, was hung separately with plenty of air circulating it. Rabbits, hares, ducks and anything else are kept separate but counted in the bag. The head keeper would make the final count and a card was filled in with the total bag for the day - 472.

The big day is over and we made our way to the gun room, where the table was full of cleaning tackle and dogs lay about wherever they could find a corner away from peoples' feet. Eventually all the guns were cleaned and put in the racks and then we could go home to supper. The day for me wasn't finished though, as I was expected to socialise with the shooting guests at the hotel later in the evening.

On the Sunday morning the keepers meet at the game larder at 10am. The employer and some of his guests came with their dogs and we would start to search the woods for dead or wounded game. By 1pm we would maybe have recovered twenty or more pheasants that would have been wasted. It saddens me to see a bird fly away and know that it is wounded. After lunch people started loading up their vehicles and each guest was given two brace of pheasants. Hands were shaken and a £10 note slipped into mine with many thanks, 'What a weekend to remember - see you soon!'

As the last car drove through the archway, our employer would ask, 'Would you care for a drink?' and a drink we would have. The van would arrive for the game which is all sorted out. Any badly shot birds were put to one side to go to my ferrets. Eventually all the game is loaded into the game dealer's van and a cheque was signed. The game dealer was called William McLure from Windermere. All that was left in the game larder was a pile of feathers of various sorts, a few rabbits, pigeons, the odd hare. The larder would have to be cleaned out ready for the next big day. On Sunday afternoon after a good meal I would have a rest and then in the evening I would be out night watching - the season had started and with it the poachers.

The day the river died

One summer Sunday afternoon I watched a river 'die'. I had set out on foot to Uddford, a quiet place on the River Eamont. Uddford Farm had been a 'putting up' place for cattle drovers as they brought their cattle south from Scotland. The house stands beside the lonning that leads to a a ford laid with stone setts, no doubt to ease wheeled traffic. The lane then goes on past Tippery Wood and on to Appleby and beyond.

The deep pool at Uddford was usually clear but that day it had a milky look. I picked my way along the rocky path, keeping my eyes on the river. At a bend I saw a pike, still upright but only moving now and then as it was carried down river by the current. It's eyes were almost white and it was discoloured. More fish were carried slowly by and just before Cave Wood the surface was covered with dead and dying fish, some floating belly up.

I had seen enough and went directly home where I phoned Jim Dawson the head bailiff for the fly fishers who rented the river from the Eden Hall Estate. Dawson came and we drove to Uddford where we found things were even worse with dead fish everywhere including eels and salmon. The water was so discoloured that we couldn't see the river bed.

The Eamont flows from Ullswater into the Eden so I headed for the salmon pool on the Eden where there was a trace of colour but nothing compared to the Eamont. The larger Eden had diluted the pollution and there were only a few dead fish but further up at Watersmeet there were trout, pike, grayling and eels all dead. I met

Jim Dawson at Uddford pool and we discussed the situation. As I was in charge of all sporting matters relating to the estate I had to find the cause of the pollution. I drove to the Cross Keys and turned left onto the A66, where the new road was being laid and a bridge put in to span the River Eamont near Brougham Castle.

Though it was a Sunday it was busy with a crowd of men and a line of concrete mixers waiting to unload. I stopped the Land Rover and went to see what was going on. In the river was a great heap of concrete - it had spewed out from a section of collapsed shuttering. The lovely Eamont was the colour of concrete as far as the eye could see. There was nothing anyone could do and eventually the water would run clear again but how long would it take?

The river was devoid for fish from Brougham Castle to Watersmeet. We never knew the full extent of the pollution and most of the smaller river creatures were also wiped out. We were stunned and the matter was put into the hands of lawyers and the environment people. The contractors promised to pay for a large re-stocking programme which eventually I helped with when three bailiffs and I introduced some new trout to the river.

The Field Trials

One year, Al Jackson, the President of the North Western Field Trial Association approached my employer to ask if they could hold the annual trials at Edenhall? My employer asked me were things on the estate favourable? I thought for a moment, 'yes' I told him, 'I reckon I can put on a good show.' The trials were to take two days to run - a 24 dog stake.

The trials would take place in October 1968 and much planning had to be done in case of bad weather or adverse winds which could spoil the days. All was in hand when the time arrived. We started the first day at Honey Pot Farm, a turnip field alongside of Lake Wood which had a fair lot of game on it. We shot over that first. During the day the winds were strong, almost gales but all went well and by 3pm we had got through a good half of the dogs. The last drive ended at Lake Wood. The guns ready in the wood, several birds dropped into the lake after being shot and so some good retrieves were made.

Later that evening I went to Edenhall Hotel where many of the trials people were staying and there we had a merry time, with much to talk about, dogs then being the main topic. As the evening went

Edenhall, 1968, the Field Trials - right to left - Arthur Sowerby, Al Jackson, president of the North West Field Trial Society and the author.

along the stories got longer and longer. The spectators were a grand lot and stayed away back when they were told. A few of these were prominent figures in the field trial world. The trial ended in a field of turnips behind the village, some birds made for Moss Wood and the boggy ground thereabouts and gave the runners up some good retrieves.

As we made our way along Gas House Lane, back to the estate yard, I was congratulated several times on a well organised trial. I must say most things had gone well for me and my other keepers. Bill Meldrum won the trial with the Queen's two Labradors. He stuffed a £5 note into my hand and told me he had really enjoyed himself and I was to have a drink on the Queen. Bill later wrote to me from Sandringham, Norfolk where he was the Queen's dog trainer. I still have that letter - it bears the Royal stamp 'ER', the envelope is thick and the notepaper bears the Royal address, Sandringham, Norfolk. I was 34 years old and a head keeper on a lovely estate. I had worked hard at keepering and done what I had set out to do.

SANDRINGHAM, NORFOLK

14th November, 1968.

Dear Brian,

    Please excuse a typewritten letter and I am sorry I have not written before this, but I have been very busy lately with Field Trials and shooting.

    I enjoyed myself very much at the recent Trials and thought you had it well organised. I enclose £1 for you to get a drink with and many thanks for the trouble you took.

    I have heard of an Alsation which you could have for £50, and you could have it on a month's trial. It belongs to John Clitheroe, Head Keeper, Bedingham Hall, Nr. Bungay, Suffolk and please write direct to Clitheroe and say whether you want it or not.

    Yours sincerely,

    Bill Meldrum.

    <u>Kennelman</u>

Mr. B. Aston,
Head Keeper,
Edenhall Estate,
Edenhall, Penrith, Cumberland.

Fuddling Chub

One day I met Dawson, the Head Water Bailiff for the Yorkshire Fly Fishers who rented parts of the Rivers Eden and Eamont from Edenhall Estates. I happened to mention the large shoals of chub in part of our private waters and said that I was concerned for the young trout.

'I'll tell you what, Brian, I have plenty of hemp seed, shall we have a go at them chub?' I told Dawson that I would be glad of his help. It was summer, the Eden was low. Dawson and I spent one morning making the bait. We had bought two fresh loaves and a large jar of hemp seed stood ready. The soft middle of the loaves was used, rolled into small balls about as big as the small finger nail and our hemp seed put into each ball. We made hundreds of balls and placed into a shallow trug, or wooden basket.

Two more bailiffs were waiting at the river when we arrived. The boat was ready and landing nets and hessian sacks were put on board. I walked up the stretch of river where the chub shoals were - hands full of bait were thrown down the middle of the river, several hundred yards of water were treated this way. 'It should take about twenty minutes to start working,' Dawson said. 'Best let the lads with the boat know.'

I climbed into the boat with Fred Curha and old Dixon. Taking the oars I took the boat into the middle of the stream and worked upstream to the head of the salmon pool. Someone said, 'There's one.' It was splashing about the edge of the river. Soon fish were splashing about all over the river. I was sweating, the bailiffs kept me busy. Evidently chub love fresh bread and feed upon it, greedily, but the hemp seed affects the swim bladder of the fish and fuddles them. That is why this method of catching chub is called 'fuddling'.

By the time we had netted our last chub we had filled three hessian potato sacks. We stayed on the water a while after the last fish was caught to see if any more would surface. On landing, the sacks were tipped out and the chub counted. I do not recollect how many were caught but some big fish were among them, weighing 4lbs or more. It was a good day's work - the young trout would have a better chance to live now.

I later buried the fish, glad to be shot of the predators. Chub kill many young trout and other small fish by surrounding a shoal and driving them to the shallow waters, then proceed to eat them. I have watched it happen and seen the small trout jump out of the water, trying to escape.

When I first went to Edenhall and anyone came to fish the river, the head keeper always went with them as gillie. Later on I used to go as well. I was being taught how the river was in all its different moods and where the fish could be caught. I had been a keen fisherman all my life so I was able to pick things up fairly quickly, for instance the names of places that held fish, such as 'being on the lies', that is behind boulders or other obstructions on the river bed.

Beech Dub was a favourite place. It was situated at the head of the salmon pool, Red Scar 'waters meet'. Boil Hole upper salmon stream and lower salmon stream were both good fast water fishing. At Langwathby Bridge there was a gauge telling the water height and if anyone was to come to fish, the gillie would be at the bridge in the early morning, to check the gauge and know whether things were good for a day's sport or not. Too high a water would mean little or no fishing that day. In summer the river would be low and choked by weed, again not much sport.

The 28lb salmon
The Eden was in fine fettle for fishing one early March. It was a cloudy, mild day - just right. I had been busy trapping and fancied a couple of hours alone by the beck. I was fishing my old heavy

The salmon pool at Edenhall.

green hart rod. The upper salmon stream took my fancy and a stoat tail tube fly was my lure. Starting below the Boil Hole I fished my way down the strong water from the bank - it was an easy cast, the water did the rest.

A pipe in my mouth as usual, having a rest, the rod under my arm, I lit it then started to retrieve the line which was close to the bank. It had snagged. Giving my rod a quick jerk, taking up any slack line, again I jerked the rod. By God, I had hooked a fish which set off. Reaching the strong water it lay there, walking downstream until I was opposite I started to put some weight on it. The fish turned and made a few short dashes downstream. I turned it easily, soon it lay in the edge just below me. It was a big fish. Wiping the tailer on, it was on the bank directly. It was the best fish I ever caught, topping the scales at 28lbs. One to remember!

Murder at Edenhall
I had been head keeper at Edenhall for about two years when the murder took place. It was spring and I had been out early as usual. Arriving at the village, in front of the four cottages on the left side, police vans and cars were parked. I was just in time to see something wrapped in a white sheet being carried from the Pennington's cottage. It was my business to know what happened on the estate so I approached the policeman at the cottage gate and asked what they were doing there. I knew the policeman and he told me, 'There's someone been killed. Did I know the people that lived in the cottage?' 'Yes, I knew them,' I said. 'Well, Mrs Pennington's been murdered.'

Later in the day the police were all over the estate looking for Mr Pennington. All the barns and farm buildings were searched, the woods were walked over, the haystacks and corn stacks looked at. I heard that the police had found an electric torch at Lady's Walk by the River Eden believed to belong to him, but nothing else was found.

Mrs Pennington worked at nights at the Hussar Hotel at Penrith as a barmaid. Mr Pennington worked at Edenhall Estate as a stockman. They would be about thirty years old at the time. Mrs Pennington, had formed some sort of friendship with a customer at work and, on leaving home, left a note for her husband saying that she was going away with this person that night. Later, about midnight the same night, Mr Pennington drove to Penrith to the Hussar

Hotel. He persuaded his wife to return to Edenhall and their home and then while they were in bed he strangled her with bailer twine.

What sort of a state he was in no-one knows. He rang the police at 4am telling them he had killed his wife and rang off. The police arriving at his home found Mrs Pennington dead and immediately a search was started. Mr Pennington's body was found in the river somewhere at Lazonby about six weeks later. The search was over, the pair of them dead. Two young children of a similar age to my daughter Lynn, were left. They were taken to the home of one of the grandparents and to my knowledge were brought up there.

Night watching

As soon as the last leaves fall from the trees, the poacher will be about, I mean the pheasant poacher, the single man or the gangs that are out to make money. Poaching goes on all year round but only in a small way, the odd rabbit, hare and fish. Later when the woods have been stocked with game, then the night poacher starts his perambulations. He will go about various estates, maybe on a bike and can be seen cycling along at dusk. He is looking and listening, stopping now and then, pretending to rest. It is easy to get an idea as to where the birds are sleeping by the racket made as they fly up to roost. I have counted the cocks then multiplied it by two and you have a good idea how many birds are in that wood.

In mild weather the pheasants will roost almost anywhere - in hedges or solitary trees. Once the weather starts to get cold and the winds and gales come, they make to the shelter of the woods where they will find feed. By the time the trees are bare, the poacher will have covered many miles and have an idea where the bulk of the game is. He will have made a note of the best ways to retreat if disturbed at his work.

November is when serious night poaching starts - Bonfire Night gives him an advantage, explosions going on everywhere, his shots will blend with the other explosions. From then on the keeper will be about. I have known poachers to be in a wood in the early evening while the keeper is sat at his supper. I would take a walk about 7pm, stand and listen, hear a shot a long way off and try to pinpoint it.

Sitting by the fire soon puts me to sleep and by 9pm I'm ready for bed but there'll be no bed until the early hours when poachers are about. Late at night I'd have a cup of tea and a sandwich, put on my boots and heavy coat and slide the .450 pistol into a pocket. My wife has seen this happen many times. 'Please Brian, don't take the pistol.' She said those words many times. I would look at her and say, 'Look, lass, they are armed. I'll be alright.' Out in the stable I would collect my gun and a pocket full of cartridges plus a pair of handcuffs. If I was crossing fields with cattle I didn't take the Alsatians.

Walking down the lane, the stars bright above, I wondered how many times I had trod the same road on the same mission. Keeping to the grass, my ears tuned, I reach Udford Farm gate. It's white with frost, my eyes are used to the dark - no moon tonight. I pull the belt of my coat tighter, it's going to be a long night. What I would give to be tucked in bed asleep. It was no good wishing, I wanted to be a keeper, and here I was, doing what keepers do, night watching.

I walked back towards my Lodge at Round End where I had a cabin for corn and other feed. I sat up on the sacks with the door open, pulling some sacks over my legs which were cold. I stayed a while, my thoughts of what the day ahead might bring. Setting off again towards Udford Farm, I was thinking it was too still a night. They, the poachers, maybe in the same mind. Did I imagine it? I thought I heard a rifle shot. It's easy to imagine things, particularly when you are straining your ears. I was on edge, hoping they would come. Let's get it over with. Each night I prayed they would come, I knew they would some time, let it be tonight.

I turned about, moving slowly, looking toward Cross Pots Rise, a wood on my left hand side, standing back one field, it would be where poachers would go. The trees were larch, a favourite roost for birds. They, the poachers, were there alright, a shot followed by pigeons in flight. Just a field between them and me. My heart started pounding, I quickened my pace, reaching the gate at the corner of Cross Potts Wood, I followed the wall. I could not be seen against the trees. The wood where the poachers were busy was enclosed by a wall. I must cross the field to reach it. Being on lower ground I had the advantage. I reached the wall and climbed over the stile, now we were all in the same wood.

I had set an alarm gun amongst the trees on the lower side of the wood. It was loaded with a live cartridge and set knee high and turned outwards instead of down. Crouching on the step I wanted to assess the situation. I had the advantage of surprise. There were three of them I was sure. I heard a low whistle, seconds later a narrow beam of light came on, then a shot, a thump as the bird hit the ground and the sound of flapping wings.

So, there were three poachers, one with the sack carrying the game, one with the torch and another shooting. They had had four shots up to now. I would wait until they shot the wood towards me. I had done this before - wait until a bird was killed close to where I sat, then when someone went to retrieve it, clout him hard then handcuff him to a tree, then fire a shot over them. It's every man for himself when disturbed by the keepers. I waited what seemed hours. The poachers were working the lower end of the Two Acre Wood. Eight shots had been fired while I sat there, these were my pheasants the bastards were killing. Right, I won't wait any longer, drastic action was called for.

Out on the field I waited, I was about opposite them. The beam came on again, I fired at it, both barrels. Not waiting I ran down to the lower end of the wood over the wall and stopped about the middle and fired two more shots about waist high into the wood. Running up the other side of the plantation I stopped again and fired two more shots. I set off again and repeated the process again at the top of the wood. My temper was getting the better of me. I was determined to do as much damage as possible to these bloody poachers. Setting off again I heard the loud report of the alarm gun, someone had tripped it. I kept running, stopping to spray the wood with shot, each fired at waist height. I was knackered with all the action.

Arriving back at the stile I sat contemplating my next move. Some of 'em may be still in the wood. They would be in a bad state, their nerves would have cracked by now. They could be living with shot in 'em. I hoped so. My gun was ready, any movement, any sound, I was determined to fire on it. I shifted myself, my backside was cold. If I crept quietly away, if there was anyone in the wood playing 'doggo', they would lie a long time. I could be home in my bed.

It was just after 2am and I had been out for four hours, over two hours at the poachers' wood. I cleaned the gun and sat a while, had a nip, wanting daylight to come. I would be back at the wood at first light. Now I must face Joan. She would want to know what was the shooting about. I had fired sixteen shots, what at? I would have no peace now for days and nights. Will daylight never come? Tramping backwards and forwards, pheasants were beginning to fly from their roosts. My mind was churning over, had I been close enough when I first shot at the torch to seriously wound the person holding it? Would they have been able to escape and maybe go to hospital. Gunshot wounds must be reported to the police. If so where had the person been when the wounds were inflicted? I knew one thing, those poachers would never dare come on my patch again for a while.

I began my search of the wood, starting by my alarm gun. The trip wire was pulled towards the outside of the wood. There was a four yard gap in the wall, the stones laying on the field, meant whoever rushed the wall was in a great hurry and could have received some shot in the legs from the alarm gun? I found one dead pheasant and nothing else. Back at the wall gap I set off towards Honeypot Farm. I found two pheasants on the field dropped by the poachers and another near a gate. I had heard eight shots, say eight pheasants the poachers had. I had now found four of them leaving them with four birds for their night's work. That day as I did my work I whistled and was happy. Tonight I would go to my bed knowing that certain of the poaching fraternity would put the word about that the keeper was wide awake and not afraid to shoot.

Later, 'phone calls were received asking was that the barmy keeper? 'Yes,' I answered. 'Well, we're coming back.' I replied, 'Aye, look sharp, ye can have some more any time.' Each night on leaving home to do my rounds I told my wife not to answer the 'phone, no point her receiving the threats meant for me. My estate was left in peace for the rest of the 1967 season. I still patrolled my ground and always would, I being the keeper and very much on my guard.

George Wilson 'shot'

I had been at Edenhall a year or two when I went to Penrith one day and met someone from Garstang. Evidently George Wilson, my under keeper, who left me due to his stealing game, had been taken on as keeper at Barnacre again.

The story I was told, was that George was shot one night during the shooting season, by poachers. The hospital where George had gone for treatment for the gunshot wound got in touch with the police as all wounds, knife or gunshot, must be investigated. At the police station, while making a statement, he said he had heard some shots at Heald Wood belonging to the estate where he was gamekeeper. He went into the wood to challenge the poachers but could not see them and started to search for them. Hearing someone moving about the wood, he shouted for them to stop. A shot was fired from one of the poacher's which struck George Wilson. He fired back and heard someone cry out as if they were shot.

The police and George went to Heald Wood to search it and no-one was found. They looked about for signs of poaching - none were found. George Wilson was questioned as to how the shooting happened. The bullet had entered his body beneath his armpit and passed out high in the shoulder or upper back.

After many hours of questioning by the police, and as there was no evidence of anyone else being involved, George Wilson finally confessed how he was shot. George had gone on to the neighbouring estate, Bleazedale Towers, owned by the Silcocks, to poach pheasants. After spending some time killing pheasants with a .22 rifle, he had left the wood. He put the rifle underneath his coat with the muzzle pointing upwards under his armpit. Evidently he was pushing his way through some bushes when something had caught the rifle's trigger and it went off. If he had not been stealing from his neighbours, he would not have had to conceal his rifle and the accident would not have happened. What the police did with George I know not. He left Barnacre and went somewhere in the south - no-one would employ a poaching keeper - not even in Lancashire.

The author and friend pictured at Fountain's Abbey, 1996.

Car poachers at Udford Lane

One Saturday afternoon during the shooting season, Jim Overs 'phoned to tell me that poachers had been seen at Lazonby Hall, the estate where he was keeper. The poachers had also been at Glasonby Estate adjoining. The keeper there, Alec Livingstone, had got the car number and had contacted all the keepers in our area.

It was a real December day, cold and dank, the frost hadn't lifted for days. I was out feeding in the woods, in fact I was in High Barn Wood which overlooked Udford Lane. It was about 3pm. Across the lane almost opposite me was a kale field which had been opened out, in other words, some of it had been carted away. Some young pheasants were picking about the kale stalks and one or two were on the wall adjoining the lane.

I watched a small car coming along the road, it was moving slowly. It took it a while to get below where I stood but there was not much doubt about it - it was the same colour and model that Jim Overs had described to me on the 'phone a short while before. The lane served two farms, Udford and Dolphenby, and you had to come the same way back - the river was the farm boundary and there was no other way out.

I could make out two people in the vehicle. It stopped by the pheasants on the wall. The birds just sat there. Now for it, I thought, but no shot was fired and the car set off again. I waited a minute then I went out of the wood quickly and ran down the field keeping behind the wall all the way to the lane. And there I stayed - if these were the poachers I was in the right place to nab them.

The birds on the wall across the road were the bait - the trap was set, just sit and wait. I was straining my ears. They would have more chances at pheasants along the road towards the farms, unless something had disturbed them. Eventually the car came in sight again, travelling slowly. At a hump in the road it stopped. The passenger got out and looked over the wall into the kale field, then got back into the car. I could see the two in the car talking. The one that had got out was pointing towards the kale opposite where I was hiding. The car set off again and stopped in front of me, the pheasants had left the wall. The pair of them got out and went to the wall. Where was the gun? I couldn't see one. They didn't see me get over the wall onto the road. I was standing beside the car and had the ignition key in my hand.

'Where's the gun?' I asked them. 'We haven't got a gun,' they said. The lads were about twenty years old. I didn't know them. 'What's your names?' 'We haven't done owt,' one of them said. 'Where do you come from?' I asked. 'Why?' 'Because you have been poaching at Lazonby Hall and Glasonby.' 'No, we haven't,' they said.

I was a bit fed up with all the talk. 'Where's the gun?' No reply. I looked at the car. I opened the door. 'Look, you two, over there by the wall.' I didn't want them close to me while I searched the car. No gun there. 'Open the boot,' I said and stood at the rear of the vehicle. A lad came and opened it, the engine was there but no gun. I went to the front. 'Open this boot, will ya?' 'I haven't got the key. That's not the right one,' the lad said. 'Well, please yourself,' I told him. 'I am the keeper here and this is a private road. Open it or I shall kick it OPEN!' I grabbed the handle and started pulling. It was locked. I stood back, I had on some heavy work boots. I prepared for a kick. 'Hang on,' said the lad with me, 'Give us the key, Michael.' His mate pulled out the key and handed it to him.

Nothing but feathers, pheasant feathers, plenty of them. I looked at the pair. 'I told ya, we don't have a gun.' 'There is a gun and by hell I will find it.' I felt under the car. It wasn't a big car, not much larger than a Minor. I walked to the rear again, staring through the back window. Everything looked alright, or was it? One corner of the leather upholstery behind the back seat had a square the size of a stamp missing, there was something underneath it.

'Stay where you are, you two,' I said. I reached inside. It was there alright and loaded. 'No gun?' I said to them. 'What are you going to do?' one asked. 'I am taking it home. If you want it back come to my house at 8 o'clock tonight. I want to talk to you.'

I gave them the ignition key and they left. I rang Harold Fell, our local policeman at Langwathby and told him about the lads and that they would be coming for their gun at 8 o'clock. The policeman was there at my home early. He put his van out of sight in my garage. It was dark and we sat and talked, the curtains drawn.

The lads were on time. I let them in. On entering the kitchen their faces changed, the Law was there to deal with them. They did not have a gun licence, nor game licence. They faced armed trespass charges, failing to give their names and addresses and carrying a loaded firearm on the road. They pleaded guilty. I do not recollect what the fine was. The policeman said it was a hefty one. One of the lads was killed about a year later in a car crash.

The Purdy Muzzle Loader

I received a 'phone call one evening in March. One of my old friends and tutor of my early days at game-keeping was at the other end of the line, Fred Dowker, whom I had been with at Rudding Park. We talked about various things, all about shooting. 'I'll tell you why I rang, Brian,' said Fred. 'The Captain is having a dinner party and we need a fresh salmon. Can you help me?' 'Yes,' I replied 'I have a 28lb fish in the stable caught this morning.' 'Can I have it, Brian?' 'Yes, of course you can have it. You have done me many a good turn over the years.'

Fred asked, 'What do you want for it?' I replied, 'tell the Captain I'll have one of the old muzzle loading guns from his gun room.' 'Aye, alright,' said Fred 'I'll come tomorrow for the fish.' I said, 'I was only kidding about the gun, Fred, the fish is yours for nowt.' 'OK, I'll see you tomorrow.'

Fred arrived at Edenhall with his wife, Mary. She went to see Joan in the Lodge. We stood by the dog pen talking. Later I showed Fred his fish which was put in his pick-up. There on the seat was a muzzle loader, a double barrelled one. I picked it up. 'It's yours, the Captain sent it to you.' 'Thank the Captain for me Fred, but he could have had the fish, it meant nothing to me.'

And so we joined the women in the kitchen over a cup of tea. We had much to say to each other. I had travelled far after leaving Fred at Rudding Park. As I looked at them both across the table, the years rolled away and I could have been back at Rudding as we used to be. Fred and Mary took leave of us. It was only then as I sat by the fire, the muzzle loader on my knee that I saw the name on the barrel flats - James Purdy, London!! Bloody hell, what a surprise, the old gun was a very early top quality one, made about 1830. Purdy were and still are, the finest gun makers anywhere in the world.

While at Rudding Park, I had wiped the old guns over, wet days were when we cleaned the guns and shooting gear. I never realised that the old muzzle loaders I then handled were by such a famous gun maker. I took the old Purdy with me to Penrith and leaving Joan to do some shopping I went to Charlie Sykes' Gun & Fishing Tackle Shop. Charlie was in a back room and John Stockdale was behind the glass topped counter. 'Can I help you, Brian?' said John. 'No thanks, John it's Charlie I need to see. I can wait a while.' My gun was in a sleeve but this wasn't any old gun.

'Now, Charlie, how's things?' I said. 'Has there been owt caught this week?' Charlie, 'I think things are a bit quiet, the water's low, need some rain.'

I laid the gun sleeve on the counter, Charlie undid the buckle and took out my Purdy. I was watching Charlie very closely. He turned the gun over a time or two, then he turned it so as to see the name on the barrel flats. He then turned the gun into better light and looked again at the place where the name was engraved. I thought I would have to take him for an operation to get my gun out of his hands! Charlie's eyes didn't leave my Purdy for a second. He was very quiet. At last, Charlie spoke, still his eyes were on my gun, 'How much?' 'Not for sale, Charlie, just thought you might like to see it.' We spent a long time, Charlie and I talking about my Purdy. Charlie like me was a keen gun collector and travelled to London where the big gun fairs took place.

As I left the gun shop the last words echoed in my ears, 'Let me know when you want to sell it.' Every now and then Charlie called at my Lodge on the pretext that he had some rifles or pistols to show me. The table was covered with all kinds of firearms at times but I knew why he was really there.

I don't know how long I kept my Purdy but in the end Charlie took possession of it. The deal included an 1853 Navy Colt, another weapon of sorts. Some cash, how much I do not remember. Out in the stable there was an old wooden gun case, the lining was missing. I happened to mention it one day in Charlie's gun shop, eventually he took possession of that too, a deal would be made that suited us both.

When Joan and I split up I sold all my firearms apart from my shot gun which I had bought as new and would not part with. Once I start writing about guns I could go on for hours and hours so many have passed through my hands. In this day and age it would almost be impossible to keep so many. It's all in the past like me. I belong in the past, I have no time for this modern age and I do not like what I now see about me.

Lassy

I heard that the new stockman at Dolphenby Farm was leaving and could not take his Alsatian with him. He asked if I could put the dog 'down'? I called at Big Wood cottage where the chap lived and asked when they were going to go. 'We shall be away Saturday afternoon. Will you attend to her?' 'Aye, you go, leave the dog there, I will come back later.' I never saw the dog, it was shut in the cabin.

Later I drove to Big Wood, the Alsatian was out in the run adjoining its cabin. It snarled at me through the wire. I stood talking to it, by God it was thin and had a job to stand. Poor thing, I thought. The gun was in the Land Rover but there was something about that bitch I liked. Each time I held out a hand she snarled. It was a real threat, she meant it. The bitch's coat was loose, some of it was already shed and lying about the run. What that loose hair hid was a starved body. Right, I thought, if I am to kill you my lass, I shall do it by kindness.

At home I prepared a meal, the same as my own dogs would get and plenty of it. Back at Big Wood, the Alsatian got the smell of the feed. Edging the pen gate open, I kept the bucket in front of me. I needn't have worried, her head was in the bucket before it was set down. Lassy, stood, her forelegs apart, gulping down the feed. All the while her hind quarters were shaking. I put out plenty of water for her, then sat and talked while the feed was finished. I left the bucket as she was still licking the last morsels from it and crept out of the pen. I returned again with two sheep heads that I had cleft in two and threw them into the run. These were soon being devoured. The noise of the bone being crunched meant there was nowt wrong with the dog's teeth.

Returning next day to Big Wood, I expected to find the Alsatian dead - blown up with all the feed of the previous day. Stopping the Land Rover and glancing at the dog pen, I could only stare. The bitch was up on her hind legs, eagerly looking at me through the wire fence, her tail wagging, evidently pleased to see me again. As I turned the vehicle round I heard her bark. Unconsciously I shouted, 'It's OK, I'm off for some feed.'

A week later I took Lassy home and installed her in my own kennels. The other dogs made a fuss of her, there was much tail wagging and snuffling. Eventually Lassy's old coat was shed - she had been groomed every day. The old hair I stuffed into the wall, where birds came and took it for their nests. Lassy made a good recovery and turned out to be quite young. She filled out and I found some stitches in her underside - she had been spayed. These I removed. Her new coat, grey/black, fairly shone. She played with my daughters and was allowed indoors at meal times and was well behaved.

Later, Simba, my other Alsatian and Lassy accompanied me many a night in my patrols. I had little to fear with them at my side. I trained Lassy for 'man work', tracking and to go for the sleeved arm. Being heavy she could hold on and 'bite' hard. She turned out a good one. Lassy had been starved, then put on death row to be 'shot', but our family thought the world of her.

The Electric Fence
I was out again on my rounds, night watching, one nasty, wet, dark night. It was an ideal night for poaching - if it had been windy it would have been even better. I had left home about 10 o'clock wishing all poachers in hell so I might be able to go to my bed as ordinary people do each night. I was worn out. Night after night I turned out to walk the lane to Udford Farm, always listening for the shot or the flight of wood pigeons leaving a wood. I stood by the milk stand a while, glad that I had my Alsatians by me - Lassy and Simba. I could just make them out as my eyes were used to the dark after the mile walk. The pair of them were listening, ears pointing forwards, no sounds escaped them. Simba wined, as he did when he was excited and Lassy nuzzled his ear.

I was glad of my old overcoat which I had cut short to a three quarter length. My hat was a good thick one made of wool and I had mittens on my hands and good, heavy boots on my feet. I was warm enough. 'Come on,' I said, the dogs came to me. I turned along the track between Udford Rise Wood and Struma Wood, the Alsatians just in front of me. My heavy blackthorn stick was under my arm and my hands in my pockets. I had a .450 British Bulldog revolver loaded in my right hand - it was comforting. In my left pocket I had a pair of steel handcuffs of the old pattern.

We crossed the field towards Cave Wood. I looked across the valley towards Hornby Hall. I could hear the river below me, and see the woods on the far bank darker than the sky. The rain was coming harder. It was a miserable night and only about 11 o'clock. High Barn Cottage would be the best place to be. I could at least keep dry there. Reaching Cave Wood, I climbed over the gate onto the field to the right of the wood, where a stone wall ran all the way to the cottage. I put my dogs on their leads as I knew that some cattle had been on that field a day or two earlier.

The wind was getting up, the rain coming in my face. I could feel my thick trousers were wet. I stood still, the dogs would tell me if and where the cattle were. No response from the dogs, maybe the cattle had been moved elsewhere? I thought if the cattle were on the field at all, they would be sheltering in the corner between High Barn Cottage and the wood. I walked out into the middle of the field, then turned back towards the High Barn Wood. The wind was much stronger out on the field and my head was down.

I heard a noise. My dogs had turned towards Struma Wood - the bloody cattle had been behind the wood. I know that the suckler cows had big calves with them and that they would chase any dog. 'Come on!' I set off at a fast walk. The cattle were galloping now and my dogs were pulling me back - Simba wanted to have a go at them. Galloway cattle being black couldn't be seen but the noise was frightening - they could have stampeded over me. I had had one accident with cattle at Mapleton and I certainly did not want another dose.

I slipped the dogs' leads and they disappeared in the dark. I set off quickly towards High Barn Wood as it was nearest. Head down against the weather I was suddenly nearly thrown to the ground - the shock caught me behind the knees. I had walked into an electric fence. My trousers being soaked, earthed the current and it seemed ages before it stopped. I was shaking all over.

Rolling under the wire I stood, the wind and rain quite soothing after the excitement of the last few minutes. I whistled for my dogs, where they had been I don't know but I know they had lured the cattle away from me. They were splattered with mud and were panting, but their tails were wagging, in fact they appeared pleased with themselves!

Poachers or no poachers, I was away home. By the time I had fed the pair and given them a good patting and talked to them, then put them up for the night, I had recovered. My clothes were put to dry, I had a bath and a bite, later a nip of whisky. I sat a long while by the fire knowing that I would be turning out again and again, regardless of the weather. That is the price the conscientious keeper pays. If I had gone to bed every night I would have lain wondering what the morning would bring?

I have walked the woods the morning after poachers have been at work - feathers on twigs, down the trees and a heap on the ground - the fruits of the season's work gone. There is nothing romantic about the poacher, he is a thief and he will take other things too. Many a night I have stood at a wood side, waiting, in fact, hoping, for them to come. Who knew what would happen with armed men roaming the woods in search of game, greedy for money? At the same moment, a keeper lies in wait, tired by nights patrolling his ground. I remember well, my blood was up when my birds were being stolen. I could be out of a job if there was nothing to shoot when my master came. I could be out of my home, where would we go? The torch came on - I fired and fired again hoping to hit the poacher. I hated him, he was worse than any fox!

Poacher at High Barn
High Barn, the cottage, had been empty for many years. The barn and house were all under one roof built of red sandstone. Some loose boxes for cattle stood in front of it and in the centre of the yard was a midden. The barn was in use and was part full of hay. I had spent many hours there during the nights when out watching for poachers. From the front of the house there was a grand view to the west to the Lake District with Saddleback and Skiddaw mountains. At the back of High Barn Cottage there were only two small upstairs windows which overlooked the east fellside towards Alston.

High Barn Wood stood almost up to the cottage, with just a track between them. If you turned your back to the house and walked along the wood side, you came to a gate. Through the gate, a ride led you to another gate at the east side of the wood overlooking Udford Lane. Douglas Firs, larch, sycamore and rhododendron grew at High Barn - in fact it was a nice wood and had some superb views from all four sides and a wall surrounded the whole wood.

I was out watching, about 11 o'clock one quiet frosty night. Just as I was below High Barn, some pigeons flew out. I stood listening. Simba was with me. I put him on the chain. He was pointing up at the wood. I heard a shot and more pigeons took to wing, passing over where we stood. Simba whined with excitement. I shushed him and he lay down. I opened the field gate and we walked along the wall side which led to the wood. It was uphill. When we arrived at the top we stopped by the gate which led into the wood. I had heard two more shots as we walked up the field.

We stayed by the top iron gate listening. Simba was fidgeting about, wanting to be away. I started to get over the gate knowing that it was fastened with wire. Simba pulled backwards and slipped his lead. I was unbalanced and grabbed the gate top rail to save myself. The gate turned over, me underneath it because it was off the hinges at the far end.

I got myself up and rubbed myself where the gate had trapped me, then lifted the gate and propped it as it must have been before. I heard a shout from inside the wood as if someone was in trouble. Simba had someone cornered, 'Hold him, hold him,' I called to my dog. All went quiet then more shouts. This time from the cottage side of the wood, I called again 'Hold him Simba.'

I set off along the wood side towards High Barn Cottage, over the gate in the field corner, turning right at the end of the wood I stood still listening. All was quiet and I didn't want to shout again in case I was near the poachers. Minutes later I walked quietly towards the cottage, coming to the gate half way along the wood side I stopped again. All was still, I wondered what had happened, where was Simba? Leaning against the wall I waited. Something had to make a noise - if the poachers were still in the wood, where was Simba? I heard a dog panting coming towards me. 'Simba,' I called quietly. The dog came up to me, he was limping.

I put my hand down to him, he was wet. I tried to see him close, but it was too dark. No point in hanging about now. We made our way home and I took Simba into the kitchen. Joan was already in bed. The wet on his coat was blood - the dog's right shoulder was swollen and there was a deep cut almost to the bone. I dressed it as best I could then gave him a feed and left him in the kitchen. I went to bed wondering what I would find in High Barn Wood the next day.

I arrived at High Barn Wood just as it was starting to get light. one or two pheasants were starting to fly from their roosts, evidently the commotion during the night had not put every bird out of the wood. Daylight was slow in coming. It looked in fact as if maybe it would be one of those winter days, cold, grey and miserable.

I walked along the field side, at the north side of the wood it had been barley, now it had been ploughed - not much to be seen there. I decided to have a look down the belt of trees that ran down the field towards the Caves and Honeypot Farm. At the gate before the farm there were some fresh boot marks. Could they have been the poachers? They could have belonged to the farm men, who knows?

It was a bit lighter by now. I made my way to the gate at High Barn Wood where Simba came to me after the commotion the previous night. The walls by the gate had been built so as the gate stood actually in the wood - the bend in the wall enabled timber to be extracted easier when felling took place. Here in a corner by the gate the wet ground was much churned up in a half circle. Outside the churned ground were the marks of a dog's paws going backwards and forwards. This then was what the shouting had been about - Simba had caught someone thereabouts. The poacher had been at bay there. The dog had evidently had hold of him and been thrown backwards and forwards in his bid to escape.

As I bent to look closer I found a piece of iron pipe, 18" long and bent slightly. One end of it was worn shiny by being held in someone's hand. So now I had found the weapon that had caused the wound on my dog's shoulder - what if the poacher had hit my dog on the head? No point in searching the wood now, I carried on with my work.

All day it was on my mind that the person who carried that piece of iron pipe had carried it a long while. Later I got hold of two walkie-talkie radios. I took one with me and left the other with my wife with instructions to 'phone the police if I should need them. The range of these radios was very short and there was much interference owing to the hilly terrain I was working in.

I was young and could be quick tempered when pushed. I hated poachers - they made my life hard. They were worse than any fur and feather vermin. I have tried many ways to make it as difficult as possible for the night poacher. He is the one that does much harm if he goes into a wood the night before a big shoot as the disturbance will spoil the next day's sport for sure. I have known keepers that hardly ever turn out watching but spend the evenings in public houses. I have heard them say, 'Oh, I never have any trouble with poachers.' Where there are pheasants perched on the trees, there are poachers and always will be. The lazy keeper encourages it. Being out and being seen at all hours is the best deterrent I know.

The villains at Big Wood Cottage

The barley was just starting to turn in the field in front of Big Wood Cottage. Some new folks had arrived there and were to work on the estate farms, so I was told. One weekend just after the new people had settled in, I happened to be on my way to the river. The young pheasants that I had put out into the wood could usually be seen out on the track that led to Big Wood Cottage. Today none could be seen, but half a dozen people were walking through the barley, strung out in line. It was obvious what was going on - they were after the young pheasants. I drove up the cornfield side and when these young fellows saw me get out of the Land Rover they started out of the corn. I asked them what they were up to and was told that they were chasing rabbits. Having told them who I was and that they had no rights to catch any game on the estate, they left. I then decided to keep a close watch on Big Wood Cottage.

I was very uneasy with what I had seen that day. the young people I had seen in the corn looked suspect. It hadn't taken them long to start chasing the game and there was plenty of it in Big Wood.

The following Saturday I was looking at the local paper where I read that the rail line through Penrith was to be electrified and the equipment was being stored at the Station Yard, Penrith. Some drums of copper cable worth many thousands of pounds had been stolen the night before, along with a transit van belonging to Frank Jackson, the knacker man from Penrith. The police believed the stolen van had been used in the raid on the railway yard.

As usual, I was out early feeding my pheasants. It was a nice warm morning, no wind and all was quiet. I finished feeding in Round End Wood and stood looking towards Big Wood. A black column of smoke rose into the sky. It was coming up from the direction of Big Wood Cottage. What was going on there at 6am on a Sunday morning? I shifted myself quickly to the Big Wood. It took about ten minutes to reach the clearing where the cottage stood - what a busy lot they were, the new occupiers.

Keeping well hidden I watched them at work. A large fire was burning in the cleared area where some drums of black coated electric cable lay. Stacked by the fire was a pile of cable cut up into short lengths, about a foot long, ready to be put in the fire. I could make out the ends of many pieces that were already burning. Black smoke was coming from the cottage chimney - they were burning it in there as well. I stayed long enough to make sure I could recognise them all again then made my way home as quickly as possible and telephoned the police. I was standing by the gate when the police and CID arrived. They took me as far as the entrance to Big Wood and let me out.

The whole gang of villains were caught while they were working, burning the stolen cable, and all were arrested. Later in the day I was down by Langwathby Bridge. In a field just below the bridge

I came across some tyre marks leading to the riverbank. The marks were of a similar type to those a transit van makes. The stolen van had backed up to the river and several drums of cable had been rolled into a deep pool. I contacted the police again and all the remaining cable was recovered. There was no reward apart for my having got rid of the villains at Big Wood.

It was a load off my mind. They were gaoled. They had only been there a few short weeks but what would it have been like had they not been found out? Had the villains burned the cable in the dark of night they might have got away with it. The early keeper like the early bird! The police never thanked me and I never received any reward or thanks from the railway people - nowt queerer than folks!

The vermin rail or gibbet

The way the keeper showed that he was about his work and doing his job correctly was by display of his vermin, killed one way or another. The 'vermin rail' as it was sometimes called was usually in or alongside a wood or on a wire fence where the victims from traps and snares or which had been shot or poisoned were hung.

Some estates paid a bonus on vermin killed. Tails were cut off or a foot and every so often the head keeper would collect these and pay the keeper his bonus. What you saw on the rail or gibbet was many weeks work by the keeper - countless hours sitting out with a gun, patrolling his beat - to account for all the vermin such as hedgehogs, rats, stoats, weasels, grey squirrels,

Dressed up for a Victorian day.

foxes, cats, badgers, carrion crows, jackdaws, jays, hawks of all kinds and owls. These were to be seen hung stinking in warm weather, to gradually decay and dry out into mummified shapes.

Badgers and other creatures were skinned and some of the feathers from bird wings brought a few bob. These were sold to Horace Friend at Wisbech, Cambridgeshire, who was a fur and feather dealer. Prices were as follows:

Otter skins	each	88 shillings
Badger skins	each	44 shillings
Jay wings	pair	1/6
Jackdaw throat	pair	3d
Starling wings	pair	2d
Stoat skins	each	1/6
Weasel skins	each	1/-
Rabbit skins	each	3d
Hare skins	each	1/-
Fallow deer skins	each	1/6
Fox skins		No sale
Mink	each	20 shillings
Moles		No sale

Later on mink made an appearance. I sold these alive at £1 each. I shot 600 starling in the winter of 1963 and received £5 for them at 2d the pair. The term vermin applied to any animal or bird that happened to destroy the game which the keeper is preserving for shooting. Later on in the season the old keepers before the First World War had no mercy on the wildlife about them. Little thought was given when a keeper could be put out of his job and his home for not having enough game to shoot.

Traps of various sizes were set wherever vermin was suspected. Many and ingenious were these traps - some as small as 2" jaws for setting on rat runs, some other traps large enough to catch badgers and foxes with jaws set at 9" or 10". The trap most used was the 4" gin trap called a rabbit trap - this was the game keeper's mainstay.

Pole traps were a round shape and used on top of a pole or stake - these were used for winged vermin - owls, hawks, jays, crows and other birds that like to sit high up to scan the land about them for prey. Snares were used in hundreds for rabbit catching, but also for foxes, badgers, cats, etc.

Poison too was widely put down - usually in eggs in the spring when there are plenty of eggs about. These were for crows, jays, magpies, etc. Desperate gamekeepers who had been losing birds to vermin would lay baits dosed with poison, particularly when foxes are feeding cubs on ground that does not belong to them and where foxes are being preserved. Some estates kept foxes for hunting and others had game for shooting - then the keeper had a right headache for the two do not mix - it's one or the other. Vermin and game do not live happily together. The vermin always win and as soon as all the game has been killed in one area it will move to the next and repeat the process.

The strange next
I often saw Joe. He was my nearest neighbour and his bungalow stood behind a low hill across the road, among a few trees. Joe Morton was a widower and a retired farmer. He was a very quiet man and kept a few sheep on the bit of land in front of his home. One day Joe was leaning on the wall and, seeing me, he called could I come over for a minute. 'Now Joe, how are ya?' I asked. 'Ho, nit so bad tha nows,' he said.

The lambing had started so I asked how they were doing at Bank Hall, Joe's old home. 'Well, that's what I wanted to see you about Brian. Andrew's having fox trouble, lost some already. He has only just got started. It's not good having early lambs up yonder. I wonder if you could do owt for him?' I knew the farm, we had been there at times for clockers.

Bank Hall lay under the fell and was isolated - just it and a small bit of another farm adjoining it with miles of the eastern fells towering over the farms - it was wild country. It was late April and I could afford a couple of days to look the fells over for Andrew. I told Joe that I would go next day and do what I could but I would not promise anything.

The weather was sunny but cold, ideal for a tramp on the fells. I looked forward to the outing. Early next morning I arrived at Bank Hall Farm. Andrew had the ewes on the low fields behind the buildings. We talked a short while and then he went back to his lambing. Gun under my arm and a spyglass slung about my shoulder, I took to the fell, climbing gradually and picking my way. I was soon a few hundred feet above the farm.

I stopped for a minute and looked about me, what a view! To the west I looked across the Eden Valley, Skiddaw and Saddleback all in snow - it had been worth the climb just to look at the view. Andrew's farm was in miniature. The sheep were blobs of white almost like snowflakes. The sun was bright and at times warm, but I had not come to look at the views. I scanned the fell side for anything that looked as though it may house a family of foxes. Still climbing and moving diagonally across the fell side, I made my way eastwards towards Appleby. Large patches of snow lay in the hollows. These I avoided as I knew that some old mine entrances were about these fells - these could be home for any foxes thereabouts.

I had left the few trees in the first hundred feet or so of my climb and shortly after the last of the thorn bushes, the fell side was bare - just boulders and coarse grass with heather patches. I stopped now and then and spied the ground. If I saw anything that could hold a litter of cubs I went to investigate. I came to a deep gill. It was full of snow, many feet deep. I reckon a house could have been buried beneath it easily. It took me a long while to skirt the chasm. By midday I had walked or scrambled about two miles and sat for my sandwiches among the heather. I hadn't found anything at all that looked as though cubs were in residence. Setting off again I turned my face to the north towards Carlisle. Again I climbed diagonally across the fell, most of it under heather and many more patches of snow. It was harder going with more snow to go around.

By 3pm I was above Bank Hall Farm again and carried on the same line for about a mile. I was a bit tired now so I turned again towards Appleby, gradually descending, stopping to spy the ground about me but there was nothing to draw me to it for an inspection. I was a couple of hundred feet above where the thorn bushes grew when something shone white in a bush. It was about eight feet off the ground and I made my way to have a look. It was worth the effort, well worth it. A carrion crow nest took up a quarter of the bush. It was completely made of bones with pieces of bailer twine interwoven. Sitting looking at the nest I wondered at its construction - thigh and shoulder bones of sheep, ribs and back vertebrae, just about every bone from sheep. Sheep wool lined the inside of the 'strange nest'. The helm winds of the east fells are well known for their fierceness yet this pile of bones built by birds had withstood them.

Making my way gradually downwards, towards the farm, my mind went back to the strange nest. The bones of at least two sheep would have been needed for a nest that size. Evidently the crows had preferred bones to the usual twigs - probably the bones were lying handy, why not use them? Arriving at the farm I told Andrew that I had not been able to locate the foxes and told him of the strange nest. He had seen it earlier and being a farmer he had not thought it queer! I made for Edenhall. What a story for my girls, they would have to see the strange nest. How Andrew managed with the fox I didn't hear. He must have done alright or I would have heard.

Farmer and keeper
One thing the keeper must not do is fall out with the farmer. I know at times he can be a pain, always on the want, but being on the land he is in a position to do much harm. Farmers allow their dogs to roam the fields and hedges in the spring when game birds are nesting, harassing the game when young among the hay and corn. At this time of year many young birds can be destroyed, not being strong enough on the wing to escape. Ducks on the ditches and boggy fields are easily killed before fledging, therefore the keeper needs the farmer as a friend.

The farmer too needs the keeper when crops are being damaged. I have been asked by farmers in the spring to shoot rooks on fresh sown fields. The rook more than pays for the small amount of seed it eats by way of following the plough and harrows. Many are the small grubs it devours. I would fire a few shots, kill a couple of rooks and hang them from a stick in the centre of the field. The farmer would know I had done my bit.

When the sugar beet is small, being just gapped out, hares will eat their way across a field, leaving the young plants lying. A lot of damage is done where hares are plentiful. I was always on the look out for hare damage and have been out on the fields early in the morning and picked up the tops of beet and turnips that were nipped off. The farmer is right to complain, his livelihood is at stake. I did what I could to keep the farmer from taking his gun and killing every hare in sight. Later in the year, pigeons gather in flocks. They descend on the fields where the corn is laid flat by the weather. Usually the keeper will know a reliable person that likes a bit of shooting, who will be willing to sit in a hide with decoy pigeons put out. This usually suits the farmer - he is getting the help he needs, the pigeons are being thinned out.

Moles are busy in the spring - they appear to be everywhere. They are the farmer's responsibility. I have seen farmers stand at mole hills, gun in hand waiting for the soil to be shoved up, then firing. Professional mole catchers were sometimes too busy to get to every farm. I have many times taken my traps and set a field where the young beet plants were being ravaged by moles working shallow runs. Deep runs at the side of field are the main runs and a trap set properly in these will continue to catch most of the year.

On one estate I know of there was a wood beside a field of corn that had laid flat owing to wet weather. A lot of young pheasants had been released. The young birds soon found the laid corn and at times a couple of hundred of them could be seen picking at it. The farmer asked his landlord to do something about it, but being a stubborn chap, the landlord did nothing.

The tenant farmer had to be careful what he did, so he asked the war agricultural people what he could do. They sent two of their pest control men who stood on that cornfield and shot any pheasants that strayed on the laid corn. In the end the landlord was sent a bill for the two men's time and the cost of the cartridges.

In another place I remember the village pond was surrounded by willows and at one end there was a mass of reeds and rushes. Moorhens lived there and bred successfully. One year a field adjoining the pond was sown with spring wheat. A dozen of these moorhens could be seen wandering about. I received a complaint from the tenant farmer via the estate office. The birds were eating all the seed corn so I must do something about it. I got a few chaps together and shot around the pond. We let it be known that X number of moorhens had been killed. The farmer, like others, must have a growl - wildlife seemed to bother 'em at times.

The mere sight of a rabbit would set the farmer cursing the bloody keeper. 'Why can't he get the damned rabbits killed down?' Before myxomatosis, rabbits were everywhere. On light soil they bred quickly and were a big problem. Where crops were being grown it was a never ending job. If the rabbits were left alone for a while, the crops were eaten back from the field edges many yards. The land was tainted with the piss and droppings. Farmers were entitled to kill them themselves or hire someone to do the job. The person doing the killing must have written permission from the farmer. If the farm belonged to an estate, the gamekeeper would demand to see the written permission, otherwise that person could be had for poaching ground game.

Rabbits have caused much trouble, and the farmer would readily agree to someone hunting them but a word of mouth agreement is not enough. The keeper maybe has never seen the chap before. He is doing his rounds and comes upon a man with ferrets, nets and maybe a whippet plus a rabbit or two. When challenged he says the farmer gave him permission. The keeper if doing his job right takes the man, rabbits and nets to the farm where he enquires of the farmer did he have permission to kill rabbits on his land. 'Aye, course he did. He's alright, leave him alone, keeper. He's doing a good job, doing what you should be doing!'

Being put down, the keeper tries to smooth the situation over. 'Would you please write on a piece of paper your permission and the chap's name. That way I won't bother him again.' 'What's up keeper? Don't yer believe me?' Keeper, 'Sorry, word of mouth's not good enough.' The rabbits have come between the farmer and the keeper. Next day the keeper turns up to start killing down the rabbits. He tries hard to win the farmer back.

When sparrows abound they are a threat to some crops such as wheat. About harvest time large flocks gather. They keep to the hedges besides the fields, descending on the corn stalks to eat corn and much damage was done if they are left alone. Farmers encouraged young lads who usually had a catapult or air gun to hunt the birds. As a young chap I had a muzzle loading shot gun and using very small shot called sparrow dust, because it was almost like sand, I spent much time shooting at these droves of sparrows. No doubt I killed many of them but still the flocks persisted. I fed the dead birds to my ferrets. Dad said that people ate sparrows during the 1914-18 War. I never tried them.

After the harvest was got in the sparrows followed the corn stacks, barns and granaries if they could get into the buildings. Sparrows were always considered fair game for the lads and many hours were spent hunting them with the 'catty' or air gun. I made wire netting traps that would catch a dozen or more when set at a feed place. Rats were always to be found about the farm buildings. Farms varied, some where over-run with them, while there were others where the farmer took a pride in his place and would wage all out war against them.

Gamekeepers set traps in every hedge and wall or ditch all year round. Many rats were caught coming and going to the sugar beet fields from the farms. Rats will infest a ditch besides a corn or sugar beet field, using old rabbit holes under a hedge, walls and drains as well. On one estate where I was a keeper, Warfarin was mixed with meal in large quantities. Two keepers working together would carry a small dustbin full of poison to where the rats were and using a long handled spoon, place two spoonfuls in every hole. I have seen us use a bin full of poison around a couple of beet fields where rats swarmed. For two days the holes were fed with Warfarin, then we missed the third day. On the fourth day when all the poisoned bait had been eaten we fed them again, that was enough to clear them.

I remember going to a farm that was infested with rats. There were some drains that were being used by them. A few chaps armed with shovels and sticks were set to watch a drain apiece. A hosepipe was inserted and the water turned on full bore. Shortly after the rats started to bolt. Several were killed, a few escaped down unmarked drains. Cats are not the answer. I have lived at a farm where many cats were but still rats abounded. The cats would sit on the window sill waiting to be fed while rats ran about below them. It is always wise to leave a stoat or weasel where there are corn stacks. They will kill and eat the rats. You seldom find rats and mice in the same stack.

Small bitch ferrets were used for bolting rats. Rat bites can turn nasty and many good ferrets have been lost that way. I have used safety fuse where there is no risk of fire. A length of fuses is shoved down one hole - if there were a lot of holes about, I would stop some of them up. Some good sport can be had with terriers and a gun. I have set a small mesh net around a poultry cabin where rats are, then set about bolting them with smoke from burning sacking or safety fuse. Snares are easily made for rat catching. Two strands of brass wire are enough with a long thin hazel wand shoved into the soil and bent over. The snare was attached and set across the rat run. It would hang them when triggered. Rats travel at speed among the corn.

Boosting the bag

Looking back, there was a bit of rivalry between keepers. I asked one keeper after a shoot, 'What did you finish up with? What was the bag?' I was told the headage of game killed, the keeper adding the shooting was nowt smart, they could have killed much more.

Later on I met a chap that was a beater that day. 'I hear that the guns were a poor lot.' The chap replied, 'There wasn't much to shoot anyway.'

I remember one keeper I worked under when the pheasants were in season. On the evening before a shoot I was sent with a .410 gun and a pocket full of cartridges to walk the boundary hedges of the estate. There were some root fields there and a fair amount of wild pheasants which were roosting in the tall bushes thereabouts. I shot a dozen birds. Later that night they were hung in a loose box adjacent to the game larder and locked up safe. The next day when the game was being hung up from the morning's shooting, the keeper sneaked my birds among the rest. A nice addition to the total bag at the day's end.

Late in the pheasant shooting season, after Christmas, usually cocks only are shot. Cribs and other catchers are put out on the feed rides for the birds to get used to prior to catching the hen birds for the laying pens. The keeper I worked with asked, 'Many cocks feeding lad?' I told him that such and such a wood was feeding well, plenty of cocks there. 'Right,' he said 'I want you to set the catchers for an hour on Friday morning. Take some sacks, let all the hens go, keep all the cocks, put 'em in the feed cabin. Say nowt, you hear?' 'Aye, alright, I'll say nowt.'

The keeper and I went with our van for the sacks of birds. Later that day he killed them. Over thirty cocks were hung close to where the game larder stood and were eventually quietly hung among the rest of the game from the day's shooting. Again they were to boost the day's bag.

Frank Siddall

I had been doing my rounds and had just left Cave Wood which was on Honeypot Farm land. It was a late November afternoon and already the light was starting to go. I followed the wall, my head down against the rain. 'Now Keeper, owsta gitting on?' Frank Siddall asked. He was leaning on the wall opposite me - I hadn't seen him, my thoughts were elsewhere.

White whiskers covered what I could see of Frank's face, a sack or sacks covered the rest of him. He was eighty years old and still pulling turnips. 'Been a bad day, Frank,' I said. 'Aye, I've seen warse many a time,' he answered. It was Friday the next day and would be a shooting day. 'Do you think it would be possible to leave this field quiet tomorrow, Frank?' I asked. 'I would think so, we hev all the feed we want now, keeper. I suppose thou will be gang for a pint toneet keeper?' 'I reckon I will, Frank, shall have earned yan by the time I get done wark.' 'Well keeper, if thou gits as much pleasure out of spending as I git out of saving, thou will be a happy man and have a lot of pleasure out of life.'

Frank Siddall was a wealthy man. The family owned three large farms and three of his nephews looked after them, all being excellent farmers themselves. I was told that each evening when dinner was over, Frank sat alone after the others departed, a piece of paper and a pencil in front of him. Frank spent the evening working out what he was worth. On the Farmers' Day Shoot, Frank would turn up and eventually ask, 'Hest a few cartridges, keeper?' His old hammer gun had seen better days, the breech leaver was held back with a bit of elastic.

I remember Frank coming up to me after the day finished. 'Here you are, Frank,' said I and handed him a brace of pheasants. 'I think it's about time I gave thee a drink, keeper.' He shoved a ten shilling note into my hand. Not so bad was it - ten shillings (50p) for eight years shooting! Frank Siddall was the old type - a gentleman, a great farmer, a quiet man and best of all, he looked after his money. But like the rest of 'em you only have it while you're alive. Frank in the end took nowt with him, it went to the three nephews.

The hatching yard and rearing field

Once the vermin has been dealt with, the rearing season was upon you and for some weeks the rearing ground was the main place of work. Even so if there was any spare time the tunnels would be looked at and I never eased up on the vermin.

Some estates rear many partridges and some pheasants, other estates rear only pheasants. I have worked on all types of estates. If I found a partridge nest that was in a place where the bird could be disturbed, I would wait until she had finished laying her nest full. You can tell when she has finished laying because the eggs will not be covered over - while the bird is still laying she will always cover her eggs. I would take all the eggs from the nest and place dummy ones in their place. The good eggs would be set under a broody bantam and then date marked on the sitting box when they would hatch. When the partridge eggs start to chip, about the 23rd day, I would put them in a woollen stocking and go to where I had taken them from in the first place. If the partridge was still sitting tight, I would gently poke her off her nest. The birds would usually only go a few feet away and stay there. Next, I would take out the dummy eggs and put the hatching eggs back. The partridge will be back on the nest very quickly. This was called the 'Euston System', as it was invented on the Euston Estate.

When sitting game eggs under hens or bantams, a hatching yard is used. An area of level ground in a quiet place where it is sheltered from the winds and weather is chosen. It should be enclosed about with wire netting about four feet high held there by strong posts and a way in left by folding the netting back. The sitting boxes are usually in a battery of six with lift up lids. Some boxes have a door that lets down at the front, while other keepers use a coop. Before anything else is done, the boxes are set out in rows. A space of four feet and then another row, four feet and another row and so on - fifty nests to the row.

Next a hole is made inside each box about nine inches across and about two and a half inches deep. This is formed with a wooden mallet to form the shape of a nest. When each box has had its nest made, we take some good hay, shake it out and line the hole, making a nice attractive nest. It can take a long while to make a yard full of them and it helps if the hay is damped with water. Next we put two or three dummy eggs in each nest. These are made of pot or china or maybe even wood.

Between the rows of sitting boxes, hazel sticks are stuck in the ground, one for each next box. The sticks have a fork on top cut that way and stand about two feet high. Each of these sticks has a tether on it and a large metal ring is placed over the stick. Before it is stuck in the ground the ring is fastened to a short piece of string or cord with a slip knot on it. When not in use the cord hangs on the forked top of the stick.

Water bowls are placed between the sticks so that four hens may all drink together. Once all that was done and the gamekeeper had plenty of eggs ready for setting, he would start to collect his broody hens or bantams. If we were going to set partridge eggs, then a bantam would cover twenty partridge eggs easily. Bantams are collected, either bought, borrowed or maybe we would use our own. The broodies are put in the sitting boxes and left for 24 hours to settle down. We fed the bantams with corn, a handful at each stick, and the water bowls were regularly washed out and filled.

At 9am as the day was warming up I would start at the end of the row of boxes, lifting the lid quietly. Usually the bantam would ruffle her feathers and start prating. I lifted her up gently, talking to her all the time. I held her with one hand, while with the other I took the cord from the forked stick and slipped the loop around the bantam's leg and put her down. Then I'd carry on along the row and do the same until all the broodies in the row were tethered and fed. It is a fine sight to see fifty hens eating and drinking. We let them off the nest for about twenty minutes and any nests that had been scratched up were re-made. After twenty minutes we put them all back on the dummy eggs. Using a shovel and scraper we would clean up all the droppings. That done, more feed is put down and fresh water put in the bowls and the next row of birds is taken off, and so on until the whole yard has been done. The work should never be rushed and the birds handled with care and talked to always. When the broodies have been down three days on the same eggs we will think about setting them proper.

Twenty-five bantams will be needed to set 500 partridge eggs - that would be one half row. On the day we set the eggs the birds are taken off the nests as usual and given a bit longer to feed as they will not be taken off the nest the next day. they will leave them 24 hours to let the eggs turn as it is called. When they have all been put back in the boxes and settled down, 500 partridge eggs were brought to the yard on trays having been sorted out. I started at the rear end of the row, lifting the box lid and gently sliding my hand under the broody I would take away all the sham eggs and give the bantam twenty partridge eggs. After closing the lid the process was repeated until the row was set with partridge eggs. The setting day is marked on the end box and the date when the eggs are due to hatch. The idea is to set one row of boxes a week until all the eggs are set.

Some estates rear many birds while others rear fewer, depending on the estate owner. He may be a keen shot or on the other hand just a casual shot, wanting just a bit of shooting for the family at Christmas. Most keepers years ago would have an oil incubator or two. These were put to use when the broodies started to hatch the eggs. On the 23rd day some of the partridge eggs would start to chip. That meant the chick in the shell starts to cut its way out of the shell. At this stage some hens start to shuffle about a bit and if so the chicks can be crushed.

The hens are not taken off on the 23rd day, but the keeper will inspect the boxes and if he finds a broody that is clumsy, he takes away all the chipped eggs and puts them in the incubator to hatch thus saving some lives. On the 24th day we went to the yard with some cardboard boxes with hay in them. These are for carrying the chicks to the rearing field. Corn and water was put out for the hens and they are treated very carefully as chicks will be tucked under their wings. The chicks ran about as soon as the mother was taken off. The chicks were caught and put in the carrying boxes and put in a warm place for a short while. When all was ready, the good hens are taken off their nests and carried in clean hessian sacks, about three to a sack, to the rearing fields.

During the time the hatching yard has been worked, the rearing field would be prepared. A good, dry field was chosen if possible, such as a meadow with plenty of clover, kidney vetch, lucerne and lots of insects and nice short grass. The coops, runs and pens are put out a few days before the chicks are due to arrive. The grass under the coops is cut short. Traps will have been placed about the field weeks before and any vermin will have been attended to.

Usually a cabin on wheels will have been towed onto the field and a stove or boiler with it. The cabin will hold all the feed for the birds, plus extra traps, cartridges and a gun, and various assortments of medicines. The keeper will spend much of his time in that field and the hut will be his second home for a while. The first lot of chicks are brought and their mothers with them. The sacks with the mother hens are unloaded first. One hen is put in each coop and the front fastened up. She will be left for a few minutes to settle down, then once she was quiet she would be given two chicks. Normally, as soon as the mother hen hears the chicks she will start clucking and maybe a bit restless. So much care and a bit of time was needed. Once the mother hen had settled down she was given the rest of her family until she had twenty chicks.

After a few hours the coop front may be taken off and the chicks let out. With coops two pieces of board in the shape of a 'V' were fastened to the sides of the coop and used for the first day. Care was taken as the chicks soon learned to get over the boards and cannot get back their mother. With coops and pens the chicks cannot wander far and with the moveable pens the keeper does not have to stay on the field all the time.

Partridge feed on the field

On the field by the cabin would be an iron boiler and plenty of firewood, plus a supply of hen eggs, usually crates of them. About fifty eggs at a time were put into a sack and the sack placed in the boiling water until the eggs were hard. They were then taken out to cool. A large mincer mounted on a table is part of the equipment of the keeper and a fair sized table with raised sides for mixing on. When the chicks were about two days old, their feed consisted of hard boiled eggs. The eggs were put through the mincer along with the shells. When enough eggs were done they were tipped out onto the mixing table with a bit of fine biscuit meal and soya meal mixed in to dry them a little. That would be the feed for the first few days.

In the second week, the feed was changed a bit. The chicks were given small crumbs of biscuit meal which were scalded until fairly soft and some fine 'greaves' - which is fine cut, dried meat boiled to make it soft and the water drained off. All this is tipped on the mixing table and rubbed through the hands with fine biscuit and soya meal to dry it off and stop the lot sticking together. When it has cooled enough it is fed to the chicks. They only need a little as they will be finding insects and seeds in the grass.

In the third week, the meat or greaves are a slightly larger size. In the fourth week a little more greaves and by now no eggs at all will be fed. In the fourth and fifth weeks some kibbled wheat and maize was added to the feed. Kibbled wheat and maize is corn that has been split so that it is the right size for the poults to eat. Between four and five weeks the partridges are well grown and are taken to where they will be released, maybe on the headland of a sugar beet field or the corner of a potato field. An open space close to some cover is what they need, somewhere they can dust themselves and feel safe.

The pheasant keeper has much the same system of work with his pheasants. The feed is similar or the same as for partridges. But when the pheasant poults are five to six weeks old and well grown, they are taken into the woods. If possible they do better on the edge of the wood as they get more sunlight.

When the poults were to be moved, tractors and trailers were laid on and a pile of hessian sacks was at hand. Pheasants are best moved in the early morning when the day is young and still cool as the birds have been shut in all night. The birds are moved in the following way. Two men each holding the corner of a sack ease back the coop and slowly put the stretched sack under the coop. Thus the hen and all the poults are now standing on the sack. Two more men then each take hold of the sack and coop and place the whole on the trailer. If the job is done correctly no poults will escape or be injured.

To the wood

Once the trailer was loaded, the tractor would go slowly to the wood that is to be their home. Men will have been busy a few days before clearing the rides on the edge of the wood of all the growth - briers, docks and the rest. As the tractor is driven along the ride, the coops complete with the sacks will be put out at intervals, facing each other across the ride. That way the mother hens can see in all directions and warn the young birds of any danger.

The coops then have the sacks slowly pulled from underneath them and the keeper standing behind the coop will quietly reach over and take off the shutter - just enough to let the poults out one at a time a while later. That done, and all being quiet, the keeper will whistle and feed the birds and give them water. There would be a cabin in the wood for storing feed and providing shelter for the keeper who would spend many days there among his birds. Lamps would be hung along the rides at night to help keep away foxes, as the first few days and nights were a worrying time for the keeper. The wood will have been trapped and all possible done to make the wood safe for the poults.

Once the birds are established in the wood or covet, some people think that this was the end of the hard work. They were very wrong. Now I speak for myself, as three times a day I would feed the young birds and all the feed was still boiled and made as attractive for them as possible. The old ways died hard on some estates where the old type of keepers were in charge. I almost lived with my birds the first month after they went to the wood.

If a keeper had to rear say a thousand birds, they were more than likely split up into three or four lots and put into different woods and each wood had to be looked after. It was a busy time - wood to get for the boiler, feed to cart to the cabin, feed to mix, traps to look at, lamps to clean and fill each day with oil and water to carry for the birds. At the keeper's home there would be dogs to exercise, feed and clean out as well as ferrets to look after. The hatching yard would be finished with by now and all the boxes taken up, cleaned and stored away. The fence was taken down and tethers bundled up and stored away with the drinking dishes and all the tackle of the hatching yard. My average working day in August and September could be eighteen hours.

Partridge driving
Partridge shooting starts on the first day of September. The big shooting estates usually allow a week or two for the later hatched birds to grow and get strong on the wing before the shoots start. I would go on my rounds, looking at my traps and watching when the corn was being cut, trying to get some idea how the wild partridges had done. If it had been a very wet spring, the weather could reduce the coveys. Cold weather, too, would take a toll on the young birds, as well as vermin and diseases. Once the ground had been assessed and a fair idea of how many birds there were, the shoots could be planned.

The estate owner and the head keeper would walk the ground to be shot over. The fields where root crops were planted were noted as was which way the partridges would be driven to make the best shooting. Shooting butts or hides had to be erected where there were no hedges to stand behind. Alternative drives had to be arranged if there was a very strong wind and the birds' flight path would alter. There was much to do. The estate staff were usually brought in to help the keeper. The places where the guns stood would sometimes have the hedge tops trimmed or if the ground where the butt was sited was rough or uneven, it would be levelled out and stiles attended to. Hazel sticks with a cleft in the top end were placed at each stand, each with a number on a card stuck in the top from one to eight. After the drive each gun would move up one number. The keeper would notify the beaters who would help him on shooting day. Most beaters came from the estate or villages close at hand. I have had as many as thirty men and boys out on big days.

Two tractors with trailers were needed - one with straw bales on board for the beaters to sit on if there is a long distance between drives. The second tractor and trailer were used as the game cart and to carry anything else which was needed during the day. On the morning of the shoot the beaters meet at an arranged place. Sticks were given out and some men would be given a white flag as well. The men with flags will be older men and could be trusted - they were called 'flank men'. The beaters went with the keepers and neighbouring keepers are usually brought in to help.

Beaters are lined out and stubble and grass fields are driven in from a large area, usually into a root field of turnips or sugar beet. This being done, the guns take their positions at the numbered sticks. The flank men would be in position and everything ready. A whistle was blown and the line of beaters moved forward, their sticks stirring the leaves of the turnips. As the partridges started to get up and fly forwards the beaters are stopped occasionally, giving the guns time to deal with them. The flank men watch carefully and any birds that try to break out at the side have flags waved at them which is enough to turn them back into the drive.

If the field is very big, birds may drop down again only to be raised again later. Where hand reared partridges have been released, these birds can form large coveys, as many as a hundred or more and get into the air together. If there are large numbers much shooting is lost. If the keeper in charge of the drive keeps the beaters in hand this can sometimes be avoided. I have seen a great covey of hand reared partridges put on the wing and never be seen again that day or ever again! Hand reared birds don't have the homing instinct of the wild birds.

As the day progressed the coveys get split up and the shooting improves. As soon as one drive is finished the keeper will gather his beaters and start walking more ground into the root fields for the next drive. About 1pm the beaters have their lunch and a bottle of beer which is provided by the estate owner. Half an hour later and away they go again, with more ground to walk before the guns take up their positions for the next drive.

After the last drive of the day, all the beaters and dog men are given their pay and go home for a well earned rest. The game cart and the keeper and maybe one or two helpers will start to sort the day's bag at the yard where everything is hung up to cool. At the end of the day the game larder is an interesting place - apart from partridges, rabbits, hares, pigeons, snipe and maybe duck - years back I have had deer as well and some vermin. Then the keeper would go to the big house and into the gun room to set about cleaning the guns. It was a busy place. Most of the guest guns would have a loader with them and they would be busy cleaning guns. After all the jobs were done - game hung, guns cleaned, the guest guns given their present of game, usually two brace of partridges -

the keeper could, with luck, wander home, his dogs trailing behind, tired out. I always fed my dogs before I fed myself and saw that everything was alright.

Appleby Fair
The fair has changed quite a bit since I first visited Appleby and there are not as many horses in the town. I first went to the fair back in 1960. It was a lively place with people arriving from just about every part of the country, including Ireland and Scotland. There were dealers along the Flakebridge Lane where horses were put through their paces before prospective buyers. The men wore brown smocks and carried long whips and usually wore a brown velour hat. There were men in breeches and gaiters with smart tweed jackets, their caps sometimes cocked at an angle over their right ear. It was typical gear of the horseman of the 1920s and 1930s.

There were potters and tinkers everywhere. Some of them were shifty looking and couldn't look you in the eye. I remember seeing two chaps with a cardboard box large enough to lay out the cards and thimbles for the three card trick - 'Find the Lady' or 'Find the Pea'. These chaps would move about among the crowds, laying out the cards and keeping a sharp eye out for the police. Anyone wanting a bit of a flutter would put their money down and the cards would be moved around. The punter chose the card he thought was the Queen but seldom won. There was always an accomplice in the crowd who would be allowed to win a game or so. He was the bait to get more people playing, luring them in for the kill.

Some of the gypsies would be carrying bundles of whips and walking sticks which could be bought for a few shillings. Women would sell coloured paper flowers from baskets on their arms and maybe carry a child on their back fastened in an old blanket. Others would sell charms and pretend to read your fortune for a bit of silver. If you laughed at them they would curse you.

There were stalls full of brightly coloured china and the huckster would shout, 'I'll give you this and this at no extra cost. Who'll be the first?' One of his mates in the crowd would shout, 'I'll have it,' and wave a £5 note in the air. Soon heaps of china were being sold.

Old harness was for sale too, laid out on a tarpaulin or blanket - bits of leather with the stitching coming undone, rusty snafel bits that would make a horse's mouth sore. There would be tug chains and snigging chains, a box with tarnished brassed and medallions, head collars and lots of gear that had lain around for years including old leather gaiters, large, small, brown and black.

A man who badly needed a shave said, 'Pick what you like.' A horsey looking man held up a dented carriage lamp. 'Twenty-five shillings,' said the scruffy dealer. 'Too much,' said the chap beside me. 'Where do you want to be?' asked the dealer. 'Fifteen shillings,' said the horsey man. 'A quid and it's yours,' said the dealer. The deal was done as they were all over the fairground.

Goats, dogs, game cocks, singing birds, ferrets - they were all for sale. In all the years I've visited the fair though, I've never seen a cat. There are too many dogs and far too much noise for any self-respecting cat. On the hill trailers and caravans stood at all angles. Some of the vans had very ornate plate glass windows with patterns on them. Inside they had display cabinets shining with all kinds of crockery and fancy ornaments and always a dog of some kind by the step.

There were hooped 'vandows' the old type of caravan of varying sizes. Some were brightly painted while others hardly had a lick of paint on them, reflecting the personality of their owners. These hooped vans were usually drawn up in a circle around a communal fire and after a few days the area would be littered with every kind of refuse imaginable. There would be horse dung everywhere and in a dry time it would smell like a farm midden - though I must say it was much to my liking!

I would watch the smith shoeing ponies at the crossroads. It was always busy there with a row of horses tethered to the fence. Some of the mares had foals with them - they were many coloured ponies with many different shoe sizes and all breeds. Not all the horses at the fair were for sale. Some of them were there for their owners to put them through their paces and show them off. Suddenly there would be a shout, 'Look out!' The crowd would part for a horse and a lad riding bareback, leaning well back, his legs thrust forwards and his body almost lying on the animal's back. 'Look out!' shouted the rider, touching his mount with a stick. Sparks would fly from shoes as the horse fought to grip the slippery road. The crowd closed again until the next rider or driver came along.

Sulkies would race up and down, passing one another at a very fast speed. They were often home-built sulkies with steel shafts which I don't like as they're dangerous. I once saw a pair of sulkies collide - one horse was badly injured. Another time an old lady was knocked to the ground directly in front of me - why she was wandering around in the selling place heaven knows.

Police were much in evidence as were the RSPCA. They do a lot to look after the animals and make sure there's no cruelty. Years ago there was much misuse of the whip and many old animals were driven beyond the limits of endurance. An animal would go down and be whipped to its feet by its owner. Thank God only now and then do we hear of such cruelty these days, yet it can still happen in some quiet out of the way place.

Occasionally a couple of lads would put on a show. They would lay a blanket on the ground and square up to each other for a fight. It was always bare knuckle fighting and spectators would throw coins on the blanket and urge the pair on. Someone kept a look-out for the police as they would arrest the fighters since bare knuckle fighting is illegal and has been for many years. If the police were spotted approaching, the combatants swiftly bolted, but not before gathering up the blanket and their prize money!

Cock fights were held usually at the far side of the fair, nearest the fells, amongst the gorse bushes. Some of the gaming fraternity would gather in the evening with the birds that were to fight. They would stand in a circle and betting would start. Once that was done the birds were introduced to each other, held face to face by their owners. Steel spurs were fitted and the cocks were thrown into the middle of the circle and the fight began. I kept game cocks among my fowls at home. They would fight naturally but with spurs on there is only one end. If the loser is not killed outright, it will suffer much and in the end both birds may die of their wounds. It is not a nice sport and was outlawed many years ago.

Today many gypsies live in proper homes or in caravan sites. Many of the potters work as scrap metal gatherers, tarmac layers or firewood sellers. They turn up each year at Appleby for their annual holiday where they meet to remember the old times and even to get married. Some of what I call the 'lower types' take weeks to reach Appleby. Their wagons can be seen camped by the roadsides on the way to Appleby. They look scruffy, unshaven and their clothes are in a bad state, as is their accommodation. Everything about them looks neglected and their ponies could do with a good grooming - some of them in their winter coats, hiding the thinness of their bodies. Ponies that have wintered badly are usually not brought to the fair but left on a farm and retrieved at some later date. These animals will be sold later in the year when they have fattened.

Appleby town seethes, at times to bursting point, especially on sunny days. All roads into the town are congested and at the bridge police stop any horses entering the town proper. Horses stand between the road and the river on The Sands, some yoked to vehicles, and crowds of men stand nearby drinking from cans and talking horses.

Lads and girls lead ponies and horses down the steep riverbank and into the river where the animals are washed. The horse is ridden into the water and swims towards the bridge and the deepest water. Back on the Sands the pony is lathered with soap and given a rubbing all over. The lad then mounts his animal and into the river again to wash off the soap. Crowds of people throng the bridge to watch the horse being bathed. It is a very ancient bridge - I wonder how many fairs it has seen and how many gatherings on the Sands? It is repeated year after year - fresh faces arrive and old ones disappear - but the tradition goes on.

In the town the few cafes that open do a great trade from early morning till late evening. The pubs that open are crammed all day and night with crowds spilling out onto the streets. Some pub owners close down for fair week and board up their windows to protect the premises. No doubt some shopkeepers cash in during fair week as all the shops that are open are busy.

Drinking and horse talke is prevalent all over the town. Fights are common when old scores are settled and there are feuds between rival families. Occasionally a caravan is burned, a vehicle smashed or tyres lashed. Some of the feuds have lasted for years and the police are never called - the travellers prefer to settle their grievances in their own way.

There is a lot of gold on show - the travelling women are fond of showing it off. They have large earrings and chains about their necks, bangles, rings and chains of gold around their ankles. Some of them must have thousands of pounds of jewellry and they wear bright coloured dresses. Some of the people must have Romany blood as can be seen by their complexion and black hair which the women often wear in braids in Romany style. I've seen stalls of clothes for children in a dazzling display of colour with frills of lace. It would be difficult to describe them as they varied so much. Some of the toddlers were wearing these fancy clothes and looked just like dolls.

Brian Aston

I remember seeing a trailer with a flat cart on it with the shafts high in the air. The cart was painted in gold, red and black and there was a large 'For Sale' sign on it. On another old lorry there were some tree branches for the gypsies to have a bonfire.

The sanitary arrangements were very basic - a few sheets of corrugated iron nailed together and stood on end formed a small compound. A trench had been dug outside and inside there were metal troughs to catch the piss and channel it into the hole outside. Anyone who wanted a shit had to do it where they could. I dread to think what the women's toilets were like. The track or rough hard core through fair hill was crowded with fortune tellers' vans each with a board outside advertising names like 'Petrolengo' or 'Gypsy Lee' - Lee was a name that cropped up everywhere. Towards the entrance to fair hill there were stalls selling hot dogs, pies, toffee apples, teas and soft drinks. All around them the ground was strewn with litter and trampled underfoot. God help the people who had to clear away.

The noise in the pubs that were open is tremendous. The men with their shirt sleeves rolled up and shirts open at the neck, some to the waist, were sweating and pouring beer down their throats as they lounged in doorways. Smoke from the bars drifts into the street where part of a pie has been trodden and kicked against a pub wall. A young man staggered out and vomited on the road.

Two policemen walked by trying to keep a low profile as the travelling people were mob-minded that night and the police were outnumbered. At the Grapes pub on the Sands it is impossible to enter the bar as a solid body of men totally blocks the doorway and spill outside onto the street. The shelters along by the riverbank were used by young people, all drinking and revelling. The shelters were used as lavatories too and were in a disgusting state. By midnight the town became quieter as people made their way back to fair hill where more drink was waiting. They would sit around fires and talk of the old days.

During Fair Week one year the Old Fox pub at Ousby had trouble with a crowd of travellers. Fred Curragh was the landlord and he was having a quiet night with some locals when a crowd of travellers descended on the place. Fred and his wife Nora were kept busy behind the bar and soon the place was fair rocking with the noisy crowd.

Eventually an argument started among some of the young chaps.

The crowd all went outside hoping to watch a fight but instead they boarded their carts and departed in the fading light. Fred was somewhat puzzled. All the beer had been drunk and all the glasses empty when they went outside for the fight. It had been a fake. He hadn't noticed that during the disturbance some of the crowd had been into his living quarters where money, horse brasses, some silver and many family heirlooms were spirited away.

Charlie Heslop was getting on in years and was keeper at Flakebridge and his estate ran right up to Fair Hill. Men and lads with lurchers ran amok over his ground but there was nothing he or the police could do. Farmers too dreaded Fair Week as horses were tethered to roadside fences and sometimes were let into fields that were due for haymaking. Fence posts were pulled out and hedges cut for firewood. Stock was harrassed by dogs and farmers were sometimes threatened. Many people wanted the fair stopped but permission had been granted hundreds of years before.

Johnny Eagles, the strong man

Close to where the smiths were working on fair hill a crowd had gathered to watch a chap of maybe 60 years old. He was stripped to the waist and had an iron bar behind his neck and was bending it. The crowd urged him on while the old chap was snorting and blowing with effort. In the end the bar is bent double and someone shouts, 'Let's see you straighten it!' Johnny shouts back, 'Let's see two of you try!'

Two young chaps stood forward and each took an end of the iron bar and went through all sorts of antics but couldn't get the bar straight. The crowd enjoyed the performance. Then Johnny challenged the anyone in the audience to bend a fresh bar but there were no takers. The strongman took the bar which was about three feet long and a quarter of an inch thick and began to beat it over his outstreched arm until it finally bent into a V shape. The crowd cheered and threw money onto a sheet. Next Johnny Eagles took a telephone directory and tore in half. There was more cheering and then he tore it in half again and more coins were thrown onto the sheet for him to collect.

Leaving Edenhall

I had been at Edenhall for about two seasons when Bob Simpson, the head keeper, died. I was put in charge of the game department as was arranged when I took the situation. It was not easy for me as Bob had been there for many years, running the estate for several previous employers. Everyone was used to old Bob, but some things had to change, not because I wanted them to but because times had changed and the ways of farming as well.

The first season I was in charge we had kept about two hundred of the old broody hens back when they were brought from the woods. We cleared the old walled-in kitchen garden, about one and a half acres of it, and made the old potting shed into places the hens could roost. As the hens were brought away from the woods they were given their freedom in the old garden which had laid derelict for many years.

Each day the eggs were gathered and when there was a full crate we sent them to the battery houses to go away with the other crates. I had talked to my boss about us not being able to get the quantity of hens when we wanted them and that if he intended carrying on the shooting in the same way as before, we would have to start looking at other ways of hatching and rearing. My employer said we could start thinking about how to go about it.

The Greens just down the wood from my Lodge would be ideal for the brooder house as there was a large open space there and it was sheltered as well. The incubator building plus garage would stand just behind the dog kennels. I had drawn the size of place we would need - there was the egg store, then the large incubator room which would house two electric Turkey Bator incubators that held 3000 eggs each. The room would also have four 250 egg Clevums & Glosters oil incubators. There would be a central washing out gully and roof ventilators.

The garage would hold two vehicles and space for pheasant feed. The whole was to be built of concrete block with an asbestos roof, sliding doors and small windows. Eddy Burne, a friend of mine on the council, drew up the plans for me. My employer was impressed by it all - plans were submitted to the council and accepted. Various contractors put in their prices for the building we proposed and in the end a chap called Crisp from Clifton, won the contract with a price of £4000.

My thoughts were of the brooder house now that the hatching was arranged for. I was looking through the newspapers one day and saw the answer to my problem. Duran Hill Camp at Carlisle was being dismantled. Having been in the Army I remembered these wooden barracks very well. One morning four of us - myself, two woodmen and another keeper - set out for Carlisle. The camp was quite big and some demolishing had started. We looked around and in the end I found what I wanted. The hut was sixty feet long and twenty feet wide, built of weatherboard with an asbestos roof. It was boarded up to window height on the inside and the floor would come up in sections. I asked the chaps with me what they thought of it. Could we dismantle it, cart it to Edenhall and rebuild it? Yes, they said, it could be done.

As we saw it that day the hut was perfectly sound and I made a note of the hut's number, etc. On the way home we talked of how we would go about dismantling and moving it. I wrote to the Ministry and made them an offer of £60, which was later accepted. I sent off my money and received a bill of sale. A haulage contractor was hired and some days later the hut was dismantled and brought to Edenhall. There were several loads - the floor being the worst to move as it was so very heavy. Once it was all on the site the rebuilding could go ahead. Work was already underway with the incubator building.

Bryson, the stonemason, soon got the sleeper walls up to carry the floor of the brooder house - the floor was perfectly level thanks to Bryson's good work. The walls went up fairly easy, but the roof took a while but in the end the hut was rebuilt. Good job we got the windows in early, the very night we finished them a gale got up and severe damage was done on the estate. Trees behind the hut were broken in two just like carrots and two woods were so severely damaged that they were never replanted. I remember that early morning, our Lodge fairly shook with one blast. Winds of 120 miles per hour were recorded at Great Dunn Fell.

The incubator building was finished about Christmas time and work went on with the brooder house for a few weeks after. Gas pipes were fitted to take gas to the eleven sections where the chicks would be under the heaters. Pens were made outside the hut - these were about eighteen yards in length, with one connected to each section inside the building. The young chicks could exercise themselves when old enough. Calor Gas cylinders were ordered, these were very heavy and four cylinders were yoked together. Two were used at a time and a gauge would tell me when the gas was almost gone. An old bath was brought and put just outside the hut door. This had to be filled by carting water from my house or a field trough.

Brian and eldest daughter Heather at 7am on the day Langwathby Bridge collapsed in the flood of 1968.

Many hours I spent in that hut on my own but in the end the job was finished. I could start to do my keeper work once more. Now that I was in full charge of the sporting part of the estate, more organising came my way. Sometimes I would be ready for my bed, when the 'phone would ring and my employer would be on the other end. He wanted to know how things were on the estate, what the men were busy doing and many other questions. 'By the way, Brian, Mr & Mrs Naylor will be coming to fish next week. Will you please look after them? See that they have anything they need.'

I was a busy man but I enjoyed it most of the time. I could fish when I wanted and shoot if there was shooting to be done, at no cost at all. When the rearing season started things went on fairly well. I got the hang of it quickly as I was young enough to make the change from broody hens to the modern incubator and brooder house system. Things looked good. Later, large release pens were erected in the woods where the birds were put.

On Saturday 23 March 1968, the Eden was in flood and the water was out as far as Toll Bar Cottage at Edenhall. A vast area was under water. A rapid thaw of the snow on the fells on the east and west sides of the valley along with heavy rain and a strong southerly wind, driving down Lake Ullswater pushed the water into the Rivers Eamont and Eden. The Eamont emptied into the already flooded Eden at Watersmeet. As the Eamont water drove into the flood it broke over the banks at Dolphenby Farm. One Sunday morning at 7am Langwathby Bridge collapsed and the river roaring down was awful to see. The old stone bridge had stood many a flood before, but this was so great a flood and so rapid a thaw, that nothing could have held it. By 3pm on the same afternoon the river was back within its banks.

I walked to our fishing hut which was intact - the water had risen to the window sills. I made a mark on the hut door and later painted the date and the year of the great flood there. Much damage had been done - some of the lower sheep fences were down and lay full length where the flood had laid them. They looked just like the sleepers of a railway track - many, many yards of them. There was much clearing up to do.

The day after the flood, I needed to drive to Langwathby. Now that the bridge was gone, it meant a long journey via Carlton and along the Appleby road as far as Culgaith, then back along the road to Langwathby. Two estate men lived there so that was twice a day I had to do that run. I had managed to moor our fishing boat to a tree on a long chain. The boat had survived the flood but it was left a long way from the water when the flood went down. Later that week the boat was put back on the river, all the men helping. I took the boat downstream as far as Stratheden, a large house on the far bank, on the Langwathby side. This done, the workmen could take themselves backwards and forwards to work. Some months later the Army brought a steel bridge from Portinscale, near Keswick, and pushed it across the river. The bridge is still in use all these years later - not nice to look at but it does the job.

A year or so before the great flood, the Eden decided to change its course on the north side of the salmon pool. If this had been allowed to happen, some 150 yards of fishing would have been lost. I talked to my employer about what I thought we should do and he agreed to it. Summer time when the river was low was the time to tackle the work. We hired a crawler track machine with a large front bucket, plus ready mix concrete which would come dry mixed and hundreds of sand bags, were ordered. When everything was ready, the concrete arrived. Several of the estate men were ready to start bagging up the dry concrete. After the sand bags had been tied up they were loaded into the front bucket of the crawler and taken across the river where I was in charge of the works there. We had dug a level foundation across the breach in the bank. The idea was to make a wall of the bags of concrete, four bags thick. The work was heavy and the weather hot. As the bags were laid the river water was absorbed into them.

By the next day they were hard. Two days of hard work went into that bank repair. After all the bags had been used the machine pushed tons of sand and gravel up behind the bags as reinforcement. It was a good job done. I know I went home that night and had a good night's sleep. If the river had broken through that bank, the salmon pool and the river above would have been useless to fish again as the level would have dropped by half. A long stretch of water would have been affected.

I had been at Edenhall eight seasons, six as head keeper and I enjoyed it. There had been problems at times, modern farming and the preservation of game do not go hand in hand. One instance comes to mind - a field of barley which was next to a wood where 800 pheasants had been released, was ready to cut. The contractor started to cut the field just before dark. I arrived on the field on the second cut. I stopped the driver and told him that many young pheasants would be among the standing barley. He told me he had to keep on cutting all night if need be, the corn had to be cut. I found the farm foreman and had a word with him, my temper was up. I rang my boss, he was away. I went back to the field by which time it was dark. The combine with lights on was still cutting corn. Now and then a bird would get up from the front of the machine to disappear into the mouth of the combine.

I couldn't sleep that night - my season's work was being destroyed not by foxes or vermin, but by our own people on the estate and a bloody machine. Early next morning I was on that field again - not a stalk of corn was standing. I started to walk the field looking for what I knew was there. I kicked the straw about and soon had about twenty dead and mutilated bodies in a sack. I left the field, murder was in my mind, that bloody farm foreman. I kept trying to reach my employer and when I finally was able to speak with him and told him my troubles, he replied, 'Well the farmers have there work do as well.' I put the 'phone down, said to my wife 'What am I doing at Edenhall? I rear the birds, the bloody machine kills them!'

Things were changing at Edenhall. At Dolphenby Farm a new 250 cow unit was being built costing around £70,000. Nearly twice as many cows would be milked there soon. A huge self-feed silage

The author today.

building enabled the beasts to help themselves to fodder all under cover. Cubicles too were installed, one for each cow. The beasts were loose at all times, apart from the period they were being milked twice a day.

Lowther Estates took over the management of the woods and the legal side of things. My employer was asking me to cut down on the cost of the shooting, on the feed and small items that were essential. What was Josie doing? Could he not help on the farm? If sheep broke into a wood, I had to repair the walls myself. In the end it seemed there was very little or no cooperation between the different departments. Money was always to be considered.

I looked back over the years - the shooting and fishing were first and foremost - the estate had been purchased with that in mind. My employer married in about 1970. His wife had a business in London and he was spending much time in the city as well, something to do with finance.

I was losing interest in the estate and started to spend more time enjoying myself - bugger the shooting. The hotel provided me with company, farmers and others who appreciated a good crack. I did a bit of drinking, maybe more than I should have, at the time I saw no wrong in it and so it went on for a while. My wife had never liked drink. Even if I had only taken a couple of pints, she thought I was drunk. Things had not been too good between us for some time. The more Joan nagged me about going out to get drunk the more I felt driven away from her. I needed some support not aggravation.

My employer said changes had to be made and I must do my best.

'Yes,' I told him, 'I shall spend time and money to rear game for you, then at the vital period you let the machine loose among them! What's the point?' We parted, I to the hotel to find some sort of comfort among the farmers and then I started an affair with one of the women at the hotel, just a friendship at first. Things being as they were, it didn't take long before I was seeing a lot of this woman. My wife soon got wind of what was happening. I didn't try to hide it and just went at it without a care. Joan gave me hell and drove me out to the hotel again. And so it went on. I out each night to get out of the way, my employer got word of my doings. What did I think I was doing having an affair? I told him that my private life had nothing to do with him as I did my job. My boss gave me a good lecture and said that I represented him on the estate while he was away and that I should mend my ways otherwise he would have to think about my employment there. Before we parted he said that he would be going away to Greece for two weeks and that I should think about my position while he was away.

Now I was getting aggravation from both sides, my wife and my employer. I was past caring. I felt I could no longer work for him and Joan made my life miserable and so there was nothing for it - back to the hotel and my affair. I was sent for by my employer on his return, 'How are things on the estate?' 'Alright,' I replied. 'Now, have you stopped seeing that hotel woman?' 'No.' 'What do you intend to do?' asked my boss. 'Nothing,' I said, 'I told you it has nothing to do with you.'

'Do you remember, Brian, before I went away what I said about having to let you go?' 'Yes,' I said. 'Well?' he asked. 'I'll tell you what Airly, I do not want your job.' Silence for a while, he looking at me, obviously a little shocked. 'And that's your answer, Brian?' 'Yes, I do not want your job.' I turned and left him.

That was our last meeting. It was the end for me at Edenhall, and I felt much better for it. I started to sell off my dogs, all my firearms apart from my A&A gun, pictures, lamps, clocks, and many items I had gathered up during my time at Edenhall. I told Joan I was going away as we no longer got on together. Where I was going I didn't know but go I must.